Archibald Forbes

Czar and Sultan

Archibald Forbes

Czar and Sultan

ISBN/EAN: 9783743332461

Manufactured in Europe, USA, Canada, Australia, Japa

Cover: Foto ©ninafisch / pixelio.de

Manufactured and distributed by brebook publishing software (www.brebook.com)

Archibald Forbes

Czar and Sultan

THE LIBRARY
OF
THE UNIVERSITY
OF CALIFORNIA
RIVERSIDE

CZAR AND SULTAN

THE ADVENTURES OF A BRITISH LAD IN THE
RUSSO-TURKISH WAR OF 1877–78

BY

ARCHIBALD FORBES

*ILLUSTRATED BY PORTRAITS IN THE POSSESSION OF THE
AUTHOR, AND BY FOUR SPECIAL DRAWINGS
BY SYDNEY P. HALL*

NEW YORK
CHARLES SCRIBNER'S SONS
1894

COPYRIGHT, 1894, BY
CHARLES SCRIBNER'S SONS

Norwood Press :
J. S. Cushing & Co. — Berwick & Smith.
Boston, Mass., U.S.A.

NOTE

The materials for this narrative are taken from several sources: from the admirable war letters written to the *Daily News* during the Russo-Turkish Campaign by my brilliant colleagues Messrs. MacGahan and Millett, the former of whom fell a victim to its hardships; from the History of the War written by Captain F. V. Greene, the United States Military Attaché with the Russian Headquarters, who was in the field throughout the war, and whose work is the standard authority; from Mr. Nemirovitch-Dantchenko's interesting and vivid *Personal Reminiscences of General Skobeleff;* from the late Valentine Baker Pasha's *War in Bulgaria;* and from sundry Russian narratives and reminiscences. I have to a considerable extent utilized some personal experiences of my own, and have drawn occasionally on my correspondence to the *Daily News*, a newspaper to which I owe what of success may have attended a career of some activity and variety.

A. F.

LONDON, June, 1894.

CONTENTS

CHAPTER		PAGE
	INTRODUCTION	1
I.	ACROSS THE PRUTH	5
II.	THE CROSSING OF THE DANUBE	21
III.	GOURKO'S RAID ACROSS THE BALKANS	36
IV.	THE SECOND BATTLE OF PLEVNA	57
V.	DREARY DAYS	83
VI.	THE CRISIS OF THE SCHIPKA PASS	91
VII.	PELISCHAT AND LOFTCHA	122
VIII.	THE SEPTEMBER BATTLE OF PLEVNA	147
IX.	THE SIEGE OF PLEVNA	174
X.	SKOBELEFF AND THE GREEN HILL	222
XI.	IN THE BALKANS WITH GOURKO	243
XII.	THE FALL OF PLEVNA	259
XIII.	GOURKO'S PASSAGE OF THE BALKANS	309
XIV.	FROM SOPHIA TO ADRIANOPLE	347
XV.	SAN STEFANO AND HOME AGAIN	372

LIST OF ILLUSTRATIONS

THE EMPEROR RECEIVES NEWS OF CRISIS OF THE SCHIPKA
PASS . . . . *Frontispiece*

	FACE PAGE
GENERAL SKOBELEFF . . .	16
GRAND DUKE NICHOLAS	22
ALEXANDER II. . . .	34
GENERAL IGNATIEFF . . .	58
PRINCE CHARLES OF ROUMANIA	148
THE ASSAULT ON THE MAMELON REDOUBT	164
THE CESAREVICH, 1877 . .	180
GENERAL TODLEBEN	192
GENERAL GOURKO .	200
OSMAN PASHA . .	260
MEETING OF NICHOLAS AND OSMAN PASHA AFTER CAPITULATION OF PLEVNA . .	276
THE "TE DEUM" AFTER THE PROCLAMATION OF PEACE .	378

CZAR AND SULTAN

INTRODUCTION

MY name is John Carnegie; I am in my thirty-third year, and, thank God, I do not know what sickness means, except for an occasional touch of Danube fever. We Carnegies are of Scotch extraction — the name will tell you that; but three generations of us have lived in Eastern Europe. My good father is still alive, hale and hearty, carrying on a commerce in grain and other products of the great Danubian valley as his father did before him, in which business my elder brother Tom and I myself are now the junior partners. My life has been quite uneventful save during one stirring and eventful year, of which I shall presently tell in detail — the year of the great Russo-Turkish War of 1877-78, at the outbreak of which I was just sixteen years old.

Before that time Bulgaria was a province of Turkey; and Roumania, on the other side of the Danube, although virtually an independent State with a German prince as its ruler, was nevertheless still tributary to Turkey. Our house did business both with Bulgaria and Roumania. Its headquarters were at Rustchuk, a Turkish fortress-town on the Danube opposite the Roumanian town of Giurgevo;

we had business offices in both towns, but my father's house was in Giurgevo and it was there where I was born. We had branches further up the river — at Sistova in Bulgaria, and at Simnitza and Turnu-Magurelle in Roumania. We liked the Turks better than we did either the Bulgarians, who were sullen people, or the Roumanians, who, though lively and smart, were not quite so honest as they might have been. The Turks as regarded commerce were slow and antiquated; but their word was their bond, and even the poorest of them had a personal dignity and self-respect which made intercourse with them very pleasant. In the days before the war, at least as regarded Bulgaria north of the Balkans, the country with which we were familiar, the Turks and Bulgarians were fairly good neighbours. The former were the dominant race, but they were not oppressive, and the Bulgarians purchased non-molestation by an occasional present to the Turkish Moullas (priests). The devils who oppressed and outraged the Bulgarians were the fierce tribes of Circassians (better known as Tcherkess) who had been driven from their own country by the Russian conquest of it, and to whom as co-religionists Turkey had in an unwise hour given a refuge within her borders. Those fiends it was whose ferocities practised on the Christian subjects of Turkey were the real origin of the Russo-Turkish war: if the native Turks and native Bulgarians had joined in exterminating those pests of the human race, you in England would never have heard of "Bulgarian Atrocities," and the Panslavists would have had no pretext for forcing the Czar to invade Turkey for the succour of the Christian subjects of the Porte.

My elder brother has twin sons who are now fourteen years of age. They are being educated at a public school in England, and during the winter vacation they annually pay us a visit on the Danube. Last winter at their own request I sent them with our head clerk, a Bulgarian educated at the Roberts College in Constantinople, on a tour through the most interesting scenes of the great war. They had spent several days at and around Plevna, in the vicinity of which they found many still unburied skeletons. They had crossed the Balkans by the Schipka Pass, investigated the scene of the stubborn defence which the Russians maintained there, followed Skobeleff's track through the snow-wreaths to worst the Turkish army around Schipka and Shenova and to compel its entire surrender, got on Gourko's trail in his combats about Eski-Zagra, and from Adrianople had pushed on towards Constantinople. On their return journey by Philippopolis and Sophia they had reversed Gourko's famous march, recrossed the Balkans, and returned to us by way of Plevna and Nicopolis. There was still a fortnight before they needed to return to Rossall; and the lads entreated of me, because they knew that I had seen much of the fighting of the great war and had known many of the leading actors in that bloody tragedy, that I should spend the evenings of that available fortnight in clothing with something of life and energy the dry bones which they had seen on their travels, and in narrating to them the "battles, sieges, fortunes," "the moving accidents by flood and field" which I had experienced during that memorable period. They are good lads, and I love them. I had packed away and, so to speak, locked up the grim memories of the war year. But they prevailed with me; and almost within sight of a part of the fighting region from our windows that looked across the great river, we sat round the great open wood-fire evening after evening while I smoked and talked, and my young nephews listened with an intentness which gave encouragement to a man who by nature is not very fluent in speech. It seems that one of the lads had learned shorthand, and with his back turned to me was sedulously taking down my narrative verbatim evening after evening, entirely without my knowledge. Since his return to England he has confessed his crime by letter. But so far from regarding his conduct as criminal, the young rascal informs me that he has written out his shorthand notes and sent the transcription to a certain Mr. Arrowsmith, a publisher of Bristol, who not only has not consigned the manuscript to its proper destination on the top of a hot fire, but has been so left to himself as to put it into print and intends to publish the work. It is not my affair; I have many faults, but I have never been accused of being a literary man, although I did perpetrate a little war-correspondence in the campaign time. My nephew's audacity has led him to demand of me that I should write a short introduction to the book which he has purloined from my lips, and I have ignominiously complied with the insolent requisition. This done, I wash my hands of the affair. Corn is my line — not literature.

CHAPTER I

ACROSS THE PRUTH

AMONG us mercantile folk the rumours of impending war, it may be imagined, were ill received. We tried hard not to believe them. But that was not easy, after Turkey's obstinate and angry rejection of the Protocol presented to it by the European powers on the last day of March, 1877. When we read that "strong in the justice of her cause, and putting her faith in Allah, Turkey had determined to ignore what had been decided without her and against her," it was clear that the Ottoman Government had resolved to throw away the scabbard. It takes two to make a quarrel; and when a fortnight passed without any manifesto on the part of Russia, we had some hope. But that vanished before the stern words given to the world by the Czar on April 24th: "Invoking the blessing of God upon our valiant armies, we give the order to cross the Turkish frontier."

The Turks had already begun to increase the defences of Rustchuk, and the reserves in the Bulgarian province were being called up to join the colours. Although no intelligence yet came of the Russians having crossed the Pruth, it seemed certain that the Danube below Galatz would soon be closed, and as we had a cargo of grain there ready for shipment, my father sent me off to Galatz on the 23rd to hurry up the ship's departure. Young as I was, I was quite a well-grown fellow, and I believe that I knew nearly as much about our business as did my father himself. The railway journey from Giurgevo to Bucharest, and from Bucharest nearly to Galatz, was quite devoid of interest. But as about midnight of the 24th the train approached the Barbosch station about six miles from Galatz, we saw the light of watch-fires along either side of the Sereth river. Were the Russians there already? we asked each other. Yes; as the train halted at the Barbosch platform there were the Russian sentries tramping up and down among the passengers and the piles of stores. There was no confusion or excitement. The refreshment-room waiter was ready with his proffer of hot coffee with as much calmness as if there had not been a Russian outside Bessarabia. Some Russian cavalry officers drinking tea in the restaurant while waiting for the train into Galatz, told me that their division had marched 65 miles on the 24th — from Kischeneff to Barbosch. Next day but one there came into Galatz the infantrymen of the 11th Russian Corps commanded by Prince Schahofskoy. I had never seen a Russian soldier until two nights before, and I looked with great interest at the infantry regiment now tramping along the dusty road in heavy marching order. The files came along in loose order straggling along all over the road, at a pace of close on four miles an hour — a long-striding, dogged, steady tramp, clumsy to look at but apparently lasting. In but few instances were the rank-and-file tall men, but they were burly square-set fellows, broad in the shoulders, deep in the chest, and clean in the flanks. They wore a sort of kepi — green with red band round it, — dark-green tunic long and loose in the skirts, and loose, baggy trousers tucked inside long boots reaching over the calf of the leg quite up to the knee. They marched with fixed bayonets; round the knapsack was a section of the *tente d'abris;* and every man carried his own kettle on the back of his knapsack, with the heavy grey greatcoat rolled and carried over the left shoulder. The men looked hard, brown and healthy. As they swung along with that great stride of theirs, they made light of their heavy kit and sang with great taste and heartiness.

Behind the infantry came a cavalry regiment of Don Cossacks, ambling along on their gaunt, wiry ponies, cocked up on a high saddle with a leather pillow on it kept in place by a surcingle. One Don Cossack was so like another that they might all have been cast in the same mould, and that in case of accidents heads, arms and legs were interchangeable. I found it pleasanter, for sundry reasons, to keep well to windward of the Cossack. Studying him as closely as his rankness permitted, I found him a sturdy, wiry little fellow of some five feet five. His weather-beaten face was shrewd, bold and knowing. His eyes were small, oblique and keen; his mouth large, and between it and his pug-nose — rather redder than the rest of his face — was a wisp of straw-coloured moustache. His long, thick, straight hair matched his moustache in colour, and was cut sheer round by the nape of his neck. He wore a round oilskin peakless shako with a knowing cock to the right, to maintain it at which angle was a strap round his chubby chin. Below the neck, as concerned his outside, the Cossack was all boots and greatcoat. The latter, of thick grey blanketing, came down below his knees; his boots came up to them. Through chinks in his greatcoat were glimpses of a sheepskin undercoat with the hair worn inside — the thermometer being over 70° in the shade. He was armed beyond all conception. He carried a long red, flagless lance with a venomous steel head; and on his back was slung a carbine in an oilskin cover, the stock downwards. In his belt was a long and heavy revolver in a leather holster, and from the shoulder hung a curved sword with no guard over its hilt. Throughout the campaign I never tired of studying the Cossack. He was not by any means a very valorous person, but he was ready for any service except that of close and hard fighting. He carried despatches; he escorted suspected spies, keeping the head of his lance within easy distance of the small of the suspect's back to be handy for skewering him if he should attempt to escape. I myself have marched at the point of the rascal's spear-head, and received occasional monitory prods. The Cossack was even placed on guard over ships at the Galatz quay to prevent their unauthorised departure. Dismounting and shackling his rat of a pony by a hobble on one fore and one hind leg, friend Cossack took up a position on the extreme edge of the jetty with his lance pointed in the direction of the ship, as if he would transfix it should it attempt to escape; and there he stood, self-contained, affable and alert. He would accept a cigarette and tender you a light in the friendliest manner, but he could not be coaxed to take his eye for a moment off the ship which was in his custody.

As soon as Prince Schahofskoy entered Galatz, he gave

orders that every ship at Braila and Galatz must depart that same evening, whether loaded or not. Our ship was ready, all forms had been gone through, and she was among the earliest to leave. But others were not so fortunate, nor could the Consuls of the various nationalities interested move the stubborn Schahofskoy, who, indeed, significantly set his watch by that of the leader of the deputation which visited him, and not less significantly hinted at speedy laying of torpedoes in the lower river. On the broad open space of the great quay of Galatz congregated most of the population of the place to watch the departure of the shipping, which was felt as the stamping of the seal of impending hostilities. But, indeed, these had already occurred, for a Turkish battery on the south bank had been firing across the river on the Barbosch bridge.

It was here in Galatz where I first met Mr. MacGahan, the famous American war-correspondent of the *Daily News*. MacGahan, with his bright sunny face, his quaint humour, his constant good temper, and his coolness which nothing could disturb, was a singularly attractive man. I loved him from the first; and no wonder, for he was kindness itself to me, a casual lad who had not on him even the weak claim of being his countryman. After a few days of delightful intercourse with him, he told me that for certain there would be no mercantile business done along the Danube for many a month to come, and he offered to show me some work which would interest me and give me fine opportunities for seeing men and things, providing my father would assent to the proposal. The old gentleman made no objections, replying to my letter simply that I must keep out of danger as much as possible. MacGahan and I were in Braila on the 10th May when a Turkish flotilla, headed by several ironclads, came out of a branch into the main Danube, and the ironclads opened fire on the partially armed Russian batteries on the edge of the town and on Braila itself. The Russian fire drove them back into the branch; but one ironclad remained under cover of some trees above which its three masts showed. Some shots from field-guns were fired at the vessel with no effect, and then two siege-guns opened. The first shot had no effect; the second dropped on the deck of the ironclad. It was supposed that the shell must have crashed through the deck into the ship's powder magazine. I saw a great flash blaze up from the bowels of the ship, followed by a heavy pall of white smoke; when that drifted away all that remained visible was the stern of the *Lutfi Djelil*, with the mizzen-mast standing on which still fluttered the Crescent flag. MacGahan and I were allowed seats in a Russian steam-launch which put out from Braila. The wreck was boarded, the Turkish flag was pulled down, and two of the ill-fated crew were rescued, the sole survivors of two hundred officers and men.

We had a stirring torpedo adventure a fortnight later. The Turkish flotilla still lay anchored in the Matchin channel a few miles above Braila. Lieutenant Dubassoff of the Russian navy determined to attack it under cover of night. He had four small steam launches, two of which were to make the actual attack; the other two were to remain in support in case of accident to either of the attacking craft. Of the latter one was commanded by Dubassoff, the leader of the little expedition, with a crew of fourteen men; the other by Lieutenant Shestakoff, who had a crew of nine. Both boats were protected from stem to stern with iron mantlets painted black and thick enough to stop bullets. The only persons exposed were the two officers, each of whom steered his own craft. MacGahan and I were aboard one of the auxiliary launches, neither of which had protective mantlets. The little expedition started at midnight of a dark and rainy night, and after an hour's steaming we were close to the Turkish flotilla. A sentry on board one of the ships challenged again and again. Dubassoff as we approached called out "Friends!" in Turkish; but the sentry fired, and thus the alarm was given. As our launch lay perhaps a couple of cable lengths away, we could hear the sudden stir aboard the ship, cries and shouts, and the loud orders of the officers to man the guns. Presently a shell came whistling over our heads; we had seen the flash as the gun was fired. Dubassoff made straight for the ship heading for its bow, Shestakoff waiting behind to watch results. Each boat, I should mention, was armed with two torpedoes at the end of long spars projecting on either bow. The torpedoes were detachable; there were fastened to them long, light chains by which they could be lashed on to any projection of the ship which was being attacked, and a flexible wire about 100 yards long connected them with the boat, where a small electric battery was strapped around the waist of the officer in command. Through the storm of wildly-aimed fire that poured from the ship, Dubassoff shot under the bow, fastened the chain attached to the torpedo on her cable, dropped the torpedo from the spar, and backed until the full length of the connecting wire was reached.

The current had carried the torpedo right under the fore-part of the doomed ship. Dubassoff caught the moment and connected the wire with the battery on his person. An instant later we dimly saw a huge mass of water shoot up into the air; as it rose it was illuminated by a terrific explosion in the din of which were mingled the shouts and cries of the Turkish crew. A gruesome rain of fragments fell into our craft, comparatively distant though it was — members of human bodies, pieces of shells, fragments of iron and splinters of wood. Dubassoff's launch was all but swamped; and he moved away, calling on Shestakoff as he passed to attempt placing another torpedo so as to make sure of the utter ruin of the Turkish ship. Notwithstanding the carnage and ruin effected by the first torpedo, what remained of the ironclad's crew fought on nobly, keeping up a heavy but random fire. The other Turkish ships struck in with their fire; but the Russian launches being all but invisible in the gloom, they blazed into each other at random and the confusion and dismay were appalling. Shestakoff darted in under the ship's stern, planted a torpedo, backed, shot the electric spark from his body-battery, and the second explosion was more terrible than had been the first. The ship sank almost immediately, nothing of her showing above water except her upper masts; her hapless crew killed or drowned, saving the few who swam ashore. Dubassoff considered that he had done enough for one night. He and Shestakoff passed under the fire of the two other gunboats, escaping unharmed, joined their consort craft from one of which we had witnessed the lurid scene, and by daylight the flotilla was safe alongside the Braila wharf. The two officers and the crews of the attacking launches received the Cross of St. George. For my part the horror of the adventure was so lasting, that for nights after I awoke shuddering in a cold perspiration with the yells of the unfortunates tingling in my ears.

By this time there had come to Braila and Galatz, as the chief points of interest for the time, a number of correspondents and artists from, as it seemed, every European country. MacGahan welcomed two countrymen in the persons of Millett and Jackson, representatives of the *New York Herald*, with the former of whom I was later to have many adventures. Mr. Villiers, the war-artist of the *Graphic*, was very kind to me; later in the campaign I was much in his company and I would go a long way to meet him again. I was glad to be able to be of some service to the correspondent gentlemen. Except MacGahan, who seemed to speak every language under the sun, and who was as glib in Turkish as in Russian and Bulgarian (which are a good deal like each other), none of them had any acquaintance with the local languages of Eastern Europe. For business purposes I had become conversant with them all, and I spent many an hour in teaching Millett and Villiers the most useful words in Turkish and Bulgarian. The campaign meanwhile progressed, as we thought, strangely leisurely. But it seemed that the delay was inevitable. The Danube was still flowing brimming full, miles of shore on either side of the main stream under water. Pending the falling-in of the great river the Russians, it seemed, were spreading themselves all over Roumania, making themselves very much at home. Mac-Gahan told me that in May there were four Russian corps actually in the Principalities, besides the elder Skobeleff's Cossack division and nine unattached Cossack regiments. The 9th Corps (General Baron Krüdener) was about Slatina in the west of Wallachia; the 8th (General Radetski) about Bucharest; the 11th (Prince Schahofskoy) along the Danube from below Galatz to Oltenitza; and the 12th (General Vannovsky) about Bucharest. I was told that three more corps were coming up in the second line — the 14th (General Zimmermann) to occupy the Dobrutscha, the 13th (General Hahn) to march forward to Alexandria south-west of Bucharest, and the 4th (General Zotoff) to Bucharest. Meantime all around Braila were camps, most of them what were called "flying camps." Their occupants were here one day and gone the next. Now it was a brigade of the elder Skobeleff's Cossacks, who put up here for a day and demanded rations, on their way to Bucharest, Kalarash, Turnu-Magurelle, or Giurgevo — who could tell? Now a regiment of Dragomiroff's stout fellows of the 8th Corps, with the mud of the Pruth valley still on their long boots; now the heavy dragoons of Prince Manueloff, big men on big horses. The masses passed outside of Braila, but a battalion, or a squadron, or a sotnia of Cossacks always made its way through the town with any amount of swagger, bands playing, or drums beating, or leading files thumping the cymbals or marching with "singers in front." Rations were waiting always for the in-marching troops, and the out-marching had their haversacks filled up. Stacks of loaves were everywhere: the grain, rye-flour; the loaves almost as dark in colour as the German Schwartz-brod, baked by the military bakers in the field ovens in the camp.

The Russians were anxious to make their left-flank bridge across the Danube in the vicinity of Braila, but so late as June 1st the river was still 15 feet above the ordinary level of that date. MacGahan determined to go to Bucharest for a time, returning to Braila when he should hear when it was likely that the bridge there would be taken in hand. He took me with him to Bucharest for service as his amanuensis. I had often before visited that city, but now I scarcely knew it again. Bucharest calls itself the "Paris of the East," and Paris was never more abandoned to an orgie of pleasure than was Bucharest in the early summer of 1877. It was throbbing in a delirium of giddy joy not less reckless than dissipated, accentuated by the clank of martial accoutrements, the clatter of sword-scabbards on the parquet floors of the restaurants, and the steady tramp of the cohorts pouring through the seething streets. Princes, grand dukes, diplomats, aides-de-camp, contractors, Polish Jews, and war-correspondents belonging to every European nationality jostled each other politely on the broad staircase of the Hotel Brofft.

In the garden-restaurant of that establishment gay Guardsmen from the Russian headquarter staff were drinking champagne as they glanced scornfully on the adjacent group of swarthy, slender officers of the Roumanian army, who had not yet retrieved their tainted military reputation by the valour they were soon to show in the fierce fighting and terrible carnage of the great Gravitza Redoubt. In a shady corner under the drooping willow-tree, sat MacGahan with myself, his loyal and loving henchman, by his side. He was telling me of a certain young Russian general named Skobeleff, an old Khivan comrade of his, of whom as yet I had barely heard although I had already met his worthy father at Galatz. As he gossiped with me about his friend over the flagon of Pilsener beer, I chanced to notice two men enter the garden-restaurant. The two were arm-in-arm. One was dressed in the plain, ugly blue uniform of a private of dragoons — a small, slight, swarthy man, with a face full of intelligence. His companion, tall, stately and blond, of noble carriage and with flowing tawny beard, was dressed in spotless white and wore the insignia of a general officer. The curious spectacle of a general and a private soldier arm-in-arm struck me, and I called MacGahan's attention to it. He sprang to his feet with the exclamation: "Why, it's the very man — it is Skobeleff himself!"

I looked at Skobeleff with all my eyes as he stood there on the garden-path, his fine face glowing with pleasure as he returned the greeting of his old friend. I thought then as a lad, as I have never ceased to think, that I never looked on a grander man. Over six feet in height, straight as a pine, the head carried high with a frank gallant fearlessness, square across the broad shoulders, deep in the chest, slender of waist, clean of flank, the muscular, graceful, supple figure set off to perfection by the white frock-coat with the decorations and the gold lace on it, Skobeleff, with his chivalrous bearing, looked a genial king of men. Presently he came and sat down by us, and MacGahan presented me to him. As he talked my eyes were fastened on his face; for he fascinated me so that I could not help myself, although he must have thought me rude. Except MacGahan himself I never knew a man so winning. No

GENERAL SKOBELEFF.

wonder that soldiers, friends, and women loved him! — it was impossible to know him, to have him smile on you with that sweet grave smile of his, and not to love him. I could not fancy this man a foreigner who sat by me talking in purest idiomatic English of that England which he knew so infinitely better than did I ; he looked to me like what I imagined an English country gentleman of the best type should look. It seemed to me that this young man — he was then barely thirty-three — had been everywhere, seen everything, done everything, and read everything. He talked all the afternoon on all sorts of subjects. We three dined together, and then we went into the empty music-room where Skobeleff to his own pianoforte accompaniment sang songs in French, German, Russian, Kirghis, Italian, and English.

Engrossed in Skobeleff, I had scarcely noticed his companion, the dragoon-private in the shabby uniform. Yet, as MacGahan subsequently told me, he was no insignificant person. He was of the best blood of Russia — his name was Prince Tzeretleff. Later I knew him well. He had been secretary to Ignatieff while that diplomat was Russian ambassador at Constantinople and London. When the war broke out Tzeretleff had abandoned diplomacy; and panting for action yet knowing nothing of war, he had taken service as a private dragoon. Skobeleff had found him bivouacking in a swamp on the Danube side and had annexed him as his orderly. Such enthusiasm for active service was not uncommon in this war among the Russian nobility. Across the Danube in Bulgaria, I remember noticing a very venerable man riding as a sub-lieutenant in a cavalry regiment. This mature subaltern was seventy-three years of age, one of the Emperor's chamberlains, and having the relative rank of a full general; the bearer, too, of a historic name, for it was his father, Count Rostopchin, to whom the sad but grand task of burning Moscow was confided when Napoleon's legions were approaching the venerable capital. The old gentleman, destitute of military knowledge, had begged a lieutenant's commission in the Hussars and he had ridden every yard of the way since his regiment had crossed the Pruth. As for Prince Tzeretleff, he, as you will be told later, distinguished himself greatly throughout the war, but the long strain wrought on his brain and a few years ago he died insane.

MacGahan had broken a bone in his ankle by a fall from his horse before the campaign began, and after this accident, although he was still one of the most active of men, he constantly limped. He needed some rest, after taking which he intended to return to Braila to study the operations on the Russian left flank. I had ventured to mention to Skobeleff that a native of Giurgevo I was intimately acquainted with the course of the Danube from Hirsova up to Widdin; and he asked MacGahan to lend me to him for a time, since he thought I should be of use in some work he had before him. MacGahan consented, and I went down to Giurgevo with Skobeleff and Tzeretleff. I should have mentioned earlier that MacGahan had told me the peculiar situation of Skobeleff in the earlier part of this campaign. He was a most brilliant soldier and had distinguished himself greatly in Asia. His latest exploit was the subjection, after hard fighting, of the Turcoman province of Khokand — later named

Ferghana, — of which he was appointed Governor. After holding that position for a year his enemies — all leading men have enemies — presented an accusation to the Emperor against Skobeleff, charging him with cruelties to the native population and embezzlement of public moneys. When Skobeleff was informed of this accusation he hurried to St. Petersburg with the papers which he believed would clear him. The Czar had gone to Kischineff to join the army. Skobeleff followed him, but Alexander's ear had been poisoned against him and he was refused an audience. The Emperor, however, knew his daring character and allowed him to make the campaign as a sort of free-lance, with the nominal position of Chief of Staff to his father's division of Cossack cavalry.

When we reached Giurgevo, I found to my surprise that the headquarters of the elder Skobeleff were in my father's house; in this very house, boys, in which we are now sitting round the fire! And it was in this very room that I found the tough old warrior and my good father — who, thank God, is still with us — placidly drinking lager beer together, while Verestchagine the Russian artist was finishing one of his paintings. For the next few days Skobeleff treated me to a few days of about the most risky amusement that the most adventurous man need covet. His employment for the time was laying torpedoes in the bed of the Danube along with Commander Novikoff, to isolate the Turkish river ironclads within circumscribed bounds. This work was done by a number of steam launches, which had been brought overland from Russia and launched in the Danube. While we were laying a barricade of torpedoes across the river at Parapan above Rustchuk in the early morning of June 17th, an ironclad came up from Rustchuk and blazed at us with shrapnel. A torpedo boat was sent after her and she scuttled home, but every man in the torpedo boat was wounded; and then a Turkish battery on the bank opened fire on us. We separated, some of the launches running up stream, some down; ultimately they were all hauled out of water and carted to Karabia, about five miles above Nicopolis, where another barricade of monitors was established. Both of the Turkish ironclads at Nicopolis came out to attempt to hinder the operations, but were driven home; and never after did any Turkish armed craft leave the shelter of the fortresses. In all, two of the ironclads were sunk, two more were captured at the surrender of Nicopolis, and the other three remained at Rustchuk till the end of the war. At the time of the crossing the Russians had about 25 steam launches and torpedo boats on the river; later they had as many as 54, policing the river and guarding the torpedo barricades. Skobeleff seemed to me to have a positive delight in drawing the enemy's fire, and he went back to his quarters radiant if he had teased the Turks into expending half-a-dozen shells in blazing at his cockle-shell of a steam launch. But indeed it was rarely that we saw quarters. Sometimes we slept in the launch among the bulrushes; other nights we would bivouac on the bank by the fire of a Russian picket, whose soup we were glad to share.

CHAPTER II

THE CROSSING OF THE DANUBE

PRESENTLY came the general move of the Russians down into the vicinity of the great river in anticipation of the crossing. Skobeleff suddenly disappeared; it was my notion that he did not like to answer questions as to where that crossing was to be. I returned to Bucharest. MacGahan had gone back to Braila, where he witnessed Zimmermann's crossing of the lower Danube on June 22nd. I found Mr. Villiers in Bucharest. He was burning with anxiety to witness and sketch the upper crossing, but nobody would tell him anything about the probable locality. He asked me to accompany him as companion and interpreter; I readily agreed, for I was as eager as himself. Knowing where the torpedo barricades were laid, I could guess that the crossing must occur somewhere between Parapan and Karabia, but that was a pretty wide word. I had heard that three Russian army corps were in and near the convexity of the great bend between those two places, but that information did not help us much. The Russian chiefs were said to have been long in doubt. At first the point was to have been from Simnitza to Sistova; then the crossing was fixed to be from Turnu-Magurelle to Nicopolis, but there was a difficulty about pontoons, and at the last moment it turned out that the first decision was also the last.

But that we could not know at the time. Villiers had received a promise from General Dragomiroff, commanding the 14th division, 8th Corps, to take him with him when the crossing should occur. But where was General Dragomiroff? we asked in vain as we journeyed from Bucharest on the morning of the 24th. Village after village, all crammed with troops, from the railway westward to Alexandria, we searched in vain for the red flag indicating the quarters of a divisional commander. The Cossack Colonel Orloff was in a charming bivouac near the village of Nieru, but he would go no further than to admit that he believed there was a General Dragomiroff in the Russian army. A major at Putinein confessed that he knew where Dragomiroff was, but frankly told us he was compelled to decline imparting that knowledge to us or any one else. We respected his reserve, but all the same gnashed our teeth. We headed for Alexandria by the nearest of the two roads from Putinein. Suddenly we were in the midst of a vast pontoon train snugly stowed away out of sight in the defile. An officer peremptorily turned us back, informed us that the valley road was "*défendu pour cause,*" and told us that Dragomiroff might be dead and buried for anything he knew. In Alexandria was the staff of the Emperor; there, too, that of the Grand Duke Nicholas the Commander-in-Chief; and more grand dukes, more excellencies, and the staffs of half-a-score generals. Every house was billeted full to the doorstep and beyond. Cossacks crammed the petty shops and grumbled at the bad exchange for their paper roubles. There was no getting a seat at the only restaurant. Yet withal singular order and quietude prevailed and there

GRAND DUKE NICHOLAS.

was absolutely no drunkenness, vodka-lover as is the Russian soldier.

I saw Skobeleff in a crowd this evening, assisting a lady out of a carriage. Now, thought I, our difficulties were over; Skobeleff would be sure to tell us where was Dragomiroff and where the crossing was to be. He shook hands in his cordial way, and I asked him both the questions, explaining that I did so in the interest of his friend Villiers. "My dear fellow," replied Skobeleff, "I assure you I haven't the faintest idea! Good-evening!" and with that he hurried away. Tzeretleff assured us that he had never even heard of any crossing. At length a happy thought occurred to Villiers. He knew Count Schouvaloff, an aide-de-camp of the Emperor and nephew of "Uncle Peter" then Russian ambassador to England, and he appealed to him. The count said that Dragomiroff was unattainable, but that he would ask General Prince Mirski, commanding the twin division to Dragomiroff's in the 8th Corps, to be of use to the English artist. Villiers promptly waited on the prince, who told him that he was marching on the following day to a point thirty versts from Alexandria, to which point he would detail an orderly to escort Mr. Villiers and his companion. We did not in the least know whither we were going. Probably to Turnu-Magurelle, was Villiers' opinion; and it seemed plausible, for during the whole of the 24th had come the sound of a heavy cannonade from that direction. It continued throughout the two following days, no doubt misleading the Turks very considerably, not to speak of the correspondents with the Russian army.

On the morning of the 25th a soldier rode up to us as

we were mounting and told us in excellent English that he was commanded by Prince Mirski to act as our escort. Russian private soldiers are rarely conversant with English; yet this man judging by his uniform seemed nothing more than a "simple soldier"—an infantry man of the 1st regiment of the 9th division mounted on a nice little grey horse. He wore the white blouse of the private soldier with the red shoulder-straps of his regiment; a bayonet hung from his waistbelt, a carbine was slung on his back, and his loose trousers were tucked into his long boots. He talked to Mr. Villiers as we rode along, and the more he talked the more I wondered to find a private soldier who had visited every capital in Europe and who told Villiers that the Prince of Wales had proposed him for the Marlborough Club. At the top of the hill he drew from his holster-case a silver luncheon-box ornamented by a coat of arms, and offered us cognac and caviare sandwiches. Soon after we had remounted there was a parting of three roads, and our escort found himself in trouble. He followed first one road and then another, and finally owned that he was at fault. We had watched his growing bewilderment with some amusement, because he had evaded our question as to what place he was taking us. I knew the country thoroughly, and at length ventured to tell him so, adding that I could not put him straight unless I knew where he desired to go. He laughed and said that Lissa was his destination; whereupon I indicated the road and we rode on. Villiers then suggested that as we had found the road for him he might be so courteous as to tell us his name, which he promptly gave as "Prince Dolgorouki." He had been in the diplomatic service, but had thrown that up to serve as a private soldier during the war. He was only a private in name and in dress. He lived with Prince Mirski and, indeed, later in the campaign saved that commander's life.

We were guests of the prince during the 26th. He was extremely kind, but still we were kept in ignorance as to the whereabouts of the crossing. Late in the afternoon Skobeleff came up at a gallop. He halted when he saw Villiers, bade us saddle and come with him, and rode forward after exchanging a few words with Prince Mirski. It was not yet sundown when we reached Simnitza, in and around which was the whole of the 14th division commanded by General Dragomiroff, who was busy with the preparations for crossing during the night.

Opposite to Simnitza, the Roumanian town on the right bank of the Danube, is the town of Sistova, then Turkish, but now Bulgarian. Sistova stands high, above and in the hollows of a precipice overhanging the river. Downstream from the place for some two miles the Turkish bank is steep, in places quite precipitous; above the crags are slopes covered with gardens and vineyards, leading up to a bare ridge forming the sky-line. The precipice ends in a deep narrow depression leading up from a little cove formed by the affluence of a small stream. At the head of this valley was a small camp of Turkish soldiers, and above the camp, on the sky-line, was a battery of heavy guns. Between the cove and the town were several more pieces, and on the height just outside the town was a small earthwork armed with a few Krupp cannon. In the camp and in the town there was probably a brigade of Turkish soldiers, not more. All this, you will understand, was ascertained later after the Russians had crossed.

About Simnitza the Roumanian bank is high; but between it and the main Danube, which here flows close to the Turkish bank, was a broad tract in places wooded with low scrub, elsewhere partly of green meadow, partly of tenacious mud, the whole just emerging from inundation. This flat was cut off from Simnitza by a narrow branch of the river, so that it was really an island. A raised road and bridge leading from the town across the flats to the landing-place on the main Danube had been destroyed by the winter floods. The Danube between Simnitza and Sistova was at this time about 1,600 yards wide and had a very rapid flow. It was necessary for the Russians to gain access to the isolated flats by a pontoon bridge across the narrow arm. The Turkish bank overlooks the Roumanian, and it was therefore impossible to bring troops forward from Simnitza in daylight. The crossing, we were told, was to be in the nature of a surprise, and it was therefore necessary to postpone the forward movement until after nightfall. Dragomiroff's division had the honour of the advance, and it was expected to make a footing on the Turkish bank by daylight. Mirski with the other division was to make a night march and be at Simnitza in the early morning to support and follow the sister division. The Grand Duke Nicholas had announced that he would take no denial; the river had to be crossed on the night between the 26th and 27th, cost what it might. The waters might be reddened but they must be traversed.

With the darkness Dragomiroff began his dispositions.

The pontoons were launched in a creek above Simnitza, and were floated down the main stream to the point of embarkation. In all there were some two hundred pontoons, boats, and rafts, with four battalions of pontoniers to work them. Forty guns were placed in position on the northern bank of the main river, to cover the crossing and silence the enemy's guns. The division numbered about 15,000 men all told. The embarkation began about midnight, and about an hour later the first detachment of craft put out from the shore and rowed towards the little cove I have already mentioned. It was a strange, weird time. The darkness was so dense that Villiers and myself, close as we were, could scarcely see each other; and the opposite bank was only just to be discerned, looming black and dark up against the hardly less black and sullen sky. Stumbling forward through mud and over roots, we struck against something like a wall, yet the wall was soft and warm. It was a line of soldiers, silent and motionless till the time should come to move. Not a light was permitted, not even a cigar was allowed to be smoked. When men spoke at all it was in whispers, and there was only a soft hum of low talk, almost drowned in the gurgle of the Danube and broken often by the launching of a pontoon-boat. I could dimly discern General Dragomiroff, mud almost to the waist, directing the marshalling of the boats close to the water's edge. The stalwart linesmen of Yolchine's brigade were manning the boats as they were launched. We got, or rather took, a passage in one of the earlier boats which put out. The strong strokes of the sailors shot it out into the stream. We could faintly discern, across the broad swirl of waters, the crags of the

Turkish bank and the steep slope above. What if the Turks were there in force? A grim precipice yonder, to carry at the bayonet-point in the teeth of a determined enemy! And an enemy was there sure enough, and on the alert. There was a flash out of the gloom, and the near whistle and scream of a shell thrilled us as it passed over us and burst among the men in the willows behind us. Shell after shell followed — from due opposite, from higher up, and from the knoll above which could be vaguely traced the slim outline of a minaret. The shells were falling and bursting on the surface of the Danube. They splashed us with the spray they raised; their jagged splinters flew yelling by us. There was no shelter; we were to stand here on the pontoon, this densely-packed mass of men, and take what fortune Heaven might send us. The surface of the Danube, flecked with bursting shells, was flecked too with craft crowded to the gunwales. There was a crash, the splintering of wood and the riving of iron, there on our starboard quarter: a double pontoon laden with guns and gunners had been struck by a shell. It heaved heavily twice, then its stern rose out of the water; there were wild cries — a confused turmoil of men and horses struggling in the water; the guns sank and drowning men drifted by us on the current down to their death. From out the trees fringing the little cove for which we were heading there belched forth now volley after volley of musketry. Several men of our company were down ere our craft touched the Danube shore. As we tumbled out of our boat with the Turkish bullets whistling above our heads, the command was to take cover close to the shore. We squatted down in the thick glutinous slime under the low overhanging bank. Already dead and wounded men lay here thick among the living. Yolchine, the fiery little commander of the advance brigade, had his orders, it seemed, only to throw out skirmishers in the meantime, and he was in a white-heat of eagerness to be advancing in greater strength. Skobeleff had come across just at streak of dawn, and he too was burning to act; but it appeared that the orders were that nothing serious was to be attempted until General Dragomiroff himself should have arrived. He came about half-past four when it was almost full daylight, and he seemed to be for the moment in rather a hesitating mood. We were within hearing of the colloquy between him and Skobeleff — Yolchine had joined his skirmishers a little way up the valley. Dragomiroff was an old soldier, but he had never seen any fighting before this morning. He was evidently nervous, said he did not much like the look of things, expressed his belief that the Turks were in overwhelming strength, and remarked that as a surprise the movement was a failure. "What should we do, think you?" he asked of Skobeleff — "You have had much experience in actual warfare." Skobeleff's answer was short and to the point. "Attack without delay," he answered: "and let me lead!" In ten minutes more a man in a white coat was scrambling up the precipitous left bank of the Tekir-Dere valley, with a whole regiment of eager infantrymen at his back. During the summer campaign the Russian troops marched and camped in white canvas clothing, more or less dingy; but they always put on their uniform coats of dark cloth to fight in. One might imagine that they "dressed" for the fray as the duellists used to do;

but it was a more practical reason which actuated the Russian soldier. The Russian ambulance service was not very alert, and it was probable enough that wounded men might lie long before being removed. The cloth coats were warmer than the canvas blouses for wounded men lying out in the chilly night season. One of Skobeleff's many singularities was that he scented himself for a battle; and no matter what the weather he made it a point to go into action in a spotless white frock-coat with all his decorations on. He always rode white chargers. He would not have it that there was any swagger in this; his explanation was racy of the nature of the man. "I do this simply," said he once, "in order that my fellows can see where I am and know whither to follow." And all this stirring morning as Villiers and I watched the scene, from the moment that Skobeleff's order echoed from flank to flank —" Get up, brothers, and follow me!"— he was always being followed eagerly for the simple reason that he was always leading.

About 10 o'clock Dragomiroff's 2nd Brigade was across the river as well as his Rifle Brigade, and then he marched on Sistova, took it in reverse, silenced the Turkish batteries, and by 2 p.m. he entered the town. The Turkish troops, who had made a pretty stout resistance considering the disparity in strength, were in full retreat, some on Tirnova, some on Nicopolis. By nightfall there were 25,000 Russian soldiers on the Turkish bank and the passage of the Danube was assured. The business had not cost the Russians very serious losses. Their total casualties were about 820 officers and men; and of these over 600 belonged to the 1st Brigade, which under Yolchine and

Skobeleff had done the hard fighting east of the creek early in the morning. Among the slightly wounded was the young Grand Duke Nicholas Nicolaievitch, the son of the Grand Duke Nicholas Commander-in-Chief of the army.

Mr. Villiers had been sketching steadily under fire from daylight until near noon. We recrossed to Simnitza, where he made up his packet for the *Graphic* and sent me off with it on horseback to the Bucharest post-office, unless I could find a trustworthy messenger in Alexandria, in which case I was to return at once to Simnitza. On the way to Alexandria I met General Skobeleff senior, marching down on Simnitza at the head of his Cossack division. I stopped the old gentleman to tell him of the bravery and the safety of his gallant son. He was moved to tears, solemnly alighted from his horse, threw both arms round my neck and kissed me warmly on both cheeks with loud sobs. The good old general always wore a huge diamond ring on the thumb of his right hand, and I vividly remember how this ring kept scratching furrows in the back of my neck while its owner was hugging me with an emotion which I respected, but with a little of the effusiveness of which I would cheerfully have dispensed. When Skobeleff senior had in this friendly way blown his nose on most of the upper part of my person, he remounted and set off at a canter for Simnitza, eager to see and congratulate his son. They were rather a droll pair. There had recently been a little coolness between them; for the old gentleman was close-fisted, while the son was rather a spendthrift and had a cheerful habit of regarding his own and the paternal purse in the nature of a joint-stock concern — a view which Skobeleff senior did not wholly share. Both now and later the father, who had ambitions of his own, had a half-serious, half-comic jealousy of his son's rapid promotion and brilliant military reputation, and was drolly savage when before Plevna he found himself actually under that young chief's command. He was especially mad in a half-serious way when Michael threatened in mock solemnity to put papa under arrest unless he forked out the money to pay for the irreverent youth's outfit on promotion to lieutenant-general. But the father nevertheless had a great pride in the son, and I more than once noticed the shaggy veteran sitting silent while he watched in a sort of complacent contentment the rapid play of the younger man's handsome features as he conversed eagerly on some subject which exceptionally interested him.

At Alexandria I was fortunate enough to find a man on whom I could rely to carry Villiers' budget on to Bucharest. When I got back to Simnitza, in the evening I found the Skobeleffs at loggerheads, Villiers sitting with them and amused beyond measure at the colloquy. It appeared that no sooner had they greeted each other than Skobeleff junior zealously urged on his parent that he should swim his whole division of Cossacks across the Danube. The old man refused. It was another thing, he said, if there were an emergency and there were no other means of crossing; but for the moment there was no urgency and in a couple of days the bridge would be ready — and what, pray, was the use of a bridge if not to cross by? The son was very angry at the paternal refusal to fall in with his proposal. His contention was that Caucasian Cossacks were fit to go anywhere and do anything, and that this glorious opportunity for proving their capacities should not be lost. Since the father was obstinate the junior Skobeleff determined that on the following morning he would swim the Danube himself, along with his special henchman, a wild Kirghis lad whom he had found a child in his dead mother's lap after a Turkestan skirmish and had adopted — a quaint, profane imp in purple-and-white dimity who never left his master in the thickest of the fight, and who was perpetually getting flesh-wounds at which he laughed — and along also with his personal escort of three Cossack orderlies. He suggested further that I should be of the party, and, it struck me, seemed rather surprised when I consented. It was not much of an exploit for one who had been swimming the Danube almost as soon as he could walk, sometimes without a horse at all, sometimes in the saddle and as often as not hanging on by the tail. Early next morning the little company started. Skobeleff swam his first charger, a noble Turcoman chestnut which he had brought from Central Asia and which was later killed in the battle before Loftcha early in September. Skobeleff, the Kirghis, and myself got safely across. The three orderlies were found some days later on an island down-stream and were buried there. It was generally considered that the result proved that in this affair the father showed more sound sense than did the son. But then the father had made his career.

It was on the afternoon of that same day that for the first time I saw the late Czar — a man of commanding stature and fine soldierly bearing, but with a cast of melancholy in his handsome wistful face. He came across the Danube to visit and thank the troops which had achieved the passage. In front of the long massive line drawn up on the crest of the slope east of Sistova in waiting for the coming of the Great White Czar, stood three chiefs — Dragomiroff, the commander of the division with which was the honour of the crossing; Yolchine, the chief of the brigade which had led and which had borne the brunt of the fighting and the loss; and young Skobeleff, who had shown the way to all and sundry. The Czar embraced Dragomiroff in the Russian fashion and gave him the Cross of St. George; he shook hands with gallant little Yolchine and gave him too a St. George to add to the many decorations already on his breast. Then he came to Skobeleff and all men watched the scene intently, for it was notorious that Skobeleff was in disfavour; yet there was the belief that his conduct of the previous morning might well have dispelled that disfavour. For a moment Alexander hesitated as the two tall, proud, soldierly men confronted each other; one could trace in his features the struggle between prejudice and admiration. It was over in a minute — and the wrong way for Skobeleff. The Czar frowned, turned short on his heel, and strode resolutely away without a word or a gesture of notice. No doubt there was still in his memory the poison of the calumnies which had blackened in his eyes the character of the finest soldier in his realm. Skobeleff, for his part, bowed, flushed scarlet, then turned pale and set his teeth hard. It was a flagrant insult in the very face of the army, and a gross injustice; but Skobeleff took it in a proud silence that seemed to me very grand. Nor did I ever hear him allude to the slight. It was not long before he could afford to be magnanimous. This despite was done

ALEXANDER II.

/

him on the 28th of June. On the 4th September Skobeleff, after having heaped exploit upon exploit, led the assault on the Turkish position at Loftcha, and drove the enemy out of that strong place, not less by his splendid daring than by the skilfulness of the tactics he had devised. On the following night at his dinner-table at the Gorni-Studen headquarters, the Emperor stood up and bade the company pledge him in the toast of "Skobeleff, the hero of Loftcha!" It is not given to many men to earn a revenge so full and so grand as that.

CHAPTER III

GOURKO'S RAID ACROSS THE BALKANS

MACGAHAN turned up at Sistova a couple of days after the crossing of the Danube there. The Turkish inhabitants of that town had fled on the day of the crossing, with everything that they could carry away at short notice. Their Bulgarian townsfolk had pillaged them as they went away, then had stolen all portables left in the Turkish quarter, and had finally wrecked it almost into tinder; at the same time defiling the mosques in the most disgusting manner. Villiers and myself had temporarily established ourselves in what had been the harem of a Turkish gentleman, since the place had at least a roof and part of a floor. MacGahan joined us there, and told us that an expedition to cross the Balkans was being organised under the command of General Gourko and that he had obtained permission to accompany it. He desired that I should go with him, in case of opportunities which might offer for me to return to Bucharest with instalments of his correspondence. I regarded myself as in effect belonging to MacGahan, who had been my earliest friend and whom I greatly loved and honoured. Another expedition was soon to start eastward towards Bjela which Villiers wished to accompany; and it was finally arranged that I should go with the latter to Bjela, and then ride southward to Tirnova at the foot of the mountains, where I should find Gourko's command and rejoin MacGahan.

Bjela is a pretty little town on the river Jantra, about midway between Sistova and Rustchuk. I was acquainted with most of its inhabitants, and it pleased me to go there again after having been for some months away from kinsfolk and local friends. MacGahan, who had all the information he asked for from the Imperial headquarters, told us that two corps under the Cesarevich's command were to march eastward to cover the Russian left flank from the Danube to the Balkans against the great accumulation of Turkish troops known to be occupying the region of Eastern Bulgaria, spoken of as the "Quadrilateral" because at each of the four corners of this area there was a Turkish fortress. The advance of this movement consisted of the cavalry division of the 12th Corps. Its chief was General Baron Driesen; the hussar brigade was commanded by General Stahl von Holstein; the dragoon brigade by a delightful old gentleman, General Arnoldi, with whom Mr. Villiers struck up a prompt friendship since both were enthusiastic artists.

The twenty miles' ride between dusty and crowded Sistova and quiet rural Bjela was delightful, through a rich grassy country studded with farm-houses and snug villages nestling in the little hollows where the streams ran and all embowered in foliage. The mass of the population had probably been always Bulgarians, to whom belonged the fertile farms and pretty gardens. Now the whole region was Bulgarian pure and simple, since the Turkish inhabitants with rare exceptions had gone away bag and baggage, either southward across the Balkans or eastward into the Quadrilateral across the Lom. Towards evening — the day, I remember, was July 5th — the head of the cavalry column was in sight of the swift-flowing stream of the Jantra. At our feet lay the rich valley waving with golden barley, the fields intersected by the sparkling river on whose banks hung village after village; in the mouth of a little cross valley on the further side of the Jantra were seen the red-tiled roofs of Bjela half hidden among foliage. But we were not yet in Bjela. Overhanging the river on the further side was an upland plateau the face of which was quite precipitous, and there were hostile indications about the river-villages and on the uplands. A squadron galloped down the slope, dashed through the stream, and was just in time to cut down a few plundering Bashi-Bazouks. A detachment of dragoons dismounted, shouldered carbines, fixed bayonets, and followed General Arnoldi across the bridge and on to the plateau; the mass of the division followed presently. The inhabitants brought out bread and salt; the priest who bore the cross tendered it for Arnoldi to kiss, as the people stood by with bared heads and eager eyes. I was promptly recognised, and Villiers and myself were soon among friends in a pleasant room looking out into a pretty garden.

Villiers had been working half the night, and in the morning he sent me back to Sistova with his sketches to be forwarded to Bucharest. I could find no trustworthy messenger and so went on myself. Travelling continuously I returned to Bjela by the evening of the 7th, to find there a strange situation. On the previous night the little town had been looted severely by the troops of the nationality which proclaimed its mission to rescue the Bulgarians from the Turkish oppression. An infantry division had followed Driesen's cavalry, and about sundown of the 6th Bjela was full of Russian infantry stragglers. These broke into and plundered a baker's shop. Two officers who were sitting with Villiers hurried down and drove away the plunderers, beating them with the flats of their swords. They heard a tumult near by, and shrieks of women; and as the officers approached a number of soldiers laden with plunder jumped from windows. The town was ultimately cleared; but the precaution was neglected of sending protecting patrols down into it and so trouble recommenced.

About 1 a.m., Villiers sleeping in his room was roused by the noise of woodwork being shattered outside in the streets. Looking out he saw by the blazing billets carried torchwise by the soldiers, that plundering was going on apace to right and left. Women were shrieking, not because of any violence offered them but because of the ruin of their property. Soldiers were revelling in a wine-shop which had been broken open, and wine was running from the casks. Over the way a butcher's shop was being cleared out, soldiers tearing at the meat. The women of the house addressed themselves to Villiers, but he was powerless. All was licence, and for the time the Russian soldier, ordinarily quiet, orderly and respectful, was a dangerous person. Presently a knocking was heard below, and the people of the house said that soldiers were breaking into the cellar which opened from the street. By-and-by there was a wild tumult about the door and a hammering for admittance, which brought Villiers down to open it. And now came the comic element in a scene which was grim and ugly enough. The proverb that stolen goods do not prosper had come home to the Russian plunderers with unpleasant promptitude. As Villiers opened the door there stood four of them in the torchlight, clamouring wildly, with bottles in their hands, a strange blackness about their lips, and a curious pungent smell pervading the atmosphere. It seemed that the owner of the houses was a woollen-dyer who used vitriol in his business, and there were a number of bottles in his cellar containing that fluid. Of these the soldiers who had invaded the cellar knocked off the necks and proceeded to imbibe the contents. The vitriol was greatly diluted and the soldiers must have had cast-iron throats. As it was, their lips and mouths were discoloured, their clothes, hands and boots were burnt, and the men were half mad with rage and pain. They insisted that the house-master was a Turk who had stored a quantity of devils' drink in wine-bottles wherewithal to poison his Russian enemies. With wild cries and threats they forced bottles into his hands and swore he should drink. He resisted successfully but had his hands and clothes badly burned. Yet they had a certain sense of discipline and order left. They recognised the "correspondent" badge on Villiers' arm and did not lay hands on him.

After daybreak the work of plunder went on with greater vivacity than ever; and Villiers went up into the camp, found a colonel, and reported to him the state of the town. A few minutes later a strong picket was marching down into it with Villiers for guide. Its officers did their work thoroughly. Every marauder met on his way to the camp was closely searched. If he was carrying liquor, it was spilled; the officer thrashed him and then made him a prisoner. A strategic movement bagged the plunderers of a whole street, some thirty-five in number, all of whom were duly searched, thrashed, and made prisoners. A permanent guard was established in the town. It was said that the townspeople would receive compensation for the damage done; but all the same the first rift in the cordiality between the Bulgarians and Russians had occurred, and the mutual good feeling never was restored.

You remember that I have just spoken of the "correspondents' badge." At first, I believe, the idea was that they should wear a certain uniform. But, as I was told by MacGahan, they objected to that, chiefly, he understood, because the proposed uniform was a bright canary colour. Then they were numbered and served out each with a huge brass badge with a number stamped on it; the badge to be fastened on the left arm of the wearer above the elbow. This badge was exactly similar to that you may have seen in London, worn by the licenced messengers who stand at the corners of streets. The French correspondents' sense of the beautiful was, however, outraged by this unpicturesque distinguishing mark. So at their instance was substituted a more dainty style of brassard, with the Russian eagle in silver embroidery on a ground of yellow silk and the word "Correspondent" in Russian characters embroidered beneath the eagle. The written permission was engrossed on the back of a photograph of the correspondent to whom it was granted, which photograph was duly stamped in brown wax with the seal of the Commander-in-Chief's headquarters. A duplicate photograph was inserted in a "Correspondents' Album" kept by the commandant of the headquarters. Once I had an opportunity of seeing this album; there were about eighty photographs in it, and I am bound to own that it was not an overwhelming testimony to the good looks of the war-correspondent profession. MacGahan, who could do anything he liked at headquarters, got me a badge and a permission in the character of his assistant, and I never experienced any difficulty in going anywhere I chose while I had the brassard on my arm and the permission in my pocket.

Villiers proposed to remain with the 12th Corps which was slowly moving eastward towards Rustchuk — he could not tear himself away from his friend, old General Arnoldi. I was due to join MacGahan at Tirnova, and I rode from Bjela to the latter place on July 9th. I found Mac-Gahan comfortably quartered in the house of a Bulgarian widow in the main street of Tirnova. It was not his first visit to that town; he had been there the summer before when engaged in his "atrocities" investigations, and had then been the guest of the widow and her pretty daughter Maritza. His room, which I shared, was a spacious, lofty apartment on the first floor looking down on to the street; it had a divan along all its four sides, the floor was covered with fine old Eastern rugs, and in one corner was the shrine or *ikon* with a lamp constantly burning in front of it. Next morning Gourko's hussar brigade came prancing through the town, bands playing, colours flying, swords drawn; Prince Eugene of Leuchtenberg curveting at the head of his command, and every officer and every trooper making the most of himself in the eyes of the "good brothers" who were being rescued by the Russians from "Turkish tyranny." We were all looking out of window at the brave show, when MacGahan suddenly gave a great shout, dashed down into the street, and was presently seen to be dragging a hussar officer off his horse by main force. This feat being accomplished, the pair were visibly hugging each other with great warmth. A word to the colonel, a direction to a trooper to look after the officer's horse, and then MacGahan led his friend upstairs into the saloon, and introduced the hussar to the widow and her daughter. He certainly was one of the handsomest men I had ever seen — tall and square-shouldered, with a well-poised head, regular features, laughing blue eyes, and a winning smile. There were lines in his face which told of dissipation and a wild reckless life; but they did not greatly mar his attractiveness. It appeared that MacGahan and this Russian officer, whose name was Andreiovich, had been close comrades in the Khivan campaign of 1873. His career had been a strange one, or rather it would have been so in any other service than the Russian. Of a noble family, he had begun his military life in the Imperial Guards. Three years of St. Petersburg dissipation ruined him outright, and as was — and probably still is — the custom in regard to officers of the Guard who have "expended" themselves, he was sent to serve in the Army of Asia. For some misconduct he had been reduced to the ranks but had redeemed his position by an act of signal valour in the Khivan campaign; and later he had been permitted to return to Europe and take service in the hussar regiment in which he now commanded a troop. These details about Andreiovich MacGahan gave me later, and Andreiovich himself was very kind to me. Meanwhile, seated side by side on the divan, the old comrades affectionately recalled many reminiscences of their Khivan intimacy; but I noticed that the subject by no means wholly engrossed the sprightly Russian. Maritza, the widow's daughter, was a very pretty girl and she knew the fact very well. She sat over against MacGahan and Andreiovich, by her musical instrument, occasionally playing a note and looking very fascinating. By-and-by I shall have something to tell you, boys, about these two which I think will interest you. Pray remind me of Andreiovich and Maritza when I am speaking about the Schipka Pass, in case I should forget to narrate the outcome of this apparently chance meeting between these two young people.

General Gourko was a very fine soldier; he was an iron man, both physically and mentally. In the coldest night of the bitter Balkan winter he never wore a greatcoat, but rode in his frock-coat when every one on his staff was enveloped in heavy furs. He was sternness itself, and exacted much from his men. They respected him but did not greatly love him; Skobeleff's men held him in their heart of hearts. It may be said that Gourko was a Russian Wellington; Skobeleff a Russian Napoleon. Gourko, after the death of Alexander II., was made Governor-General of Poland, which post, I believe, he still retains. A couple of years ago I met a Polish gentleman in Jassy, and asked him how Gourko was held in Poland. "Poland," he replied, "has been governed in its time by some rare devils. She has known Mouravieff; she has been under the gouty hoof of Bariatinski; but Gourko is the most mercilessly savage Governor that any living Pole can remember." His command for this trans-Balkan expedition consisted of 8,000 infantry, 4,000 cavalry, and 32 guns. Starting from Sistova on the 3rd July he had marched slowly enough until he reached the vicinity of Tirnova on the 6th. He took the ancient capital of Bulgaria on the 7th with a brigade of cavalry and a single battery. His entire loss was two men. The Turkish garrison, numbering over 3,500 men, ran away in panic towards Osman Bazaar.

Gourko quitted Tirnova on the 12th, having been relieved by a division of the 8th Corps. He cut loose altogether, carrying his supplies on pack-horses and his only wheeled vehicles were his artillery. He was to find and to cross by an unfrequented pass over the Balkans; debouching from the mountains he was to move westward to Kezanlik and attack the Schipka Pass from the south on the 17th, on which day according to the preconcerted arrangement troops from Gabrova would co-operate with him by attacking it from the north. As I spoke both Bulgarian and Turkish like a native, MacGahan lent me to Prince Tzeretleff, to whom had been confided the whole of Gourko's intelligence department, the pioneering of roads, discovering passes, &c. While charged with this responsibility the Prince held the rank of Cossack sergeant, having been promoted from private and transferred from the dragoons to the Caucasian Cossacks. The roads to the foot of the Balkan acclivity were easy enough; to find the unfrequented pass, by the unexpected issue from which of Gourko's force all Turkey south of the Balkans would be suddenly surprised, that was the problem. It was curious that what the local people did not know, we found in Moltke's book describing the Russo-Turkish War of 1828-29. He refers to a pass between the Schipka and Slievno passes, but speaks of it as impracticable for an army. In reality there are at least three intermediate passes, but it seemed that the pass of which the Prince had heard of by the name of the Hainkioj Pass was probably the one to which Moltke referred; and it we proceeded to explore, disguising ourselves as Bulgarian peasants and tramping on foot. We had very unpromising accounts of this pass. It was rarely used either by Turks or Bulgarians because of its reputed difficulties and because it was said to be a haunt of brigands. But we found a man who had been through it with an ox-cart two years previously. Where an ox-cart could go, Tzeretleff argued, wheeled guns could go. We tramped along it, finding pleasant villages on the way and a hearty welcome everywhere. The village of Voinis, some 18 miles south of Tirnova, lay snug in the bosom of a delightful little valley. We sent back word that there was no difficulty so far, and went on 15 miles further to Parovci. The track hereabouts became rugged and wild and the gorge was narrow and extremely rough. But the pioneers were close behind us making the foot-trail into a more or less decent road. Parovci turned out a nest of brigands, but they proved not only friendly but zealous. Their chief, who claimed to be a prince and had swagger enough for an emperor,— the Czar sent him a decoration for his services,— was invaluable to us. The brigands went to work on a section of the track; when the troops presently passed they were most helpful and kept the secret of the advance inviolate. For eight miles beyond Parovci the gradient was almost precipitous and the guns had to be dragged by the infantry, the road being much too steep for horses to be of service. Beyond the summit the descent was both steep and rough to the mouth at Hainkioj, some 12 miles further on. We tramped down to within sight of the village of Hainkioj, where we saw, not half a mile distant, a Turkish camp which the local Bulgarians told us contained only two companies of Turkish regulars. Returning to Parovci, we were conveyed by our brigand-in-chief in his araba back to Voinis, around which village most of Gourko's force had gathered to wait for the word to advance. This was on the evening of the 12th. Next morning the column, in advance of which Tzeretleff and I trudged with an exhilarating sense of success, moved on to Parovci where our brigand-in-chief entertained Gourko and his staff in quite a sumptuous style. In the afternoon the head of the column crossed the divide and bivouacked a little way south of the summit. On the morning of the 14th General Rauch with 200 Cossacks surprised the little Turkish garrison in its camp just inside the mouth of the pass. The Turks ran off eastward to the village of Tvarditza at the southern mouth of the Elena Pass where there was also a garrison, and the joint forces, some 2,000 men in all, turned back and had a little fight with two Russian battalions which were following. In the end all the Turks went east to Slievno, and the Russians seized both camps full of arms and ammunition with very trivial loss.

Next day Gourko remained halted at Hainkioj, assembling his troops as they came out of the defile. The only accident which had occurred during the passage of the Balkans was on the steep descent from the summit where two guns with their teams rolled down into a ravine. Strange to tell, not a horse was injured and both guns and teams were recovered. But poor MacGahan had come to grief. I have already told you that he had been lame since before the war began; the injured ankle-joint had been encased in plaster-of-Paris and it was amazing how pluckily he limped about with this encumbrance. He would not be dissuaded from going with Gourko's adventurous expedition. Up in the pass his horse slid over a bank and fell on his rider, so that the half-set bone was broken again. But although now unable to put foot to ground, MacGahan resolutely declined to be invalided. He quietly had himself hoisted on to a gun-carriage and so contrived to go through the whole raid, in the course of which, helpless as he was, he was in the heart of several actions and once narrowly escaped falling into the hands of the Turks. He was all the same constantly cheery and full of quaint humour. He would not let me stay by him on the gun-carriage, which during the march to Kezanlik was mostly in the rear. He gave me his horse and bade me go forward with the Cossacks, see any fighting that occurred, and bring the details of it to him to be inserted in his correspondence. He told me, as I have already said, that there was a strong Turkish force on the summit of the Schipka Pass, and that it had been arranged that this position was to be attacked simultaneously on the 17th: on the north by troops advancing from Gabrova, and on the south by Gourko from the village of Schipka at the southern foot of the pass.

Gourko left part of his force to hold the mouth of the Hainkioj Pass in case he should have to retreat by that route; and on the morning of the 16th he started on the 20 miles' march to Schipka with about 8,000 men and 16 guns. At Uflani, about nine miles from Hainkioj, fighting began. Our road was barred by some 3,000 Turks posted in rear of a little stream. The Turks fought splendidly, that I will say for them. For hours they held their own in spite of Gourko's immensely greater strength. At length, assailed in front and their right flank at the same time turned, they fell back fighting as they retired. Gourko's loss was about 60 men. How obstinately the Turks had fought was proved by their losses: they left 400 dead and they must have suffered heavily in wounded. Their stubborn resistance wrecked the projected Russian combined operation which was to have come off on the 17th. Gourko's troops were so exhausted by their long fight that the force had to spend the night 10 miles short of Schipka. At daybreak of the 17th we were on the march again; but again, when about half-way, a Turkish force was found athwart our path, and although it was but three battalions strong the fighting lasted for several hours. By noon Gourko was in the beautiful village of Kezanlik, in the centre of the gardens where grow the roses from which the inhabitants distil the finest attar of roses in the world. So fatigued were the troops that the force did not reach the village of Schipka until sunset, when it was too late to attack the pass. The night was a regular orgie of plunder by the Cossacks and Bulgarians. Most of the Turks had already fled hurriedly from Kezanlik and Schipka, leaving the bulk of their belongings in their houses. Gourko had no provost-marshal and Prince Tzeretleff undertook the duty. The way he used his Cossack whip on the marauders was a caution. I saw him cut half-open with it the face of a Greek interpreter to one of the brigade commanders, a person who passed for a gentleman but whom the Prince found dividing spoil with Cossacks in a Turkish house.

In the course of the night Bulgarian spies who had crossed the Balkans by obscure footpaths brought in the tidings that Russian columns from Gabrova had attacked the Turkish positions in the pass on the previous day, and had been beaten back with heavy loss. MacGahan told me later that the business had been a muddle, for which Prince Mirsky, commanding the 9th division (8th Corps), was chiefly responsible. There was only a single regiment available — about 2,400 men with six guns. This force was split up into four distinct columns and the only wonder was, MacGahan said, that the Turks, who were entrenched on the summit of the Schipka in a strength of about 5,000 men with twelve guns, had not annihilated the weak Russian columns in detail. Gourko had not kept tryst, having lost a day as I have told you. MacGahan's opinion was that he should now wait until he had communicated with the Russians northward of the pass and arranged with them a combined operation; but, added he, Gourko was furious with anger and chagrin and was about to attack immediately single-handed.

He did so; but, with that contempt for the Turks which in the early days of the campaign was general in the Russian army, he attacked in very inadequate force. He might have struck with 5,000 men; instead of which he climbed the steep woodpaths and deployed against the Turkish positions with but two battalions of riflemen. The firing had barely begun when the Turks sent out a flag of truce. The "cease fire" was sounded on both sides; a number of Turkish officers followed the white flag and a party of Russian officers went forward to meet it. Prince Tzeretleff was of this party, and as I had been with him all the morning I now accompanied him. A short conversation in French was held between some of the Turkish and Russian officers, and the former spoke of capitulation. Suddenly the Turkish officers turned and hurried back to their lines; Turkish bugles sounded the "open fire" and a number of bullets came whistling by and over us. The Russian riflemen, excited by this treachery, charged the Turkish trenches with a rush and carried parts of the outer lines; but they were too weak to penetrate to the main works on St. Nicholas Hill and retired down the mountain into the village of Schipka.

Next day was full of sensation. The Russians were to attack the Turkish positions both from north and from south. But the Turks had determined to decamp; and to gain time for their withdrawal they practised a neat deception. The Pasha sent to Gourko a letter tendering his surrender. It was agreed that the capitulation should take place at noon. Meanwhile Gourko sent some stretcher-bearers up to the scene of the previous day's fighting, to bring in the wounded. Prince Tzeretleff took charge of these bearers and I went with him. To our intense surprise, as we reached the crest we found the Turkish position entirely abandoned. We advanced cautiously, fearing foul play. There were no wounded men to be carried down. On the hill-slope we found many Russian corpses headless and mutilated in a ghastly and abominable manner. Inside the main works, in front of where the Pasha's abandoned tent still stood, was a pile of Russian heads: the mouths of some open and black with the tongues cut out; other mouths filled in an atrocious manner. It was a ghastly sight. To this day I sometimes dream of it and awake shuddering.

Tzeretleff sent me back into Schipka, bidding me hurry, to tell the general of the disappearance of the Turks and of what sort of legacy they had left behind them. He scribbled a pencil-note on a leaf from his pocket-book, which I handed to the aide-de-camp on duty at the door of Gourko's headquarters. Presently I was called in and was examined by the general in a series of short abrupt questions, the answers to which he invariably cut short before they were finished. Suspecting treachery he had sent forward a reconnoitring party, which on its way up I had passed as I hurried down; and there now stood on the village street a couple of battalions which it had been intended to send in support of the reconnoitring party. Gourko called for his horse; his staff gathered around; and mounted on MacGahan's horse I took the liberty of joining the general's following. Gourko ordered the two battalions forward and himself started at a hard gallop, which very soon was checked by the steepness of the ascent. As we approached the position there was quite an outburst of surprise. The reconnoitring party had gone away to the left, presumably on the Turkish trail. But the camp, strangely, was full of men! Were the Turks still there? "No," shouted a staff officer; "look at the Russian flag!" And sure enough there was the double eagle floating from the staff on which yesterday we had seen the Crescent-banner flying.

Young Skobeleff met Gourko at the exterior trench. Yes, it was that wonderful man who had "nicked in" adroitly and made himself master of the Schipka Pass! — in the attempt to carry which every other officer had failed — Mirski, Darozhinsky, the young Grand Duke Nicholas, Gourko himself. Gourko looked very black and was grumpy in the extreme, while Skobeleff in the blandest manner told him of his good fortune. He had not a great deal to narrate for he had not fired a shot. He had quitted Gabrova in the early morning with two battalions of infantry, four guns, and some Cossacks; climbed the pass by the road, advanced successively from one line of trenches to another, finding each and all empty; and finally had attained to the heart of the Turkish position on the St. Nicholas Hill without encountering any defenders. He had arrived about an hour after I had been sent down into Schipka by Tzeretleff, and when Gourko came up his command were still shuddering and crossing themselves over the mutilated remains of their comrades.

MacGahan had accumulated a great budget of correspondence. I should have told you before that in the Russian army there was no postal service and that what postal service there had been in Bulgaria before the war had been broken up before the Russians crossed the Danube. The correspondents had thus either to be their own couriers back to the post-office at Bucharest, the nearest place where there was any certainty of quick and sure despatch, or in the alternative to have with them, or to find on the spot, persons who would serve as couriers. If they acted as their own couriers they had to leave the front and might miss important events. If, again, they hired couriers, many despatches went astray. The messenger having been paid in advance, might merely start and halt for copious raki in the next village — he might be honest but stupid; while it was possible, especially in the Balkans, that a messenger could not be found on any terms. Colonel Burnaby of *The Times* accompanied Gourko's raid, which lasted more than a month. During all that time he never found an opportunity for forwarding a single letter, and he brought back to Bucharest a pile of correspondence which by that time was out of date and of which I believe he had finally to make a book. I was by way of being MacGahan's secretary; but I thought it no discredit to act as courier for him, or when not required by him for any other gentleman of the English or American Press. I was in no want: I had my father's house to go to; but in the arrest of all commerce the firm of course was earning nothing. I was quite willing to make an honest living in the kind of service of which I have mentioned; indeed, for the sake of the adventurous life and the opportunities for seeing fighting and the inner as well as the outer life of warfare which my companionship with correspondents gave me, I should have been quite content to give my services without fee or reward. MacGahan desired that I should leave him at Schipka and hurry to Bucharest with his budget of correspondence. He intended remaining with Gourko, who, he had the belief, was determined to sweep on through the Tundja and Maritza valleys to the capture of Adrianople. The main Russian army would follow fast on Gourko's track now that the Balkans were conquered; and MacGahan did not in that event anticipate any difficulty in sending his correspondence back to the base from wherever he might be. I was very anxious to remain with him, because he was my first and best friend and also because of his lame condition which necessarily hampered him not a little; but it was my duty to obey him. General Skobeleff had told me that he was returning to Gabrova on the following day and that I might go with him. The same evening he came down into Schipka to visit MacGahan, and bidding adieu for the time to my kind master and friend I returned with the general to the camp on the top of the pass.

I may briefly summarise Gourko's subsequent adventures. He sent a detachment by way of Eski Zagha to strike the Yamboli railway about Karabunar, which after some resistance destroyed several miles of line, and then returned to Eski Zagha after having been within 70 miles of Adrianople. Another detachment rode to a station on the main Philippopolis railway, where it destroyed a stretch of line, cut the telegraph, and did other damage. Meanwhile, although Gourko did not know it, Suleiman Pasha's army, having been removed from Montenegro, was now being sent up from the sea-coast by train and was marching on Eski Zagha and Yeni Zagha. At both places Gourko fought desperate battles with inadequate forces against the Turkish army by this time numbering over 40,000 men, and finally was forced to retreat. No reinforcements could be sent to him, and he had to withdraw the mass of his troops through the Hainkioj Pass which he had always kept open, the Bulgarian Legion taking position to hold the Schipka Pass. His total losses had amounted to nearly 1,000 men. He had deservedly earned great distinction, and was the only Russian commander in the war who showed skill in handling cavalry.

Up on the summit of the Schipka early in the morning of the 20th a solemn funeral service was performed over the great trench in which were buried the mutilated Russian dead; and then Skobeleff's little force, which I accompanied, marched back to Gabrova. Buying a pony there, — the little horse cost me about an English pound and carried me well on many a long journey, — I rode fast to Sistova, crossed the Danube, and took train at Giurgevo for Bucharest. Here I found Villiers who had come back to post his sketches, which went to England by the same mail as carried MacGahan's budget.

CHAPTER IV

THE SECOND BATTLE OF PLEVNA

VILLIERS had been at the Imperial headquarters in Bjela, where General Ignatieff had told him that Osman Pasha was at Plevna with a great Turkish army; that he had already defeated a Russian force sent against him; and that he was about to be attacked again towards the end of July by a much stronger force under the command of General Krüdener. Ignatieff had given Villiers a letter of introduction to Prince Schahofskoy who was to co-operate with Krüdener, and he was just starting on his journey in the direction of Plevna. Villiers was very glad to have me with him because I knew the country and could interpret for him; and by the morning of the 27th we were once more on the Bulgarian side of the Danube, jogging through the grassy country on our way to Poradim, where we understood were Prince Schahofskoy's headquarters.

We found him there sure enough, but he was in a most boorish humour. He owned that Ignatieff's letter of introduction compelled him to receive the English artist; otherwise, he frankly said, he would have sent him away since he hated both correspondents and artists. With that he turned to his dinner which he ate in a ditch. We looked wistfully on for we were dying of hunger, but he offered us neither bite nor sup. We had become ravenous and had designs on Schahofskoy's leavings, when Villiers was accosted by General Count Protassoff-Bakmetieff, a grand old soldier who had been at the Salisbury Plain autumn manœuvres in 1872, when he and Villiers had met. The count took us to his tent and fed us with the best he had, talking about England as we ate. The battle was expected for the morrow. Count Protassoff told us that the whole Russian force allotted for the attack on Plevna amounted to about 30,000 infantry, with three brigades of cavalry and 160 guns. Krüdener would have a whole division in front, with a brigade in reserve. His field of action was on the right of the half-circle enclosing the Turkish positions. Schahofskoy's intended position was on the left, with two brigades in his fighting line and a third in reserve. Osman had entrenched himself strongly and was believed to be in greater strength than were the Russians. Krüdener, it was said, did not at all fancy the task laid upon him and had even remonstrated against the risk of failure which he apprehended; but he had received a peremptory and even angry order from the Commander-in-Chief to obey his instructions without delay and not bother the headquarters with any more querulous croaking. Krüdener was now said to be furious: he had the full belief that he would be beaten, — a belief which the event justified, — but he was resolved to put in his last man; and as regarded himself, he would rather prefer that he did not come out of the business alive. Indeed throughout the camp there was little of that excitement of anticipation which I had observed in the evening before the crossing of the Danube. The Russian officer, subject

GENERAL IGNATIEFF.

of a despot though he is, has a habit of speaking his mind; and before this battle the Grand Duke Nicholas' ears would have tingled had he heard the comments made upon him.

On the afternoon of the 29th there was a great council of war in Schahofskoy's Camp. Krüdener drove over from his own quarters and was greeted rather sourly by his brother corps-commander. The council was held in the farm-yard of a Bulgarian house. The generals and leading staff officers gathered into the wide clay-floored porch under the spreading roof, and there, standing in a group, pored over maps and no doubt discussed the plan of operations. The other officers stood about the farm-yard or sat on the shafts of waggons, waiting for the detailed instructions to them which would follow on the settlement of the general dispositions. It was a fine opportunity for studying the divers types of Russian officers. I am not good at description, as you young fellows have no doubt found out by this time: but Villiers had a rare faculty that way as well with his pen as with his pencil; indeed for the matter of that I used to think that he wrote better than he drew. I will read you a cutting from a letter of his to the *Graphic*, in which he touched off to the life the types of warriors forming the various groups. "Here one sees the grey-bearded, hard-faced old major, who without interest has fought his sturdy way up through the grades with long delays, much hard service, and many wounds. He was an ensign in the Crimea, and was afterwards forgotten for heaven knows how many years in some corner of the Caucasus. To-day he is only a major, but he has half-a-dozen decorations, and please God he will gain another to-morrow if he has the luck to stand up. He is as hard as nails and would probably prefer to live on biscuits and commissary beef rather than on champagne and French cookery. There is little in common between him and this tall, stately, grizzled general, an aide-de-camp of the Emperor: a man of the Court yet who has never forsworn the camp: a man who will discuss with you the relative merits of Patti and of Lucca; who has yachted in the Solent and stalked red-deer in the Highlands; who wears his decorations, too,—some of them earned in the forefront of the battle, others honorary distinctions as marks of Imperial favour. He can gallop, can this young Hussar in the blue and gold; he can cut the sword exercise and sing French *chansons;* he can pick up a bottle of champagne between his teeth and holding it there let the contents run down his throat; he would give his last cigarette either to a comrade or to a stranger like myself; he has the portraits of his mother and his *fiancée* in his bosom, and in his secret heart he has vowed to win the Cross of St. George to-morrow. I don't know that I quite like Lieutenant Brutokoff even yet. I know that the first time I met him I disliked him down to the ground. His manners—well, he had none to speak of; and his voice was a growl, with a hoarseness in it that came straight from schnapps. He did not look as if he washed frequently, and he was the sort of man who might give some colour to the myth that the Russian has not yet quite broken himself of the habit of breakfasting off tallow candles and train oil. But he turned out a good sort of a fellow on further acquaintance, and I never knew him without a tot in his flask and a hearty readiness to share it."

The Second Battle of Plevna

This same night young Skobeleff came galloping into the camp from Tirnova, with an order from the Grand Duke that Prince Schahofskoy should hand over to him the temporary command of the Brigade of Caucasian Cossacks comprised in the latter's command. The Prince, Skobeleff told us, was excessively angry, and told him he could go to the devil and take the brigade with him. It seemed he had threatened to put Skobeleff under arrest for what he called "impertinence," but in the end had thought better of it. Before sundown on the following day he had to own his obligation to Skobeleff for preserving him and his whole force from being destroyed.

The night between the 29th and 30th was spent with tents struck and horses saddled in readiness for the order to advance. It had rained all night and the morning was very dismal. Villiers had caught a chill and in common with everybody else we were wet through. In the drizzling dawn good General Protassoff sent us some coffee and eggs; he had no bread, he sent word, but the coffee and eggs were a great deal better than nothing. He himself came to us later, looking very grave. He told us that information from the reconnoitring parties had come in to the effect that the Turks in the Plevna position were in greater force than had been believed — that their strength was now estimated at 40,000 as against the Russian 30,000; and that the prospects were not favourable for an inferior force assailing a superior force in strong and prepared defensive positions. The advance began at 6 a.m., the cavalry leading. The Russian troops were in good heart. As the infantrymen went swinging past the general without knapsacks and carrying only greatcoats and haversacks, they cheered vigorously and seemed ready for anything. We rode alongside the leading regiment, and after a march of about two hours we were on the upland in front of Pelischat whence the Plevna region lay before us. We were near the apex of a great horseshoe closed in at the heel by a wooded valley running north and south in the centre of which, we were told, lay the town of Plevna; and as the clouds broke and the sky cleared we could discern above the encircling trees its white minarets on which the sunlight was glinting. On the long ridge forming the northern section of the horseshoe we could discern the tents of the Turkish camps, and towards the curve of it nearest us there lay the Gravitza redoubt, of which later the world was to hear much. Now it did not seem very formidable — merely a rough parallelogram the long sides of which lay north and south; all of defence that was visible consisting of a rough bank of earth with a ditch at its outer foot, a few guns here and there behind the earth-bank and a good many Turks inside the work. That northern ridge, we were told, was the section of the attack belonging to Krüdener. To our left front as we looked towards Plevna, there stretched a long ridge forming the southern edge of the great central horseshoe. It was spoken of as the ridge of Radischevo, the name taken from that of a village lying in the hollow behind it; and this ridge of Radischevo, we were told, was the ground allotted to Schahofskoy. When he should have moved forward and occupied it, the top of the horseshoe from which we now looked down would be denuded of troops, with the result that the attacks of Krüdener and Schahofskoy would have no link between them and would in effect be independent of each other. Protassoff spoke of this as a great evil, rendered necessary, however, by the wide circumference of the Turkish positions and the comparative weakness of the Russian forces.

The area enclosed within the ridges bounding the horseshoe was not a flat space. Along its centre from east to west rose a considerable elevation reaching back all the way to Plevna and rising as it approached the town. Disposed along the summit of this elevation which sloped downwards both to north and south, were Turkish earthwork redoubts; looking through his binocular Villiers noted three of these, which he said were full of men and were armed with guns. It was altogether a strange scene. The Turks out yonder in front of us seemed perfectly quiescent, save for working parties here and there in the trenches and about the parapets. Schahofskoy's people for the time played the part of curious and inoffensive spectators. Some of our gay young staff officers would have it that slow old Krüdener had not yet got out of bed. But Krüdener was wide awake and close at hand. It was the Turks who in effect told us so, for from where we were he was not discernible. At about half-past eight the guns of the Gravitza redoubt opened fire. We were not their mark — we were too far away. Smoke rose to the eastward of the redoubt and the cannon-thunder came to us on the wind. Krüdener's artillery were in action, playing all it knew on the Gravitza redoubt.

Villiers and I had remained behind to watch the beginning of this artillery duel while Schahofskoy's force was marching leftward into the deep valley behind the Radischevo ridge; and we now rode sharply to overtake our friends. All Schahofskoy's force was comfortably ensconced in this valley waiting for events. Further westward, beyond the termination of the Radischevo ridge and upon the Loftcha road, Skobeleff, we were told, was covering Schahofskoy's left. In the village of Radischevo it seemed that there were still some Turks. They were but a handful of marauding Bashi-Bazouks, against whom a company was sent. The Turks stood their ground and were promptly bayoneted to the great joy of the villagers who had suffered much at their hands. After a while, under the direction of Colonel Bischofskoy, the general's chief of staff, twenty-eight guns were brought up on to the crest of the Radischevo ridge and came into action. The infantry moved up closer towards the foot of the reverse slope and into the glades about the village, about which were falling many Turkish shells which had flown over the ridge crowned by the Russian artillery. It was strange to witness the peasant villagers standing in scared groups in front of their cottages, shuddering as the shells crashed into the place, while the children were playing about the dust-heaps without any sense of their danger. Villiers and I, leaving our horses in the village, dodged up to where the batteries were in action and lay down between two guns to watch the scene. From this point of vantage we looked right down into the Turkish positions. Several guns in the earthwork about a hamlet or farmhouse which seemed to us to be the most advanced of the Turkish works on the central elevation, were vigorously replying to the Russian cannonade. The work stood on a knoll with a smooth slope falling away from it in three directions, north, east, and south. On its right were more redoubts all the way to the edge of the broad valley in which the roofs and spires of Plevna sparkled in the sunshine from out a circle of verdure. The place had an aspect of serenity strangely contrasting with the turmoil of the cannon-fire raging in front of it. It seemed so near that a short ride might bring us there to the breakfast we needed so badly; but thousands of men were to die and many months were to elapse before the place was accessible to others than Turks. As we lay and watched, men were falling fast round us by their guns; for the elevated position was greatly exposed and the Turkish practice was most uncomfortably true.

Now and then a staff officer would come along and sit down for a little talk. I remember especially a chat with Count Keller, a German officer in the Russian service with whom Villiers had made acquaintance in Servia. Count Keller was not sanguine. Krüdener was still hammering away at the Gravitza redoubt with his cannon. Five hours Keller thought was rather too long for an artillery preparation. It was time that the old fellow was putting in his infantry, and ascertaining at the point of the bayonet whether that infernal earthwork was impregnable or not. Caution was all very well; but no battle was ever won by sheer artillery fire. What he, Keller, was afraid of was that Schahofskoy, who was already in a white-heat of impatience, should act rashly and attack with his infantry in advance of co-operation from the side of Krüdener. In that case there would be the mischief to pay; the whole force was too small for the work put upon it, and how much more so would be one-half of that force? "I fear it will be a *schlechtes Tag*, gentlemen!"

said the count, as he rose and descended the slope behind us.

Keller was but too right in his apprehension as to Schahofskoy's impatience. Presently that chief came up the slope from the village, to see for himself how things were going. As he reached the sky-line the Turks clearly marked the mounted group, and a regular hurricane of shell-fire was directed upon it. Three officers were killed on the spot. Schahofskoy promptly rolled out of the saddle, letting his horse take its chance, and crept forward into the little depression in which we were squatting. His eyes were blazing and his face was flushed, as he swore most vigorously in the strong colloquial Russian of the common soldier. He looked at his watch. It was a few minutes past two. No sign of Krüdener. Schahofskoy turned his head with an oath and shouted to Colonel Bischofskoy, his chief of staff, who was lying down behind him: "Bring up the 125th and 126th Regiments at once! Quick!" These were the two regiments belonging to the brigade of his own army corps which he had brought with him from Tirnova; the rest of his command, the 30th division belonging to the 4th Army Corps, had crossed the Danube only a few days previously and had never been in action. General Tchekoff, the gallant chief of the brigade, came up the slope at a canter and told the prince that his two regiments had been chafing at the forced inaction and were already on the advance. We heard them cheering as they came sweeping up the slope with a swift swinging step, marching in company columns the rifle companies leading. Just before reaching the crest the battalions deployed into line at the double and crossed it in this formation, breaking to pass through the intervals between the guns, quite impartially treading over Villiers and myself — the general had risen and was standing against a tree, saluting the men as they streamed past him. The artillery had heralded the advance of the infantry by an added rapidity of fire; as the latter passed the guns there was a brief cessation; and then the gunners fired all they knew as soon as the infantry had passed the crest and were descending the further slope, and while they were crossing the intervening hollow to the assault of the Turkish position. The Turkish shells crashed through the ranks as the regiments pressed forward, and men were already down in numbers; but the long undulating line pushed on through the undergrowth descent and then tramped steadily over the stubble fields below. No skirmishing line was thrown out in advance. The fighting line retained the formation for a time, till what with impatience and what with men falling it broke into a ragged spray of humanity and surged on swiftly, loosely, and with no close cohesion. It was a stern rush of fighting men on which we looked down with eyes fixed and intent — a helter-skelter of men impelled by a burning ardour to get forward and to come to close quarters with the enemy calmly firing on them there from behind the shelter of his earthworks. Conscious of their defective weapon, the Russians had been holding their fire while as yet at the long range where the Turkish rifles struck them down in sections; but now all along the face of the advancing infantrymen burst forth spurts and splashes of musketry fire. The jagged line sprang onward up the maize-covered slope, gradually assuming a concave formation. The Turkish position was neared; and now we held our breath. The roll of rifle-fire was incessant, but yet mastered by the fiercer and louder turmoil of the artillery above us—for we had gone halfway down the slope behind the fighting men. The ammunition waggons came tearing up to the cannon with fresh fuel for their fire. The guns redoubled the energy of their cannonade. The crackle of the musketry fire rose with a sharp continuous peal. The clamour of the cheering of the fighting men came back to us on the wind making the blood tingle with excitement. A village was blazing on the left. The supports that had been held back lying down on the reverse slope were now hurried over the brow and down the hither descent, up which wounded men were beginning to trickle past us limping and groaning. We could see the dead and the more severely wounded lying where they had fallen on the stubbles and amidst the maize. The living wave of fighting men was pouring over them ever on and on. The gallant gunners above us who had been standing to their work with a will on the shell-swept ridge, now at the word of command ceased firing all at once, lest they should hurt their own people now close to the Turkish trenches. The Turkish cannon-fire began to hesitate in that earthwork over against us there. More supports streamed down with a louder cheer into the Russian fighting line. Suddenly the disconnected men were drawing together. We could discern the officers signalling for the concentration by the waving of their swords. The distance was about 100 yards. There was a wild rush headed by the colonel of one of the regiments. The

Turks in the shelter-trench held their ground, firing steadily and with terrible effect into the advancing assailants. The colonel's horse went down, but the colonel was on his feet in a second and waving his sword led his men forward on foot. But only for a few paces: he staggered and fell — he was a dead man.

From where we sat we could hear the tempest-gust of wrath, half howl half yell, with which his men, bayonets at the charge, rushed to avenge their gallant dead chief. They were over the shelter-trench and over the parapet and down in among the Turks like an avalanche. Not many of the Turks in that redoubt got the chance to run away from the gleaming bayonets wielded by muscular Russian arms. The first redoubt was taken; only the Turks had got away ten guns, leaving but two in the Russian hands. But the Russian soldiers were not content with the capture of one Turkish redoubt. There was another near the one taken, nearer to Plevna and like the first also on the summit of the central elevation of which you will remember I have already spoken. Schahofskoy's soldiers, full of pride in their first success, went at this. The Russians are poor skirmishers — at least they were so in 1877; for aught I know they may have improved greatly since then. They used not to understand taking cover and suffered accordingly. Napoleon was wont to say of the Russian soldier that it was not enough to kill him; after having done so you had to go up and knock down the corpse. The men we were now watching went on in close order and deep formation against the terrible fire which the Turks poured into them. We could see through the telescope the latter standing behind their defences on which were laid their breech-loading rifles. Each man had a heap of cartridges by him and he slipped cartridge after cartridge into the breech with inconceivable rapidity, closing it with a turn of the hand, pulling the trigger, and then throwing open the breech again. It was all done with a minimum of exertion and no aim was taken; but there were three tiers of fire and the fire-zone must simply have been alive with bullets. Nevertheless the Russians bored their way through this solid torrent of missiles, carried one after another the intervening shelter-trenches, and steadily if more slowly fared forward.

Schahofskoy would no doubt have acted wisely if he had contented himself with holding the position his troops had captured so brilliantly until he should learn something of Krüdener's situation; but there was great temptation for him to prosecute his success. It is true that the already captured position was clearly not to be compared, whether in natural or artificial strength, with the strength of the second position, an isolated mamelon, as Kellar afterwards called it, with batteries on the swell behind it. But Schahofskoy determined to go for it and his troops were not the men to baulk him. The order "Forward!" was sent and was received with cheers. But the first impetus was out of the brave fellows. They hung a good deal in this second advance, exposing themselves recklessly and falling fast but not getting on with the original dash. Schahofskoy called up half of his reserve brigade and sent in the 118th Regiment (4th Corps) to take part in the attack; at the same time ordering two of his batteries into a position close by the already captured redoubt.

The new blood told at once. There was a brisk forward movement — the momentary hesitation all gone. The Turks evidently noticed the advent of the reinforcements. I observed through the glass a couple of Turkish officers on horseback standing behind the parapet of the second redoubt and watching the oncoming Russian masses. They rode away at a gallop and presently came back with what seemed a regiment of Turks at their horses' heels. I cannot tell you how the affair happened, so sudden and mixed-up were the swiftly-passing events; but all of a moment there was a final spurt of white smoke all along the lip of the Turkish parapet, through which were visible swarms of dark-clothed men scrambling over the ditch and up the outer slope of the work. On the crest of the parapet itself there was a short but sharp struggle. Then we saw a crowd of men in lighter blue in full flight across the great stretch of vineyard behind the redoubt. Schahofskoy's men had taken a full half-hour to accomplish the short distance between the two redoubts; but at the last they made quick work of it and now they were in possession of the second as well as of the first redoubt. The effort had cost them dear. The 126th Regiment had led both assaults: its losses, as afterwards ascertained, were 725 men killed and 1,247 wounded — a total loss of about 75 per cent. of its strength!

The Russians, then, at about half-past five of this bloody afternoon had carried two of the Turkish redoubts; but their tenure was very precarious. Krüdener made no sign. The Turks had not run far away from the second redoubt, about the northern and western faces of which they hung obstinately while the Turkish cannon from further rearward dropped shell after shell into it with extraordinary precision. About six o'clock the Turks pressed forward a heavy mass of infantry to its recapture. The defence was stubborn, but the Moslems were not to be denied; and spite of the stubborn Russian resistance, they re-occupied the redoubt by half-past six.

Then the Turks had it all their own way; for they brought forward great quantities of fresh troops, whereas Schahofskoy by seven o'clock had not a man in reserve. One of the brigades of the 30th division had early inclined to the left, heading in the direction where the spires of Plevna were visible. It was a rash movement, for the brigade was exposing a flank to the Turkish cannon in the central elevation; but the goal of Plevna was a keen temptation. There was no thoroughfare, however. They would not give up, and they could not succeed. They charged again and again till they could charge no more for sheer fatigue; and then the stubborn gallant fellows stood leaderless, for nearly all the officers were down, sternly waiting death there for want of leaders to march them back. The last reserves had been thrown in only to swell the slaughter. And then the ammunition failed, for the carts had been left far in the rear; and all hope died out of the heart of the most sanguine as the sun sank in lurid glory behind the blood-stained and smoke-mantled field.

The Turks struck without stint. They had the upper hand and were clearly determined to show that they knew how to make the most of it. Through the dusk they advanced in swarms into their original first position, and recaptured their two guns which the Russians had taken in their first assault but which they had found no opportunity to withdraw. Turkish shells now again began to whistle and yell over the Radischevo ridge and to crash into the village behind, by this time crammed with wounded men. The streams of wounded were incessant. The badly wounded lay where they fell and were butchered ruthlessly by the Turkish irregulars, who swarmed over the battle-field and smote and spared not. We saw them at their devilry when the moon rose; and in the hot still night-air we could hear, and shuddered as we heard, the shrieks of pain, the futile entreaties for mercy, and the yells of blood-thirsty fanatical triumph.

The Russian defeat was complete. The remains of the army came sullenly back — companies that had gone down 200 strong returning by fives and tens. For three hours there had been a steady current of wounded men up from out of the battle to the reverse slope of the Radischevo ridge which Schahofskoy still held on to grimly — back into comparative safety. All around us the air was heavy with the low moaning of the wounded who had cast themselves down behind us to gain relief from the agony of motion. A crowd of maimed wretches had gathered around the fountain at the foot of the slope, craving with a longing which you may thank God you will never know for a few drops of the scanty water.

In this dreadful hour I could not but admire Schahofskoy. In the crisis of the fighting he had been close to us and Villiers had made a sketch of him as he stood with set face and terrible eager eyes, the working of his lips and fingers belying his forced composure. Now that the day was lost beyond remedy he was cool and resolute. To protect his wounded and rally what remained of his force, he was determined to hold the ridge to the last extremity. He ordered his bugler to sound the "Assembly." Men gathered to the sound singly and by twos and threes, many bleeding from flesh-wounds yet willing still to fight on. But it was barely a company that came together; it seemed as if the rest of the army was quite dispersed. The company was disposed along the ridge in open order to show a semblance of force against the enemy. But the numbers were too scanty to afford even a pretence of covering the front. "Gentlemen," said the general to his staff, "we and the escort must take part in holding the front; these poor wounded must not be abandoned!" Through the growing darkness one could watch the streaks of flame fore-shortened close below us; and nerves tried by a long day of foodlessness, excitement, fatigue, and constant exposure to danger, quivered under the prolonged tension of endurance as the throbbing hum of the bullets sped through or over the straggling line. The Turks had early got our range, and we could watch the flash of flame over against us and then harken to the scream of the shell as it tore by us. Schahofskoy still hoped that belated troops would come back out of the Valley of the Shadow of Death down below us; but he was disappointed. Meanwhile the ambulance work was going on apace. The wounded were being carried back from the reverse slope into the comparative safety of the village in the valley behind — merely a comparative safety, for the shells reached it freely.

Cavalry was brought up to line the ridge and cover the village thronged by the wounded; and about nine o'clock

Schahofskoy and his staff quitted the front, threading their way through the prostrate wounded who still lay thick on the reverse slope. I joined the party at the invitation of the general's chief of staff. He was anxious that Villiers also should accompany the headquarters; but I had to tell him that I did not know where Villiers was. In the confusion of the dusk he and I had lost each other. He was ill and faint; the strain of excitement and the sight of the slaughter had sickened him. I searched for him without cessation, — along the ridge, on the slope, and down in the teeming village, — but with no success. He was leading his pony when we were whirled asunder; and I thought it possible that he might have ridden back to Poradim, intending to sleep there. I could do no more, and was fain to go away from the environment of blood and death with good-natured and friendly Colonel Bischofskoy. As we rode at a walking pace through the moonlight a cynical young lieutenant came alongside me and remarked in an undertone: "We are following a general who has lost his army going in search of an army which has lost its general who now, to make the day's loss complete, has lost his way." The last statement, at all events, was true enough. Nobody knew in the least where we were. The Cossack escort constantly brought in alarms of Bashi-Bazouks and Tcherkesses swarming in upon the scattered and retreating troops. At length about one in the morning we turned into a harvest-field, and making beds of the reaped corn commander and Cossack rested under the stars. But we were not even then allowed to have our sleep out. Before sunrise an alarm came that the Bashi-Bazouks were upon us, and we had to rouse and tramp away.

At Pelischat, where we found ourselves in the morning, some troops were rallying and news came in to the general. Krüdener, it seemed, had fought hard although with no more success than Schahofskoy. His final attack on the Gravitza redoubt was made at sunset with his whole force and with great desperation — a general officer was killed within 100 yards of the redoubt. His artillery remained in action all night, the infantry gradually withdrawing under its cover. Krüdener's messenger owned quite frankly that their attack had been a total failure: "Judging from appearances," he added, "your people have fared no better!" The only honours of the day rested with Skobeleff. With the Caucasian Cossack brigade and a single battalion of infantry he had got close up to Plevna and opened fire on the place with his four guns. Of course he was driven back, but he had made a successful diversion in favour of Schahofskoy; and all through the day and into the night he maintained an unequal fight, and successfully hindered the Turks from occupying a hill from which they could have taken Schahofskoy in flank and destroyed his force. Skobeleff had been able even to carry off his wounded; and although his losses had been extremely heavy he had made good his retreat, and here he was at Pelischat in great spirits, and offering to Schahofskoy to go back and seize the Radischevo ridge that same day and hold it until further orders. Schahofskoy growled at the cheery man like a bear with a sore head. Skobeleff took the rebuff quite complacently and asked Schahofskoy for orders. The prince sullenly told him to go where he chose and get killed in any way he might prefer. "Thanks, Excellency," returned Skobeleff, as he turned on his heel; "I shall have all the more freedom to do a stroke of independent business on my own account."

The Russian loss at Plevna on the 30th July, I was told afterwards, amounted to 7,300 men in a total of 30,000 engaged, of which number 2,400 were killed in action or slaughtered as they lay wounded. This latter fate had begun to perturb the Russian soldiers; for my part I was surprised that they continued to take the risk so resolutely. For when a man was once down there was no longer any hope for him; he was in effect a dead man already. Indeed his situation was worse even than that. A dead man is dead and out of his pain; but the poor fellow brought to the ground by such a comparative trifle as a broken ankle, unless he adopted the expedient of putting himself to death then and there as many did, had to lie and await the torture and mutilation which he would certainly have to endure before some Turk, more humane than his fellows, should give him the death-stab. I have watched the ghouls at their work, coming out with a rush and a shout after the fight, and robbing, mutilating and murdering with a hellish zest. I should tell you, however, that it was not the Turkish regular soldiers who committed those atrocities, but the Bashi-Bazouks and Tcherkesses who hung about the Ottoman armies under subjection to no discipline and left to their own devices. The responsibility for the actions of those murdering savages nevertheless attached itself to Turkish commanders, who could have prevented their practices had they cared to do so and who could not but have been aware of the barbarities they habitually committed.

Neither at Pelischat nor at Poradim could I get any tidings of Villiers. An officer told me that he had last seen him on the previous evening in the village of Radischevo, attending to the wounded. Then there came in the dreadful intelligence that in the night the Bashi-Bazouks had got into that village, where they had fallen upon the wounded and butchered them without mercy. In the hope of meeting Villiers or learning something of him, I rode back to so near Radischevo that I was fired upon by Turks on the outskirts of the village. In that direction, then, I could do no more. My last hope was that he might be ahead of me on his way to Bucharest, making for the post with the sketches with which he had filled his book on the day before; and I turned my pony's head towards the Danube. At Sistova, still no tidings of him, nor in Simnitza. The station-master at Giurgevo, who knew him well, assured me that had Villiers passed through he would certainly have seen him. I really brought the tidings of the Russian defeat to Bucharest, although rumours of it had got there before my arrival. MacGahan I found in Bucharest back from Gourko's raid, very lame and quite worn out with hard work and poor fare. He was, indeed, quite prostrate for the time, and I was greatly concerned about his condition. But ill as he was, he had no thought but of his duty to his paper. He took me into his room and asked me to write down some account of the battle of the 30th to be telegraphed to the *Daily News*. I told him that was quite above my powers; but that if he liked I would tell him by word of mouth everything that I could recollect and that he could write out my narrative in his own style. I believe

I talked to him for a couple of hours, he making a note now and then; by the evening he had written what seemed to me sufficient to fill a whole newspaper. Then he took a cab and drove to the telegraph office with his budget. In ten minutes he was back again. It was the only time I ever saw MacGahan in a passion. It seemed that in the Bucharest telegraph office there was a Russian "censor" who read all the messages that were sent in and stopped such as he did not approve of. When MacGahan brought him the account of the defeat which he had put together from my disconnected narrative, the "censor" refused even to look at it. "Not a word to be despatched about any Russian mishap!"—that was his short and firm ultimatum. So MacGahan brought back his sheets in great disgust.

"By George!" he suddenly exclaimed, "I had quite forgotten. I know how we can do the trick after all!" Then he told me a curious thing. He and his colleagues of the *Daily News* quite early in the campaign had foreseen that occasions might occur when the "censor" in Bucharest might refuse to sanction the transmission of intelligence adverse to the Russian cause. To meet such a contingency they had established a pony-express across the Carpathians from Ploiesti in Roumania to Cronstadt in Transylvania, a province of the Austrian Empire. That service had never been used, no occasion for it having arisen; but it was still maintained, and Mr. Cross, a *Daily News* man who always remained in Bucharest to receive despatches from the front and forward them, sent money weekly to meet the expenses of the service. MacGahan now bethought himself of this expedient; and "Carnegie," said he, "you must start at once by train to Ploiesti, and thence take the pony-express over the Balkans." I was not half rested and was full of anxiety about Villiers; but I sort of belonged to MacGahan and he could not ask anything of me that I would not willingly undertake.

There was a train from Bucharest in an hour. I ate something, pocketed the despatch, put on a waistbelt with a number of ducats in it to defray the expense of the journey and of the telegram, bade good-bye to MacGahan and started. I was in Ploiesti by midnight, took a carriage there for the first 10 miles towards the mountains, found the successive ponies just where I had been told by Cross that they were, kept each in succession at a steady canter during its 10 miles' stage, and reached the Cronstadt telegraph office at eight o'clock of August 3rd. I handed in the budget, showed the telegraph superintendent the gold I had to pay for it, and then went to breakfast. When I returned the message was already counted — it was several thousand words long, and its transmission was well begun. MacGahan had written very legibly, and the operator, who was a German, fortunately knew some English and said he found no difficulty in the manuscript. So I paid, — the sum was about £400, — made the operator a present of a box of cigars, tipped the superintendent handsomely, and by eleven was fairly on the road back to Bucharest. I believe I knocked up two or three of the ponies, but MacGahan said the *Daily News* didn't mind that. Anyhow, I was by his bedside in Bucharest before midnight, having ridden 160 miles, made the two railway journeys and undergone considerable delays, in twenty-eight hours. "Good business!" said MacGahan, as he turned on his pillow and went to sleep. I followed his example after having eaten a hearty supper. I was young, keen, enterprising, and weighed under ten stone in those days, my lads; it was the light weight that enabled me to cover 160 miles in eighteen hours on rats of ponies not worth a couple of pounds apiece.

But there was still no news of Villiers, and tired as I was my sleep was broken by apprehensions about him. Next day we were sitting at luncheon in the hotel garden, — Colonel Wellesley, Mr. Kingston, MacGahan, and myself, — and the talk was of Villiers, because we all knew him, and to know Villiers was to love him. I wonder whether that good fellow and pleasant companion is alive now? — if he is I am sure that he cannot have lost the memory of those adventurous days of 1877 when he used to sit in the bullet-fire and placidly sketch. I think he was about the coolest under fire of all the cool men I knew in those days, and they were many; yet, although he did not mind a big dog, he was always in mortal terror of a little one. He owned to me once that he broke off an engagement with a charming girl because she would not send her pug out of the room when he came to pay her a call!

It was a dreary meal. The question discussed was, whether the time had or had not yet come when a telegram telling of Villiers' disappearance in ominous circumstances should be sent to his parents, whose address I happened to know from having carried letters to post addressed to them. Colonel Mansfield, the British Minister to the Roumanian Court, joined the group, and his advice having been asked he judged it best that another day should be allowed to pass. Suddenly, just as Colonel Mansfield was speaking, I heard a familiar voice call out: "Waiter! quick! Something to eat; I'm beastly hungry!"

It was Villiers! We all jumped up and crowded around him, asking him questions and making snatches at his hand. "What's the row with you fellows?" he asked with surprise. "I know my nose is twice its proper size and there is no skin on it; but that is the sun. I may be rather a holy show, what with dirt, and sun, and dust; but I'm blessed if I know why you keep staring at me and grabbing at me!" He became pacified when he found that we were not amusing ourselves at his expense, but he insisted on eating and drinking before he recounted his experiences.

Villiers had helped the surgeons in Radischevo until he grew tired, and he was asleep in an ambulance waggon, to which he had fastened his pony, when the Bashi-Bazouks entered the village. A young surgeon had sprung on the box in the very nick of time and had driven the vehicle out of their reach just as the Bashi-Bazouks came yelling after it brandishing their knives. It was a very near shave — a "close call" was MacGahan's expression — the quick action of the young surgeon had unquestionably saved Villiers' life. He had come out safe from that pandemonium of rapine and slaughter, and had got to Bucharest in time to shout for food and to save us the task of telegraphing to his parents apprehensions which would have plunged them into grief.

CHAPTER V

DREARY DAYS

AFTER the battle of Plevna of July 30th, I should tell you that the Russian advance in Bulgaria was brought to a standstill. It became certain that the 200,000 men with whom the invasion was originally begun — and, indeed, it was said that a considerable proportion of that 200,000 were soldiers only on paper — were inadequate to carry out the original plan of campaign. Turkish armies were on both of the Russian flanks. Five corps were engrossed in trying, not very successfully, to protect those flanks; one corps was away in the Dobrutscha; and the only remaining corps, the 8th, could not cross the Balkans and march on Constantinople single-handed. Since the campaign began the Russians had lost in killed and wounded about 15,000 men and unquestionably double that number of sick. Their total strength in the first week of August was probably, all told, about 120,000 infantry, 12,000 cavalry, and about 650 guns of all sorts. It was therefore decided to order up from Russia the Guard, two divisions of Grenadiers, four divisions of the Line, and one Cavalry division — in all about 120,000 men and 460 guns.

Meanwhile the Russians were to undertake no offensive operations, but were to remain as quiescent as their enemy would allow them to be. They held in Bulgaria a region from the Danube to the Balkans about 80 miles from north to south; from flank to flank about the same distance. On their right flank was Osman at Plevna with some 50,000 men; on their left flank Mehemet Ali with 65,000 men; beyond the Balkans and threatening to cross the mountains, Suleiman with 40,000 men. It was reckoned that the Turks had in the field nearly 200,000 men; and I have always wondered why, during this interval of paralysis which the Russians had to endure, the Turks did not combine to go in upon them and heave them bodily into the Danube. That they could have done this had the Turkish armies co-operated with each other and had possessed any enterprise, every Russian officer at the time ruefully admitted.

In this period of quietude, the idea occurred to Villiers of going to the Russian headquarters and making for his paper some portrait-groups of the most important persons of the Imperial suite. MacGahan was still invalided and he gave me permission to accompany Villiers. The Czar was now in Bjela. Villiers and I had been there before when the little town was yet clean and sweet, and when its inhabitants were comparatively guileless. Now things were very different. You could not look at a meal — and a bitter bad meal too — under a rouble; and it was well for us that we had brought Villiers' waggon and tent, for every hole and corner of Bjela was crammed. The streets were foul to a degree; the air was tainted thick and heavy with filth and rotting offal. The Great White Czar was in residence there; yet no one in authority took the trouble to set the lazy men of Bjela, who were doing nothing but get fat on their exactions, to the task of scavenging the stinking place.

The Emperor was living in the middle of the town, in the enclosed yard of a dismantled Turkish house which the Bulgarians had gutted when its occupants fled. A high wattled fence surrounded this yard, in which grew a few mangy willow-trees that afforded a trifling shade. The offices were in the battered Turkish house. The Emperor lived in two officers' tents communicating with each other by a canvas-screened alley-way, up in a corner of the yard under the willow-trees. In the centre of the yard was the large dining marquee, in which his Majesty joined at meals the officers of his suite and such of the foreign military attachés as were not in the headquarters of the Commander-in-Chief. He breakfasted alone in his own tent, where he worked all the morning with Miliutin the Minister of War; Ignatieff the diplomatist; Adlerberg the chamberlain of the palace and the Emperor's foster-brother, and other high officials who solicited interviews. From his camp in Bulgaria Alexander strove hard to administer the affairs of his huge empire whose capital was many hundred miles distant.

You will understand, my lads, that all those particulars, which may perhaps interest you as telling you how simply an Emperor may live on campaign, I only gathered at second-hand from people who knew personally of their correctness. By-and-by, though, you will find me telling you of an actual interview between the Great White Czar and my insignificant self.

To continue. Luncheon was served in the great marquee, and all the suite were wont to gather in the yard for conversation a short time in advance of the precise hour. The Emperor came out from his own private tent, shaking hands with the nearest members of the suite and greeting always the foreign attachés as he passed into the marquee. His seat was in the centre of the right-hand side of the table, usually with old General Suwaroff on one side of him and General Miliutin on the other, the foreign attachés sitting opposite. The greatest simplicity prevailed in the fare served at the Imperial table; three courses were the rule at dinner, and champagne was given only on exceptional occasions. When the time for coffee came the Emperor gave the signal for smoking, and immediately the marquee became filled with a cloud of cigarette smoke. He was wont to talk freely at table, directing most of his conversation to the foreign officers opposite to him, and very often, especially when addressing Colonel Wellesley, the British military attaché, his tone was that of what you and I, not being emperors, might call "chaff."

No elaborate precautions to outward seeming were taken for the Emperor's safety, living here as he was in the midst of a curiously-mixed population of wretched Bulgarians and prowling Turks — for all the Turks had not quitted Bjela. His only escort consisted of a handful of the Cossacks of the Imperial Guard, on duty at the entrance of the yard in which he lived. He drove out every day attended by an escort of a dozen of these; and he would make the round on foot of the hospitals in the environs of the little town accompanied by a single companion, a Cossack following a little way in rear. He spent many an hour in talking with the poor ailing fellows in the miserable apologies for hospitals which the half-wrecked Turkish houses afforded; and they used to claim that his kindly presence did them more good than all the attentions of the military doctors. Once during a drive Alexander's eye fell upon a wretched company of Turkish fugitives among whom were many women and children, lurking in a wood. He at once alighted and went among them, and by the assurance of his protection he succeeded in prevailing on them to return to their homes in Bjela, where he had them supplied with rations until they were able to do something for themselves.

MacGahan, the Republican citizen, had a great respect and pity for the Emperor who was an absolute monarch. He once wrote a character-sketch of Alexander which struck me so much that I copied it and have preserved it to this day. Pray, Tom, hand me the writing-case from that table. Yes, here it is. It will not weary you for it is not long. You will of course understand that the Emperor survived MacGahan: " In many respects Alexander II. is a grand man. He is absolutely free from that corruption which is the blackest curse of Russia, and whose taint is on the nearest relatives of the Great White Czar. He has the purest aspirations to do his loyal duty towards the huge empire over which he rules, and he never spares himself in toilsome work. He takes few pleasures; the melancholy of his position has made sombre his features and darkened for him much of the pleasure of life. For he has the bitterest consciousness of the abuses that are gradually alienating the subjects who had been wont, in their hearts as on their lips, to couple the names of 'God and the Czar.' He knows how the great nation writhes and groans; and he, absolute despot though he is, writhes and groans no less in the realisation of his powerlessness to cure the evil. For although he is honest and sincerely well-intentioned, there is a fatal weakness in the nature of Alexander II. True, he began his reign with an act of masterfulness; but, later, unworthy favourites have gained his ear, his family has compassed him about; the whole vast *vis inertiæ* of immemorial rottenness and obstructive officialism has lain and lies doggedly across the hard path of reform. Alexander's aspirations are powerless to overcome the dense, solid obstacle; and the consciousness of his impotence, with the no less disquieting consciousness that it does behove him to cleanse the Augean stable of the Russian State, has embittered the later years of his life."

I hated this stay of ours in Bjela, and longed to get away from the poisonous place. Villiers was down with malarial fever in our tent on the upland — we had not ventured to take up quarters in the town in every spare corner of which lay putrefying dead horses and the entrails of slaughtered cattle. The natives did not seem to be affected by the tainted air, but the illness it produced affected the Russian soldiers very much, already predisposed to sickness as they were by over-fatigue and bad food. The most serious disorder from this cause manifested itself, however, among the members of the Emperor's suite. General Ignatieff was dangerously ill of gastric fever; old Prince Galitzen very nearly died of the same disease, and every one of the Emperor's five general-adjutants were disabled from duty. The Emperor himself never wholly recovered the effects of this long stay of his among the nastinesses of Bjela.

There was a general thrill of joy and relief when on August 10th the order was issued for the Imperial headquarters to leave Bjela and move about 20 miles westward, to a village named Gorni-Studen, nearly equidistant between Bjela and Poradim and about half-way between the Danube at Sistova where the bridges were — there were two now — and Tirnova up among the foot-hills of the Balkans. Gorni-Studen was a very small place, rather a hamlet than a village, but it stood high; and on a hill-top was a fairly good house which had belonged to a Turkish gentleman now a fugitive and which became the residence of the Emperor for several weeks. Most of his suite lived in tents on the slope and in a pleasant garden a little way off. In this garden a Bucharest hotel-keeper set up a restaurant in a marquee, where he poisoned his compulsory customers with abominable fare at a tariff which made my hair stand on end when I once ventured in and called for a modest chop. Villiers and I did not contribute much to swell the plunder of the headquarter caterer. In the well of the waggon a good supply of tinned food had been stored before leaving Bucharest. Villiers had a very good, although rather stupid, servant, who could cook very well and who had a wonderful faculty for finding poultry and lambs in a country where all supplies were believed to have been exhausted.

At Gorni-Studen Villiers recovered his health and had great success with his portraiture. The Emperor himself gave him a sitting for a sketch, and he "did" Ignatieff; General Stroukoff, one of the handsomest and bravest officers in the Russian army; Orloff the Cossack chief;

the Montenegrin colonel with the impossible name — a handsome giant with a moustache a foot long and a uniform encrusted with silver ornaments; Colonel Wellesley the British military attaché and many others. On the hill-top opposite to the Emperor's hill were the headquarters of his brother the Grand Duke Nicholas the Commander-in-Chief. He and his people lived in tents very comfortably. Among his staff officers was a handsome young fellow who was afterwards to make a great name and attain a high position, and yet later to abandon the advantage he had so gallantly and skilfully attained, to make an unequal marriage which consigned him to private life, and to die in early middle-age after a remarkable career. He was then simply Colonel Prince Alexander of Battenberg, but two years later Europe knew the young man as Prince Alexander of Bulgaria; and his skilful generalship and personal heroism at Slivnitza were among the surprises of the time. Young as you are, boys, you must be familiar with the career of Prince Alexander, whose subjects in a sense you and I were from 1879 until he was kidnapped by traitors in August, 1886, and to our sorrow held that honour and duty called on him to abdicate.

CHAPTER VI

THE CRISIS OF THE SCHIPKA PASS

IT was on the early morning of August 22nd that General Ignatieff came into our tent, and informed Villiers that Suleiman Pasha was "hammering with forty battalions at the Schipka Pass, the garrison of which was only twenty companies strong." This was great news: there had been no fighting to speak of for three weeks, and the *Graphic* had written to Villiers that it did not care for more portraits but was anxious for more battle pictures. We left waggon and tent under the charge of the driver in the garden on the Gorni-Studen hill, and were on horseback within twenty minutes after Ignatieff had left the tent. Our ponies were fresh, the weather was not unpleasantly warm, the road was fair and through a pretty country, and we were hurrying to see important and perhaps decisive fighting. We regarded ourselves as in rare luck, blessed Ignatieff, and cantered on in exuberant spirits.

Leaving Tirnova well on the left we set our faces towards Gabrova, the town lying at the northern foot of the Schipka Pass. For great part of the way we abandoned the high road with its clouds of dust and long trains of creaking provision-waggons, and rode by the narrow hill-tracks, which at once shortened the way and made it pleasanter. We threaded glen after glen, climbed steep after steep, passed through sweet-lying village after village, all bowered in foliage. We rode through thick woods whose dense foliage shaded us from the sunrays; by wimpling streams on which were rushing mill-races; and then came the cool splash of the water over the moss-grown water-wheel, and the scent of balsam and thyme from the miller's garden fringed by willows whose tresses dipped into the stream. We rode through verdant meadows, our horse-hoofs trampling the rich grass; and by fountains from whose carved face sprang a jet of clear cold water, grateful alike to parched throat and burning temples. We skirted vineyards where heavy masses of dark-green foliage but half-screened the clusters of grapes just beginning to soften into ripeness; by orchards over whose fences the plum-branches nodded heavy with yellow and purple globes; by snug detached farm-buildings, each one the residence of several families all closely related to each other and forming a kind of little tribe. And so by devious tracks we came back into the valley of the Jantra, and found ourselves looking down into the picturesque town of Drenova which lies on the banks of that rapid stream.

In Drenova, where we rested a couple of hours, we found, also resting, the 55th (Podolsk) Regiment, on march to reinforce the Schipka. Villiers and I both recognised the colonel of the regiment, Duhonin, as having seen him on the morning of the crossing of the Danube. The blood was then flowing down the blade of his drawn sword from a bayonet-wound on the right wrist which he had received in leading the assault on the height above the Tekir-Dere creek. He gave us tea and told us all the news. It appeared that so early as the 18th Suleiman had been demonstrating against the Hainkioj and Elena passes, and that on the same day his advance had reached Kezanlik near the southern foot of the Schipka Pass. Radetski, commanding the 8th Corps, was at Tirnova when these tidings came in. He immediately ordered a regiment from Selvi to hurry to the reinforcement of the Schipka; but deceived by the demonstration against the Elena Pass he had marched there with part of Dragomiroff's Division and the 4th Rifle Brigade. Finding all quiet in that region he had returned to Tirnova on the 21st, and now, on the morning of this day (the 22nd), in spite of their fatigue, he had put on march two brigades with orders to push energetically to the Schipka. It was the leading regiment of that force on which we had chanced here in Drenova; and there we left it, hurrying on to reach Gabrova before sundown. Before arriving there we heard the cannon-fire away to our left front; it died down partly as the darkness fell.

In Gabrova we got all particulars as to the situation on the Schipka. General Darozhinsky, who was in command of the force of 5,000 men all told — the 36th Regiment and the Bulgarian Legion — which consisted the garrison of the Schipka, had seen from the pass on the 20th Suleiman's whole army of 40 battalions deploy on the plain at his feet. The Russian general, not a very energetic man we were given to understand, had a sort of chain of defensive positions along the road crossing the pass, and those he had manned thus: One battalion behind St. Nicholas, $4\frac{1}{2}$ battalions along the "Central Hill," $3\frac{1}{2}$ battalions as a reserve on the "isthmus" between the Central and the St. Nicholas Hills. He had in all 30 guns, which were allotted to the respective positions.

He had made his dispositions just in time, and the Turks were exceptionally prompt. On the morning of the 21st they had established a battery on the Berdek Hill on the Russian left, and at noon assailed with desperate fury the left flank of the St. Nicholas position. Again and again with fierce shouts of "Allah!" they charged up almost to the muzzles of the Russian cannon, but were steadfastly repulsed with heavy losses. Their attacks lasted until after sundown and their final rush was made in the moonlight. Recoiling from the staunch defence they maintained a heavy fire throughout the night at close range. On the following morning they confined themselves chiefly to artillery fire and the development of their positions until by nightfall, in spite of the Russian fire, they had established batteries in front, on either flank, and, indeed, all but in the rear of Darozhinsky's position. Their infantry were in full occupation of both the flanking spurs, and their cross-fire and that of the Moslem guns swept and searched the whole of the bare central saddle held by the Russians, while the road in their rear was threatened from both sides.

I daresay you youngsters consider those details as very dull and dry, and I do not deny that to follow them demands close attention. But if you really want thoroughly to understand the sort of fighting which occurred in the Schipka Pass at this period of the campaign — and you have assured me that, from what you saw there with your own eyes, you would have given anything to have had with you some one who was actually on the spot when that fighting was going on and who could tell you everything from his own recollection — you must keep firm in your mind those dispositions I am describing to you and trying to make as simple as possible.

We were up by daybreak on the morning of the 23rd. Before then we had been awakened by the sound of the renewed cannonade — if, indeed, it had stopped at all during the night. As the gusts of cannon-thunder came sweeping down the ravines and eddying along the quaint old streets of Gabrova, the townsfolk gathered in anxious groups and whispered with pale lips. It had volumes of awful meaning for them, that sullen booming up on the Schipka yonder, not three hours' climb from their doors. While the Russians stood their ground up there, the pale citizens were safe; but let them be worsted, and a few short hours would see the leaders of the hordes of murderous Tcherkesses riding down the old main street, with the fierce lust of blood in their cruel eyes. For the Russians to be worsted signified Gabrova in a blaze; and meant, too, the letting loose of a swarm of savages on the vast masses of fugitive people through whom we had passed the day before, and who were bivouacking in every field and under every tree from Gabrova to Drenova. For the Bulgarians, then, each moment was an agony of suspense. When we reached the pass, Russian officers owned to Villiers that for once in their reckless lives they felt the burden of an awful responsibility in the remembrance of those poor fugitive women and children crowded in the valley below. We were sure that the Russian soldiers were fighting all the more stoutly because they realised how much depended on their staunchness. We had seen the good fellows we had fallen in with the day before empty their haversacks into the laps of hungry

Bulgarian women and children, although their charity left themselves foodless without a guess when they should eat next. We had seen them grope into their pockets, fish out the poor copecks which they had been saving for schnapps and tobacco, and bestow the coppers on the gaunt children of the fugitives, with some word of rude jocularity under which was real tenderness.

Leaving Gabrova in the pale half-light of the dawn, we made forward along the beautiful romantic valley of the Jantra through beech-forests in which were many clearings and little villages. The roar of cannon high above us — it seemed in the very clouds — swelled in louder and yet louder volume as we drew nearer; and wounded men were already trickling to the rear, a sure token that the fighting had been warm and close from its very commencement. Suddenly the road left the Jantra valley and bending sharp to the left struck up the mountain-side. The steep ascent lasted for about three miles. The road was extremely tortuous, having to turn, twist and wriggle to take advantage of the rugged ground. Very steep in places, it was quite practicable for vehicles, having been reconstructed by the pioneers during the Russian occupation. Patches of the old road remained, avalanches of boulders hurled in heaps over fixed jagged rocks. About $3\frac{1}{2}$ miles from the foot we reached the "Karaula" — the hut which had been the Turkish custom-house. At the little khan a few hundred yards further on, was the dressing-place of the third line, whither, after having their wounds roughly bound up in the fighting line, came such soldiers as were able to walk. This place and its vicinity were already thronged with severely-wounded men, among whom was an extraordinary proportion of officers. Two colonels were being brought in as we passed.

We halted here for a little time, while Villiers made a rough sketch of the ground in our front. It was apparent at once that the Schipka Pass, as you must have recognised when you crossed it, was no pass at all in the usual sense of the word. There is no gorge, no defile. It probably is so termed simply because at this point there happens to be a section of the Balkans of less than the average height, the surface of which from the Jantra valley to the village of Schipka is sufficiently continuous to afford space for a practicable road. The ground on either side of this continuous saddle is depressed in some places into shallow hollows, in others into cavern-like cups, and the ground on either side of the road presents a wild and broken jumble of crag and ravine. The highest point of the pass is at the St. Nicholas Hill, where the road crosses the summit; but this central hill was flanked on either side by a mountainous spur higher than itself and so commanding it, as well as having the command of the central saddle by which the road attains the summit. The Turks held both those spurs, whence their fire flanked and swept the central Schipka ridge. It was this which constituted the weakness of the Russian position on the Schipka. The Turks could and did descend from the flanking spurs, struggle through the intervening glens, and climbing on either side up the steep of the central ridge, they were trying to join hands in rear of the Russian position on the road running along the backbone of the saddle towards the summit.

It seemed to us, as we stood gazing, that the Turkish

cannon-fire we saw in action commanded the whole Russian position, in front, on both flanks, and even from its rear. Up to the main entrenchment on St. Nicholas Hill was a distance of about two miles, and every foot of the road seemed exposed to fire. It was not a pleasant prospect, but there was no alternative, and fortunately for the time there was not much musketry fire; so we started. Dead men lay about the road rather ominously; shells burst rather closer than we liked, and bullets kept striking the road about us and ricochetting viciously. I don't care to talk about that tramp; I know I was very thankful when it was over. The worst nuisance was that at commanding points Villiers would stop, serenely sit down, bring out his sketch-book, and betake himself to drawing some group that caught his fancy, or some battery over against him which, as like as not, was actually trained on himself. I own that at those junctures I lay down behind a rock — not that this was any important protection, because of the thoroughness of the Turkish cross-fire. Once inside the chief redoubt, Generals Darozhinsky and Stolietoff — it was the latter who in the following year was the head of the Russian mission to Cabul which brought about the Afghan War of 1878–79 — received us very cordially. They were short of most things — short of food, short of water, shortest of ammunition; but there still was tea, and that was served. The firing died down somewhat in the late afternoon, but a dropping fire was maintained until after sundown. A tent was assigned us and we were advised to lie down without delay — the prostrate attitude was recognised on the Schipka as the safest. All through the night the Turkish batteries maintained an intermittent fire to which the Russians made scarcely any reply, their ammunition being almost exhausted. The situation on the morning of the 23rd even I, quite inexperienced in war as I was, could not but realise to be all but desperate. The Turkish infantry were now in full possession of both the flanking spurs: it was clear to us that the Russian position was well-nigh entirely surrounded; the narrow ridges along which ran the high-road by which were connected the little hills held by the Russians, were now wholly exposed to the Turkish cross-fire at a range of from 1,500 to 2,000 yards.

Darozhinsky wore a very sombre face as he called Villiers and myself to drink a glass of tea with him in the early morning. Stolietoff was more cheerful, but that was the nature of the man; he owned with a laugh that he expected us all to be dead men before many more hours should have passed. At six o'clock began the Turkish onslaught, the cannon-fire covering the rushing advance of the infantry. The assaults were furious and concentric: as one attack was hurled back another was immediately made by fresh troops. I could not but smile at Villiers' devotion to his own particular duty; but the smile was melancholy enough — for, to tell you frankly, I had not the least hope that the sketches he was working on so calmly and assiduously would ever reach the *Graphic* office. I did not believe that a man of us would ever quit the Schipka alive. Noon came with no pause in the strife; the worn Russians and Bulgarian Legion still fought on staunchly. But the odds were cruel. Darozhinsky, as he came back panting from heading a counter-attack, owned that the end was very near — the fight was too unequal between his 7,000 Russians and Bulgarians, and the 25,000 Turks who were besetting us on every side. Stolietoff came up and the two generals wrote what they believed to be their last message to their master the Czar. It was a short and simple message coming straight from the hearts of brave and loyal soldiers who had done their best and could do no more. Darozhinsky read it to Villiers and I well remember its tenor. "We are all but surrounded," thus it ran, "by a force more than thrice our strength. The men are spent; the ammunition is all but done. We shall hold out to the end and fight till we die." The despatch was entrusted to a Bulgarian to be carried back to Gabrova and thence telegraphed to Gorni-Studen. Darozhinsky had little hope that the man would get through; but the Bulgarian was confident in his knowledge of the by-paths.

He departed. The fighting continued. Villiers resumed his sketching. The Russians were fighting against hope and simply bracing themselves to die hard. The reserves were engaged to the last man. "Look at them!" said Darozhinsky with melancholy pride, — " how they hold on, the brave fellows! They have been under a constant cross-fire for forty-eight hours, they are blistered by the fierce heat, they are parched with thirst, they are weak for want of food, and yet they do not quail or grumble!" But an hour later he owned that the long strain was at last telling. The wounded who could move were going rearward to the field-hospital in so great numbers as to create among the yet unwounded men the impression that a general retreat had been ordered. And this moment of confusion and wavering was promptly chosen by the Turks for an attack in force from the western flanking spur towards the high road in rear of the Russian position, while at the same time another column from the eastern spur moved down to join hands with it. The final crisis was imminent. Colonel Lipinski, gathering about him a few ragged companies of trusty soldiers, rallied them to face the oncoming Turks with feeble despairing volleys; but their efforts availed but little against the hordes climbing the steep slope to gain the road, give the hand to the co-operating column, cut off the retreat of the Russians, and pen them up in their narrow and exposed position.

Never to my dying day shall I forget that thrilling hour. As the afternoon shadows were falling, Darozhinsky and Stolietoff, with Villiers and myself by their side, stood in the Turkish fire on the parapet of the central entrenchment. Along the bare ridge above and below us lay the grimed, sun-blistered men, beaten out with heat, fatigue, hunger and thirst; reckless in their despondency, that every foot of ground was swept by the Turkish rifle-fire. Others still doggedly fought on down among the rocks, forced to give ground but doing so with sullen reluctance. The cliffs and valleys echoed with triumphant shouts of "Allah il Allah!" The glasses of the chiefs scanned the visible glimpses of the steep brown road leading up from the Jantra valley, through copses of dark green and masses of darker rock. Stolietoff cried aloud in sudden access of excitement, grasped Darozhinsky by the elbow, and pointed down the pass. Through the glasses the head of a long black column was plainly to be discerned against the reddish-brown road-bed. "Now God be thanked!" uttered Darozhinsky solemnly: he was a dead man twenty-four hours later. Both chiefs bared their heads and crossed themselves. The troops about us sprang to their feet; they too had descried the long black serpent coiling onward up the brown road. Through the hanging pine-woods there flashed a glint of sunshine that danced on the bayonets and inspirited the soldiers.

The Turkish war-cries were drowned in the cheering which the wind carried from the sore-pressed defenders of the Schipka to welcome the comrades hurrying to help them. As the dark serpent-like column neared the rearward position, it struck us all as a strange kind of reinforcement, as seen from where we stood. A big man on a big horse rode in front; behind him followed, to all appearance, a column of cavalry! Stolietoff burst out laughing. "Cavalry in the Schipka!" he snorted; "deal of use horse will be among these rocks! Are we Russians all born idiots, then?" But Stolietoff was an impulsive man and he presently took back his hasty words. The big leader was brave old Radetski, the corps-commander; his following was a rifle battalion which he had mounted on Cossack ponies and hurried forward, himself at its head. The rifle brigade to which the battalion belonged — the same rifle brigade which had fought so hard under Gourko in his daring advance and bloody retreat — was close up behind; it had marched thirty-five miles straight on end without halting to cook or sleep, and was now climbing up from Gabrova burning to come into action. But Radetski did not wait for the arrival of the brigade. He struck promptly with the battalion which was already to his hand. He dismounted the nimble riflemen from the Cossack ponies and formed them up; and then he sent them with a rush down into the rightward valley on the flank of the Turkish mass threatening to enclose the position. By this time the old chief had been joined by Darozhinsky and Stolietoff, whom Villiers and I had accompanied — Villiers and he were old friends since before the crossing of the Danube, and Radetski greeted him warmly. The staff-officer who was with the chief, and who headed the attack of the rifle battalion, was none other than the Captain Andreiovitch who was MacGahan's Khivan comrade and with whom, you may remember that I told you, he had foregathered again in Tirnova at the beginning of Gourko's raid. Andreiovitch was a major now; he had distinguished himself greatly in the cavalry action at Eski-Zagra, and when Gourko's expedition returned to Tirnova Radetski had posted him to his own staff. Presently I shall have something more to tell you about this Andreiovitch.

Before the charge of the Russian riflemen the Turks gave ground. The riflemen, Andreiovitch at their head, chased the Moslems through the valley strewn thick with the dead of the previous fighting, hunted them fiercely up the opposite wooded ascent, carried their advanced trenches, and drove them into their fortified position on the Bald Mountain. Radetski himself waited by his mountain battery in action till the rifle brigade came up, and then marched it forward under the long gauntlet of the Turkish fire, dropping a company here and a half-battalion there, until with what of the command was still at his back he entered the St. Nicholas redoubt along with Darozhinsky, Stolietoff, and ourselves.

A single weak brigade was not in itself a very strong succour; but Radetski was able to tell that Dragomiroff with his whole division was hurrying on at best speed.

The Turks seemed to realise that their opportunities were on the wane, and they attacked again and again with great fury. But now the Russians, although suffering heavy losses, confined themselves no longer to the defensive; for they knew that for them there could be no safety, far less elbow-room, until the Turks should be driven from that ridge which loomed so threateningly on their right flank. The firing weakened before sundown, and at length we had something which could be called a meal. Radetski had brought up a two-wheeled baggage cart which contained proviant as well as baggage. There was no lack of cooks; the general was good enough to invite Villiers and myself to be his guests with Darozhinsky and Stolietoff, and in contrast to the gloominess of the day the evening was very cheery. Radetski had a fund of quaint humour of the old-fashioned type. He was not a man of great culture nor was he supposed to be a great strategist, but he had a well-deserved reputation for dogged hard fighting; and I remember to have heard that critics of the war reckoned him next to Gourko and Skobeleff. As to that you will believe that a civilian like myself cannot speak; but I can tell of many a pleasant hour spent in the company of the fine old chief over glasses of tea. I have heard British officers who knew both men, say that Radetski and Lord Napier of Magdala resembled each other in features and figure in a most extraordinary degree.

Early on the morning of the 24th General Dragomiroff arrived with his leading brigade consisting of the Podolsk and Jitomer regiments, which had marched thirty-eight miles on the previous day. The Podolsks he left in reserve and they later in the day assailed without success the Turkish flank on the Bald Mountain spur. The Jitomers he led forward along the road under the heavy fire which the Turks maintained on it throughout the day. Villiers, to whom he had been very kind in Roumania and at the crossing of the Danube, went down to meet the general, and I accompanied him; we encountered him about ten o'clock while he was ranking his soldiers in preparation for an attack. He was shaking hands with Villiers when he was struck by a bullet in the knee-joint. There was no surgeon present and Villiers, who had learnt some surgery in the Servian campaign of the previous year, cut away the trouser and, assisted by myself, set about bandaging the wound. The general had fallen when hit, and the soldiers had carried him into the cover of a shallow shelter-trench where he lay in comparative safety. It was clear that the wound was serious: the knee-joint seemed quite shattered and it was impossible for us to do more than to bandage the joint and have him taken down to the field-hospital some distance to the rear. A stretcher was made of rifles and soldiers' greatcoats and he was slowly carried down along the exposed road. Two of the bearers were shot down on the way. Dragomiroff throughout was perfectly cool and composed. He was an elderly man, rather stout and of florid aspect, with a large expanse of bald head. He had long been a professor in the St. Petersburg Military Academy and had a great reputation for strategical knowledge; but this was his first campaign and before this morning he had been in action only once — at the passage of the Danube, where his dispositions were regarded as having been very skilful. The two surgeons at the field-hospital wanted to amputate the wounded leg then and there. But Dragomiroff refused them permission to their great disgust; and the event justified him. He returned to the army before the end of the war, in possession of both legs; but he limped badly on the one that had been wounded, and the distortion, he feared, would be permanent.

Suleiman was no doubt aware of the arrival of reinforcements to the garrison of the Schipka, and probably believed that more were coming. In the meantime he hurled forward a number of battalions on the errand of attempting the conquest of the St. Nicholas defences. Success there would have been ruin to the Russians; for the St. Nicholas Hill was the key of the position. The Turks rushed to the assault with extraordinary dash and enthusiasm. As they came on, I for one, I well remember, believed that it was all over with us. The lithe rushing swiftness of those Turkish warriors was at once beautiful and terrible. We lay and watched the issue of a conflict which was sure to be desperate— Villiers the indomitable sketching as he lay. The foremost regiment was commanded by an Englishman who wore a Norfolk jacket and cord breeches. That of itself, you will say, did not make him an Englishman. No; but you could have had no doubt on the subject had you heard with what vigour he swore in our vernacular. We learned later that he was not an Englishman after all, but a Scot named Campbell, a brave soldier of fortune who was afterwards killed fighting in South Africa. At the moment I thought I could recognise the Highland accent as he cheered on his men and hurled objurgations on the

Russians. Straight at the Russian trenches he led his ardent Moslems, who carried them with a rush at the point of the bayonet and then mingled with the Russian defenders in a wild affray in which the bayonet and clubbed rifles were the only weapons used. The hand-to-hand struggle lasted for many minutes; but in the end the steadfast Russian doggedness held its own, and those of the Turks who had survived the close conflict of cold steel were heaved back over the parapet by dint of main strength. We went into the interior of the position after the Turks had retired. They had been in it for no great length of time, but the place was like a shambles. No quarter had been asked or given; and when the Russians were ordered back into the trenches they had to kneel in actual blood. Campbell was among the few survivors of his command: the mass of the battalion remained in the Russian position, but no longer alive.

There was no respite. Throughout the day the deep valley separating the ridge on which ran the road from the higher wooded ridge of the Bald Mountain further to the right, was the scene of constant hard fighting. About noon we crept up to the edge of the central ridge, and taking off our white caps, looked down on the scene below us. The Russian riflemen were up among the trees of the Turkish mountain-face, leaving the rocky bottom behind them strewn with killed and wounded. The Russian stretcher-bearers were behaving admirably, picking up the wounded under the hottest fire; and indeed not a few of them were themselves among the wounded. As to the progress of the Russians up in the forest little could be discerned, so thick was the cover; but the evidences were that the fighting waved to and fro — now the Russians and now the Turks gaining ground. Occasionally the Russians at some point would be hurled back out of the wood altogether, and through the glass we could mark the Turks following them eagerly to its edge and lying down there while pouring out a galling fire. It seemed a very even thing: the Turks and Russians were alike full of fight and neither gave any signs of succumbing. The Russian riflemen, finely-trained skirmishers, were great adepts at taking cover, and the Turks skirmished as dexterously as if they had never done anything else from infancy; but the soldiers of the Brianski Regiment of the line did not seem to know how to escape exposure. They obviously had no thought of quailing; but they stood up in the open somewhat helplessly and accepted punishment doggedly. No doubt their casualties were heavy.

To the onlooker there is something exceptionally terrible in a fight in a wood. One can see nothing save an occasional flash among the dark foliage and the white clouds of smoke rising above it like soap-bubbles. Hoarse shouts and cries come back to one from out the mysterious gloom. How was it to go? Were the strong-backed Russians with those ready bayonets of theirs to end the long-drawn-out fight with one short, impetuous, irresistible rush, or were the more lissom Turks to drive their clumsier adversaries out of the wood backward into the fire-blistered open? Who could tell? The struggle went on; the clamour of it still rose up into the serene blue sky. Wounded men came staggering from out among the swarthy trunks and sat down in a heap or crawled on towards the ambulance men. The riflemen and Brianskis were not progressing, and the Turks were gaining strength. "See," cried Villiers, "yonder on the sky-line are Turkish reinforcements coming along their ridge towards that bare patch close to their mountain battery on the edge of their right flank!" It was determined, while the riflemen and Brianskis continued to fight on where they were, to push an attack across the neck of the valley on the Turkish batteries on the "Woody Mountain." Two battalions of the Jitomer Regiment were ordered on this service. They quitted the Russian central position, and marched in company columns across the comparatively smooth ground at the head of the valley close to the summit level of the range. The Turkish mountain-guns punished them heavily; and as they went on they suffered severely from the hostile Remington rifles. But they pushed onward to the forest-edge at the foot of the ascent. The crisis of the day's fighting had now arrived. For us as spectators there remained nothing but to gaze into the perplexing mystery of forest. There were some evidences that the Russians were gaining ground as well on right as on left. The Turkish position on the peak of the "Woody Mountain" was assailed, but unsuccessfully; yet Radetski in the final result had gained considerable elbow-room on both his flanks. The struggle ceased for the time at sundown. Villiers went to the general and asked him whether he considered that on the day's fighting he had bettered his position. Radetski was oracular. "The Turks," said he, "will no doubt renew their attacks to-morrow with fresh troops, and probably do so for a good many morrows. But I am a tough man, and," he added, "with God's help, I shall hold on here till I am ordered away. But this is a very sad night for me. Poor Andreiovitch went out with the Jitomers when they advanced to the attack, and word has just been sent in to me that he is missing. He was last seen up in the wood within a short distance of the enemy's battery. The Jitomers fell back several hundred yards and he did not come back with them. You know that the Turks make no prisoners, and you know also what they do to our wounded. I count the poor fellow a dead man, and—and," said the old warrior as the tears ran down his face, " I had come to love him as a son."

Andreiovitch had spent the preceding evening with us and, because we were both MacGahan's friends, had given us his confidence. Before he had left Tirnova with Gourko he and the pretty Maritza, the widow's daughter with whom it seemed he had fallen in love at first sight, had grown mutually tender. When he came back, promoted and covered with honour, she had confessed that her heart was his and had plighted her troth to the handsome hussar. He had wanted, he told us, to get married then and there, so ardent were his emotions; but Maritza, though in love, had not wholly taken leave of her senses and had prevailed on him to wait until the war was over. It was not two hours ago, when the Jitomers went out, that we had shaken hands with Andreiovitch, as with a smile in his eye and a cigarette between his lips he lingered one moment to give us a message in case he should not come back. And now he had not come back and it was almost a certainty that he never would come back.

Villiers had determined to remain on the Schipka till something decisive should occur. But he had an envelope full of sketches for which the *Graphic* would be hungering, and he determined to send me down with them to Bucharest with instructions to return with all speed. I left him in the twilight, travelled down the pass to Gabrova, and from thence made haste through the darkness on my way to the Danube. All my thoughts as I rode were about poor Andreiovitch. I do not hesitate to tell you that I fervently hoped our poor friend had been shot dead; for the warfare in which the Russians were engaged had in it a feature of savagery at which I shuddered. But I knew that in common with all Russian officers at the front, Andreiovitch carried a dagger with which to take his own life in case of finding himself too severely wounded to get away and left without chance of removal by the Russian stretcher-bearers. I made a detour into Tirnova on the melancholy errand of breaking to Maritza the sad tidings regarding her betrothed. Minutes were of importance to me, and I left the poor girl in a dead faint in her mother's arms.

From a stable-keeper in Tirnova I hired a fresh horse, leaving my tired pony with him; and I hurried on to the Imperial headquarters at Gorni-Studen, which place was on my direct road to the Danube at Sistova. It was an understood thing with the English correspondents during this war, that whenever they had seen or heard of any event of importance and were within reasonable distance of him, they should report to Colonel Frederick Wellesley, the British military attaché in the camp of the Czar. I was not a correspondent, but I was the messenger of correspondents; and besides Villiers' instalment of sketches I carried his hurriedly-written notes of what we had seen on the Schipka Pass, which I was to desire Colonel Wellesley to read before I should carry them on to Bucharest to be sent to the *Graphic* by telegraph. Wellesley lived in a tent in the staff officers' square on the slope near the Emperor's house. He read the notes, looked at the sketches, asked of me a good many questions, gave me some food, and let me go. I was remounting when General Ignatieff came round the corner. He knew me very well from having seen me often in the company of MacGahan and Villiers; and he called out in his "boat ahoy!" manner: "Where from now, Mr. Carnegie?" "From the Schipka Pass, your Excellency," I replied — "I left there at dusk last night."

"The deuce you did!" exclaimed Ignatieff excitedly. "You have beaten all our messengers by hours: you must see the Emperor and tell your tidings to him!"

Now, as you know, I have not been exactly brought up among Emperors; but nevertheless I have a sense of decency, and I knew that a man ought to wait on an Emperor in his Sunday clothes. I was not a man, but a mere lad; I was not a correspondent, but merely the humble friend and general-utility assistant of correspondents and artists. I hadn't seen any Sunday clothes, or Sundays either, for three months; and I was conscious that my aspect was disreputable in the extreme. I had been wearing clothes originally white for over a fortnight, night and day. The black of my saddle had come off on to them with great liberality, and they were spotted with the blood of poor wounded Dragomiroff. I was all over about half-an-inch thick with dust, and the dust on my face was relieved by fiery sun-blisters. I had not washed

for three days, for on the Schipka we had been short even
of drinking-water; and I altogether felt a most degraded-
looking subject of that great empire on which the sun
never sets. But Ignatieff insisted that the Emperor in
the circumstances would by no means stand upon ceremony. He went in and awakened his Imperial master,
who had been asleep; and he presently ushered me
through the Cossack Guard into the dingy alcove which
seemed to be the Emperor's receiving-room. His quarters
were in a battered Turkish house, the balcony of which,
where I was to be presented to his Majesty, was enclosed
with common canvas hangings. There was not even a
carpet on the rugged boards. A glimpse into the bedroom from which the Emperor came showed me a tiny
cabin with mud walls and a little camp-bed standing on a
mud floor. His Majesty, who was quite alone, received
me with great kindness, shaking hands and paying me a
compliment on my speed as a courier, which I told him
was my present avocation. He was gaunt, worn, and
haggard, his head sunk between his shoulders, his voice
broken by nervousness and by the asthma that afflicted
him. In the following summer I saw his Majesty at a
great State function in his capital — a very Emperor,
upright of figure, dignified in every movement and gesture,
arrayed in a gorgeous uniform and covered with decorations. A glittering Court and suite thronged around the
stately man with devoted and respectful homage. The
dazzling splendour of the Winter Palace was the setting
of the sumptuous picture; and as I gazed on the magnificent scene, I could hardly realise that the central figure of
it in the pomp of his Imperial state, was of a verity the

self-same man in whose presence I had stood in the squalid Bulgarian hovel — the same worn, anxious, shabby, wistful man who, with spasmodic utterance and the expression in his eyes of a hunted deer, had asked of me breathless questions as to the occurrences and issue of the fighting.

I told him that I could make him understand these much better if I had a sheet of paper on which to draw a rough sketch of the ground. It seemed that there was no map of the Schipka Pass in the Imperial headquarters. He said at once: "Ignatieff, go and fetch paper and pencil." Ignatieff went, and the Emperor and myself were alone together, standing opposite each other with a little green-baize table dividing us. He was so good as to ask me a few questions about myself, remarking that I was very young to be a witness of scenes of bloodshed and death. He asked very earnestly about General Dragomiroff; and when I told him that Mr. Villiers and myself had been with him when he fell and had applied the first bandaging to his shattered knee, he was much moved and again shook me by the hand. I asked him to permit me to read Mr. Villiers' notes taken during the fighting, adding that it would be better that I should do so when I had sketched the ground with which they were concerned. Ignatieff returned with a sheet of foolscap. I was but a poor draughtsman, and my chart, I am sure, was very rough and crude. Then I read the notes, pointing as I did so to each position as they referred to it, and where they seemed obscure, adding some explanations from my own recollection. The Emperor was not only very patient, but gave me the conviction that he was deeply interested in my poor and disconnected narrative.

He was again much moved when I spoke of the conduct of his troops — when I said that I could not have believed, had I not seen it, that men could have endured so much and dared so much. He wanted to know about the losses. Of them I could tell him merely that to me they seemed awful; that in places the dead lay in heaps; that Generals Darozhinsky and Petroceni were killed, with many other officers; and that the wounded suffered beyond conception. When I spoke of the dead he crossed himself fervently over and over again, and went into his bedroom for a few moments, beckoning that I should wait. When he came out again, it flashed across me to repeat to him the encouraging words which General Radetski had spoken to Mr. Villiers before the latter had sent me away. His face cleared, and he said in a low voice: "Brave old Radetski!" and then he repeated the old warrior's words — "Please God, I shall hold on until I am ordered away." He was so good as to ask who was Mr. Villiers of whom I had occasion to speak, and bade me say to that gentleman that he would be glad to receive him when next in his camp. Then he thanked me for my information, hoped that all would turn out well, did me the honour to present me with the Order of St. Stanislaus with the crossed swords, and desired that I should go with General Ignatieff to the camp of his brother the Commander-in-Chief on the top of the opposite hill. As I bowed on retiring he again shook my hand, and said he was much obliged to me.

Ignatieff conducted me through the mud up to the headquarters of the Grand Duke Nicholas. He and his staff lived in tents; not, however, the usual canvas tents, but in Turcoman kibitkas of thick felt stretched on a framework of laths. The Grand Duke was bluff, noisy and rather abrupt. I simply said that the Emperor had desired me to read to him Mr. Villiers' notes, which I did. He seemed impatient while I did so. He appeared concerned when I told him that Generals Darozhinsky and Petroceni had been killed; and he remarked: "I hope old Radetski won't get himself killed!"—not in a very feeling manner. He asked me what seemed the tone "up yonder." I thought the best way to answer him was to repeat what I had heard General Radetski say to Mr. Villiers before I left. "Ah," he exclaimed, slapping his thigh, "that is the right tone! I hope to God he will be as good as his word!" Then he asked me whether I could tell him what was the feeling as to reinforcements. It was not likely that a person in my circumstances could inform him on that point; I simply stated that I had heard Colonel Duhonin say that the Schipka could never be safe unless a whole army corps was allotted for its defence. He spat on the floor angrily, and then, swallowing a great glass of wine, exclaimed: "An army corps! What is the use of talking about an army corps when I don't know where to find so much as a spare battalion?" He dismissed me curtly enough, I thought, since it was to oblige him, not myself, that I had gone to him, and since the visit was delaying my journey. As I left the kibitka Prince Alexander of Battenberg said to me in very kind tones: "Mr. Carnegie, I am sure that after your long ride you must be very tired. I have taken the liberty of sending your horse over to Colonel Wellesley's groom, who will take charge of it until you return; and my carriage is outside, waiting to take you down to the Danube." There spoke the true and courteous gentleman! I felt beholden to him for a most kindly and thoughtful service, and accepted it thankfully. The vehicle was a "troika"—a light open carriage drawn by three black stallions abreast; the centre horse, taller than the other two and more powerful, was a fast trotter; the two side horses went at a gallop with their heads fastened down and bent outward by a rein. The driver was an imposing person, in fur bonnet encircled by peacock feathers, long blue caftan and flaring red sash. He used no whip, held the reins tight in both hands with squared elbows, and carried me along at the rate of 10 miles an hour. The superb coachman accepted with condescension my humble baksheesh. I hurried across the Danube, travelled athwart the plain to Giurgevo, caught the train for Bucharest, and Mr. Villiers' sketches were in the post-office and his notes on the wires within twenty minutes after my arrival.

I took the liberty of sleeping for once in the course of some six weeks in a comfortable bed with actual sheets; but on the morning of the 27th I was on my way back to the Schipka. At Gorni-Studen I picked up my hired horse, rode him to Tirnova, returned him to his owner, and received my own pony. I found no Maritza in her mother's house. The latter told me sadly that on the morning after my previous visit she had started for the Schipka, refusing the mother's companionship because of the sure absence of such comforts as those to which the old lady was accustomed. Reaching the Schipka, I found Villiers drinking tea with Radetski in a leafy wigwam on the Central Hill. The fighting had ceased on the evening of the 26th and both sides were now standing on the defensive, although the Turks maintained their positions on the two commanding spurs and picked off the passing Russians on the high road to the number of forty or fifty a day. Indeed, when I found Radetski and Villiers they were drinking their tea under a dropping fire, which they did not seem to mind. After five days of almost uninterrupted fighting both sides were very much as they had been at the beginning, but for the slaughter; the Russians had lost about 4,000 men. The Turks were said to have had over 8,000 wounded and about 3,500 killed. During the first three days the garrison had suffered intensely. Their only food consisted of a single day's biscuit ration in their haversacks at the beginning. The heat was cruel, radiated as it was from the rock; but there was no water nearer than three miles away, and all that could be had was that brought back in their canteens by the stretcher-bearers returning from the field-hospital. The fighting was maintained day and night, for the moon was at its full; the poor fellows caught mere snatches of sleep as they lay on the ground they were holding. They were always under fire — not merely during assaults; for the Turks with one trifling exception commanded every point of the Russian position; and even in a spot supposed to be in some degree safe General Darozhinsky was shot dead. The whole region was abominable because of the stench of decomposing bodies, and the sight of their dead comrades sickened the living.

Villiers was quite ready to make his farewell to the Schipka and it was settled that we should depart on the morning of the 29th. Most of the wounded had been sent down to Gabrova; but I found in the stone hut which had been the field-hospital poor Maritza attending two soldiers so mangled that they could not be moved. She had in her possession her lover's uniform, all torn and soiled with blood and clay. The sorry fragments had been found in a little hollow somewhat wide of the line of attack and retreat, and there lay beside them a naked corpse whose state was such, after three days' exposure to sun and weather, that no identification was possible. Maritza steadily refused to believe that this body was that of Andreiovitch, but she was alone in her convictions; and, indeed, the name of "Major Michael Andreiovitch of the 9th Hussars," had been included among the "killed" in the supplement to General Radetski's despatch. I tried in vain to persuade Maritza to return with us to her mother. Her pretext for refusal was her duty to the poor broken fellows whom she was nursing; but it was not difficult to perceive that she still hoped against hope that her lover might yet be restored to her. The Gabrova woman who was sharing the nursing duty promised faithfully that as soon as the two wounded men were dead — they were beyond recovery — she herself would accompany Maritza down to Tirnova, and would not leave her until she was in her mother's arms. So I bade a sad farewell to the poor wan-faced girl, so changed since the still recent days of coquetry; and Villiers and I departed to another section of the theatre of war, where amidst the carnage of Plevna I did not lose the memory of the tragedy now associated in my mind with the once gay and laughing Maritza.

I must finish her story here now — it does not end in a tragedy after all. It was in the Podo Mogosoi of Bucharest in the following April, that to my unutterable surprise I met Maritza walking arm-in-arm with Andreiovitch, he in civilian dress and walking very lame with the support of a stick. "Yes," said Maritza, all her archness restored; "this fellow one morning in the end of January coolly sauntered into our house in Tirnova, limping on crutch and staff and with one leg supported by a strap round his neck, condescended to kiss me, and then sat down and demanded vodka. Since then, I may inform you, I have amused myself by marrying him. I've told you all that is important; he must give himself the trouble of recounting the minor details." We went into Brofft's restaurant and then Andreiovitch told his strange story, which I believe I can give you almost in his own words: —

"During our attack on the 'Woody Mountain,' a Turk and I were at close quarters when a bullet shattered the bone of my leg and I rolled aside into a hollow, dragging along with me the Turk whom I killed with my dagger. Averting faintness by resorting to my flask I first bandaged my leg, and hoping to escape the fate which so many of our poor fellows underwent, I tore off my uniform, stripped the dead Turk, and contrived to work myself into his garments. All night I lay there uninterfered with, but suffering great agony. Early on the following morning there passed close to me going towards the front, a tall man dressed partly in the uniform of a Turkish officer. I was about to risk it and call to him, when he tripped over a root and as he recovered himself I heard him distinctly mutter 'D——n!' That satisfied me he was an Englishman and I addressed him in your language. He was most kind. His name was Campbell and he commanded a battalion in Suleiman's army. He got a stretcher on which I was placed, Campbell's Turks who carried me believing that I was a wounded countryman too ill to speak. Campbell accompanied me down into Schipka village, where he handed me over to the care of the British surgeons of the Red Cross. They treated me with the greatest skill and care, but months passed and I was still on my back. Suleiman marched westward about the new year, leaving Vessil Pasha at and about Schipka with some 40,000 men. You must have heard how Radetski, Mirski, and Skobeleff came wallowing through the snow ten feet deep on the Balkans in January last; and how Skobeleff, after a desperate struggle for the possession of the Shenova redoubts, received the surrender of Vessil and his whole army. That evening I ceased to be a wounded Turk and became a lame Russian — good for no more soldiering, worse luck. When the track got beaten over the pass, I found a Turkish pony on which I rode to Gabrova and thence down the valley to Tirnova. I may incidentally remark that Maritza didn't in the least expect to see me any more. But one fine morning she went to church with me all the same, and came out Madame Andreiovitch; and now we are on our way to Russia by short stages, when I shall be compelled to make things excessively unpleasant to my respected father if he does not behave handsomely to us."

So, lads, that is the true and eventful story of the pretty Maritza of Tirnova and her true lover, the once rackety Andreiovitch. They sometimes write to me to this day, and they jointly testify that they are very happy.

CHAPTER VII

PELISCHAT AND LOFTCHA

IT was quite a relief to leave behind us the tainted atmosphere and the squalor of the Schipka Pass. Mr. Villiers had not eaten a decent meal for more than a week; he had never taken his clothes off, and water was so scarce on the Schipka that he had been able only twice to wash his hands and face and then only in the driblet of water which a soldier's canteen held. I had brought up for him from Bucharest a change of clothes and some clean linen which I had left in the inn at Gabrova. We bathed in a pool in the Jantra, he got into clean garments, and then we sat down to a meal which, although plain and served roughly enough, was at least clean and wholesome.

He had lost touch of the course of events during the week spent up among the bullets and rocks of the Schipka, and he was now desirous of visiting the Imperial headquarters at Gorni-Studen, in order that he might see Colonel Wellesley and learn from him what were the state and prospects of the campaign. But we knew the road to Gorni-Studen from Gabrova by way of Drenova and Tirnova so well, that he determined to make a detour from Gabrova to the south-westward about Selvi, a region which he had not previously visited. Our route was through a very picturesque country which had not been in the least devastated by war. The inhabitants, Bulgarians though they were, had nothing of the sullen stolidity characterising the race in other districts. Their houses were comparatively clean and the same could be said of their persons; they were clearly excellent farmers and they resembled the patriarchs of old in the abundance of their flocks and herds. We had heard at Gabrova that the Bashi-Bazouks had been in Selvi, and we knew too well what was likely to be the aspect of any place which had been visited by those ruffians. But it turned out that no Bashi-Bazouks had been in Selvi; there was a Russian brigade in occupation, or rather it was encamped beyond its outskirts. The village was by far the brightest and most smiling little place we had found south of the Danube. It contained many good houses the interiors and exteriors of which were clean and picturesque. There were flowers everywhere in the village gardens, vines and blossoming creepers covered the fronts of the pretty dwellings, there were busy little shops thronged with customers, and there was a really good little inn the landlord of which knew how to cook. So charming was Selvi that we should have been glad to spend a day or two among its amenities, but for Villiers' anxiety to gain intelligence. We slept in great comfort at the little Selvi hostelry and next morning took the road leading to Gorni-Studen. On the way, shortly before reaching that place, we passed two separate brigades marching on Selvi. The soldiers were fine strapping young fellows, and their clothes showed little of the wear and tear which by this time was apparent in the troops of the original invasion. Villiers, entering into conversation with some of the officers, was told that both brigades belonged to the reinforcements which had been ordered up from Russia, and that they had crossed the Danube only a few days previously. The line brigade was the 2nd of the 3rd Division, and the rifle brigade was the 3rd. The officers were very anxious that a battle should occur soon in which they might hope to take part, and they were greatly disgusted when we told them that at Selvi there were no symptoms of imminent fighting.

Colonel Wellesley, as always, was most kind and pleasant. He took copious notes of all that Villiers had to tell him about the Schipka Pass; and then he explained how things stood at the headquarters and elsewhere. The Russians were making great preparations for the third and, as they hoped, the final effort to drive Osman and his Turks out of Plevna and Loftcha — this latter place was to be first attacked. Of the reinforcements from Russia two complete divisions had arrived. The Roumanian army had been crossing the Danube during the whole of the month, and was now in Bulgaria in its full strength of 30,000 infantry, 4,500 cavalry and 126 guns. It consisted in all of three divisions, one of which was the reserve. Colonel Wellesley had visited the Roumanians and thought well of them; but he had found that in each brigade there was but one line regiment, the other two consisting of militia or, as they were called, Dorobanz. I knew something of the Dorobanz; they were simply peasants clad in sheepskins instead of uniform and wearing sandals instead of shoes. But they were stout active fellows who could march all day and then dance all night. Colonel Wellesley spoke highly of the Roumanian artillery; the weak point, he thought, was in the officers, who, accustomed to a life of idleness and dissipation and destitute of confidence in themselves, might default in constancy if the fighting should be prolonged.

Villiers asked the colonel about poor old General Pouzanoff. This officer, one of the richest noblemen in Russia, had held the command of the 30th Division, which took part in the battle before Plevna of July 30th. Before the fighting began he disappeared altogether and was seen no more until the morning after, when he was found at Poradim in great distress of mind. Of course he incurred much obloquy and was freely denounced as a coward. We remembered his coming into our tent on the afternoon before the battle, and that, having introduced himself, he had spoken in a very soldier-like manner of the impending battle. His last remark as he left us was still in my memory: "I hope God will give us all strength to do our duty as becomes Russian soldiers." He was an old man, this was his first campaign, and we heard later that both his brigades had been taken out of his hands, that he then quite lost his head and hurriedly quitted the field. Colonel Wellesley told us of a fine trait in the not very amiable character of the Grand Duke Nicholas, in sending the poor broken old man away with a fine mixture of arbitrary assumption of profound medical knowledge and of genuine kindly feeling for a man in misfortune. "I observe, general," said he, "that you are very ill, and I am sure that there is no chance of your recovering your health without returning to Russia." "But," remonstrated the general, "I am not ill at all, your Imperial Highness. I was never in better health in my life." "Allow me, please, to know better. I can see that you are ailing seriously, and I must recommend you to recover your health in the bosom of your family."

On August 31st we rode in pouring rain from Gorni-Studen to Poradim, a village of which our recollections were the reverse of pleasant, but where, as Colonel Wellesley had informed us, were the headquarters of the army gathering for the third attempt on Plevna. As we rode past one of the half-subterranean dwellings of which the straggling village of Poradim consisted, we heard a sound which struck us as familiar. It was a voice uplifted in comic song, and the voice was the voice of MacGahan. We shouted, there was a rush upon us of ferocious Bulgarian dogs, and then appeared Mac-Gahan in a red silk shirt, riding-breeches, and brown boots. Glad to be out of the rain and yet more glad to meet the genial American, we followed him inside. We found ourselves in a regular nest of correspondents. In this underground hole, besides MacGahan, were Mr. Jackson of the *New York Herald*, Mr. Frederick Boyle of the *Standard*, and Mr. Dobson who was MacGahan's companion; all waiting with more or less impatience until the fighting should begin. Some of the gentlemen had been here for a fortnight. The filth and squalor of the place were abominable. It was overrun with mangy dogs and dirty children. The hovel was entered by a damp and slippery descent, at foot of which one entered the low-roofed mud-walled principal room which the correspondents occupied. There was no chimney; a hole in the roof let out the smoke and let in the sparse modicum of light. The only furniture was a Turkish table and a water-jug. The cooking utensils, such as they were, belonged to the gentlemen; the Bulgarian outfit consisted of two earthenware plates, two huge wooden spoons, and a dirty iron pot. The dull saturnine Bulgarian peasant would sell nothing; he steadfastly refused to deal although money to triple the value was laid down before him. No! what was wanted — and he had plenty of hay and corn, of cattle, sheep, and poultry — had to be taken without his consent, and then he churlishly pouched the money.

The place was already full enough, but Villiers and myself were taken in and treated hospitably. We came empty-handed on horseback; MacGahan had lost his waggon and servants as usual, but Mr. Boyle travelled luxuriously. His waggon contained considerable creature-comforts, and his man "King," who called himself "a Yorkshire Turk" and who spoke all languages equally badly, looked after the proviant and did the cooking. The day we arrived was turkey-day. King is on the alert. Seizing the moment he catches a turkey — to the fury of the owner, who subsides on the instant when he sees the bird is headless, and placidly accepts a franc. This formula of giving refusal, I find, is a regular thing, is gone through every day, and has come to be accepted as a matter of course. King skewers the bird with a stick and puts it on the fire, legs all abroad and feathers frizzling. There is a sutler over the way who sells bacon in slices and a concoction which he calls wine for which he charges famine prices. The dessert habitually consists of a roly-poly pudding in which Crosse and Blackwell's jam is a luscious ingredient and earns for Boyle the donor a store of blessings. Then follows unlimited tea, for some one has a samovar, and it is drunk out of glasses with a modicum of sugar held in the mouth, but, alas, there is no lemon.

Skobeleff, returning from a visit to the Trojan Pass and from a series of reconnaissances against Loftcha, came in to dinner, full of energy and frankness as usual. He was followed by two of his Caucasians carrying a bucket of soup, the general's contribution to our meal. The soup was that on which, with his black bread, the Russian soldier chiefly lives, whether in the field or in barracks. I have often tried to analyse it, but never with success. Mr. Boyle went into the question closely, and this was his report: "Its essence is all sorts of meat, its accidents cabbage, pumpkin, onions when they can be foraged, and in a general way everything that the company can pick up. Grapes are much esteemed, crab apples and wild pears have their value, maize is rightly held to be a most desirable ingredient. If, in looking for these, a soldier finds anything whatever that may strike his fancy, he pops it into the soup—say, a weasel, a bunch of love-apples, a crow, a chilé, or a melon. The compound is not nice, but many a time have we paid the company cook a rouble for a portion."

On the morning of the previous day (August 30th) the Turks from Plevna had made a furious attack on the Russian position in front of Poradim, and the battle, although it did not last long, was one of the most hardly fought combats of the war. Lame as he was, MacGahan had been a witness of the fierce and stubborn struggle; and after dinner, as we sat or lay drinking tea, he gave an account of what he had seen to General Skobeleff. I listened, as you may imagine, with the greatest interest and attention, and the same night wrote out my recollections of what I had heard not two hours before. This is what MacGahan had to tell: —

"We first heard the sound of distant cannonading about half-past six in the morning, and most people thought the demonstration — for it was regarded as nothing more — was against the Roumanians on the right flank. No reports came in, and becoming impatient, I mounted and rode to the front, three miles distant, where was the left flank of the entrenched position facing Plevna on the east and north. As I rode towards Pelischat I met great crowds of Bulgarian refugees fleeing from the vicinity of the fighting; and the ambulances were already coming back with the wounded. The vine-clad hills between Pelischat and Sgalevitza, further northward, were covered with heavy cannon-smoke, and the fierce bicker of rifle-fire mingled with the thunder of artillery so loudly as to show that if the Turks were merely making a demonstration it was a very violent one, to say the least of it. Just to the right of Pelischat a Russian battery was in energetic action, throwing shells over the ridge a mile in front, which exploded out of sight in the direction of a Russian redoubt which I knew to be there. It was clear, then, that the Turks were in possession of this redoubt, and that the Russian left had been thrown back on the trenches in front of Pelischat. Galloping forward to an elevation just left of that village, I found there some officers who told me that the redoubt I have mentioned had been taken by the Turks at the beginning of the fight, retaken by the Russians, and finally was again in

Turkish possession and was now being furiously shelled by the Russian batteries.

"I had not been on the hillock five minutes when suddenly the crest of the ridge in front grew black as with a line of ink drawn across the clear sky. Through the glass I discerned this black line to be the Turkish army, preparing for a direct assault on the Russian positions after its initial success in capturing the advanced redoubt. The ridge it held commanded that occupied by the Russians from Pelischat to Sgalevitza, and the distance between the two ridges was something over a mile. General Zotoff, who was the Russian commander, had manned the trenches in front of both those places and the space between them with four whole regiments — about 10,000 men — had brought three batteries into action, and had ordered up his reserves. In less than five minutes after crowning the forward ridge the Turks began to descend the hither slope straight in our direction, leisurely and without firing, not in masses or lines but scattered and diffused. They came down about half-way in this manner, the Russian shells all the time tearing up the groups they formed in the most savage manner.

"Just as I was thinking of clearing out the Turks brought up their right shoulders, their front bending nearly half-left, and, while the Russian infantry-fire was now punishing them heavily, they went at the Russian trenches about half-way between the two villages with shouts of 'Allah!' opening fire at the same time. As they rushed forward they descended into a little intermediate hollow and were lost to my view for a short time, while the Russian trenches smoked and flamed and a storm of bullets poured down upon the Turks struggling onward through the hollow. This lasted from fifteen to twenty minutes, during which time a fearful loss of life must have occurred. Then we saw the Turks begin to withdraw, carrying off their wounded as they went. But the brave fellows had not yet enough.

"They had scarcely withdrawn out of range of the Russian fire when they hardened their hearts and came on again to the attack. Scourged by shot and shell they plunged gallantly down into the valley of the shadow of death, to struggle there amid smoke and fire in a death-struggle of giants — for, Skobeleff, no man knows better than yourself that there is nothing to choose between Turk and Russian on the score of bravery. Dozens of Turkish bodies were found on the very lip of the Russian trenches. The gentle slope, on the crest of which those trenches were, was literally covered with dead. I counted seven in a space of not more than ten feet square. The battle here was terrible; the Turks were again repulsed and again retired out of fire. You will hardly believe me when I tell you that the indomitable Turks went at it yet again; but it is the fact that they did so. To us who had watched the two preceding assaults this third effort seemed sheer madness, because we could see that the Russian fire never slackened an instant and that the Russian line never wavered; while we knew, also, that the Russian reserves were waiting behind ready to fall on at the least sign of wavering on the part of the troops in the trenches.

"The scene of carnage was again repeated, but the struggle now lasted only for a few moments. The Turks, completely broken, withdrew sullenly, firing and taking time to carry off their wounded and indeed many of their dead. Still they held on to the redoubt which they had earlier captured and upon which they fell back with the apparent intention of retaining it permanently, but they were not allowed to remain long in occupation of that work. The Russians followed up with a murderous fire, and then six strong companies went at the redoubt with the bayonet and swept the Turks out of it like a whirlwind. Very soon the Turks were in retreat everywhere; the Russians regained the whole of their advanced positions and pursued the Turks some distance with cavalry. The Russians, engaged and in reserve, were about 20,000; their loss was about 1,000. There were probably about 25,000 Turks with about 50 guns; their loss we reckoned roughly at 3,000 men killed and wounded. No prisoners were taken on either side."

In talking the matter over, neither Skobeleff nor MacGahan could divine what was the object of Osman Pasha in making this attack. In the words of the former, it was too strong for a reconnaissance and too weak for a serious attack.

That same night Skobeleff — who had come from Loftcha merely for the day to consult with General Zotoff in command here at Poradim in regard to some difficulty which had presented itself to Prince Imeretinsky who had the superior charge of the Russian forces about Loftcha — left on his return to his quarters at Kakrinka, on the east of Loftcha, a ride of about 18 miles. "I believe," said he, "that there will be wigs on the green to-morrow in front of Loftcha. Do any of you fellows care to see the fun? If so, saddle up and come along!"

Boyle had no horse available, Jackson did not ride, Villiers was oppressed by a pile of unfinished sketches, and when Skobeleff came from Zotoff and shouted — "Who's for Kakrinka?" MacGahan and myself were the only volunteers. I own that I wanted to see what Skobeleff called "the fun" — that was one reason why I went; another was that MacGahan was still very lame, and quite unable to get out of any difficulty on foot if any accident should occur to his horse. As we rode along in the darkness, I listened in great surprise to Skobeleff's animated and bitter talk. "I've a good mind," said he to MacGahan, "to desert and join the Turks — I am so mad with our idiots of the headquarter staff. I don't speak of the Grand Duke Nicholas — he is a mere figure-head and has about as much notion of conducting a campaign as I have of the differential calculus. Old Nepokoitschitsky, the chief of staff, is a mere sergeant-major, and has learned nothing since the Crimean war in which he distinguished himself by bull-headed personal bravery. The man who is responsible for all our follies and troubles is that pedantic Professor Levitsky, the assistant chief of staff. It was he, for instance, who as soon as it was known that a Turkish army was marching down the Danube from Widdin, should have sent out reconnaissances to watch it, which should never have lost touch of it until a Russian army was ready to meet and fight it before it could threaten our right flank. Nothing of this nature was done, and the Turks were actually in Plevna and fortifying their position before we were aware that they were within 20 miles of us. That was bad enough in all conscience; and our blundering and stupid neglect in not occupying Plevna in advance of the approach of the Turks has wrought us mischief of which we cannot yet know the final result. But one thing is certain, that as soon as we knew of the occupation of Plevna by the Turks we should immediately have seized and held Loftcha. And this for two obvious reasons. With the Turks in Loftcha it is just as impossible for us to cross the Balkans as it would be if we had retaken Plevna in the attempt of July 30th. The possession of either point — of Loftcha as well as of Plevna — equally hinders our advance southward of the Balkans. I hope that in a day or two Loftcha may be ours. But even so, while Plevna is held by the Turks we still remain pinned down to the region northward of the mountains.

"And, again, just look at the mince-meat which Levitsky has made of the army while waiting on the defensive for the reinforcements which are now arriving! Divisions, brigades, and even regiments have been cut up, parcelled out, and sent to all the points of the compass — dispersed in order to patch up a hole here and close a crevice there, to such an extent of dislocation that their reunion will present the greatest difficulties. Just look, for example, at the 14th Division, which we consider the best in the army. A part of it is at Osman Bazaar, another about Elena, a part at Khaini, a part at Selvi, a part at Tirnova; all points far apart and having no tactical connection with each other. Its commander is left at Tirnova with a couple of battalions, his fine division dispersed in fragments all over the face of the country. All this dislocation has arisen from Levitsky's miscalculation of the important defensive points and the force required for each point; and then from his efforts to remedy the miscalculation in a hand-to-mouth fashion by grabbing troops wherever he could find them — a battalion here, a regiment there — hurriedly to strengthen the threatened and weak positions. These blunders of Levitsky stare every one in the face — personally I wonder that he has not been man enough to go out and hang himself. But no — he still blunders along with all the self-complacency in life; and if the Commander-in-Chief has found him out by this time, as he surely must have done, he has not given himself the trouble to send him home to his congenial duty of instructing cadets."

Skobeleff rode on for a couple of versts in silence, occasionally muttering to himself. Then he broke out again: "The Russian soldier is beyond all praise — he is a trifle stupid, but he is brave and staunch and he does not know what a panic means. Our weakness is in the officers. They are frank enough. You will hear them honestly confess: 'Ah, if we were but half as good as our soldiers, the Russian army would be the best in the world!' Our senior generals are nearly all bad, veterans although a good many of them are. I will tell you how this came about. After the Crimean war there was in Russia a very strong and bitter feeling against the army in consequence of the surrender of Sevastopol, and the conclusion of what was regarded as a discreditable peace. The popular feeling was so strong that the Government yielded to it, and indeed neglected the army. The service thus became unpopular, and the best and bravest of the officers who had distinguished themselves in the war — the men who were capable of profiting by the experience gained, who had become splendid officers in the stern ordeal of battle — became disgusted and indignant at the treatment they received, and resigned their commissions. Those were the men who should have been the generals of to-day. When they retired their places were taken by men of an inferior class, whose want of means prevented their retirement, whose want of education hindered them from adopting civil professions, or whose thick-skinnedness made them indifferent to neglect and reproach. And these are the men who are our generals to-day. You, MacGahan, have eyes in your head, and you have been with us since we crossed the Pruth. I ask you, of the sixty or seventy generals of brigade, division or corps commanders, have you yet seen one man who has given proof of exceptional talent, who has risen high enough above the level of mediocrity to challenge attention, who has begun to make any sign as being the man of the future? Well, yes, as you say, you have seen Gourko, a man of great energy and a brilliant handler of cavalry, but he had to come back through the same pass in the Balkans as that by which he had gone out. Dragomiroff? — well, he is a sensible elderly gentleman who is earnest enough, and his dispositions for the crossing of the Danube — no great exploit — were quite satisfactory; but he himself should have been across earlier than was the case. Radetski? — a grand old war dog, yes, and knows about as much of strategy and tactics as the sergeant-major of one of his regiments.

"In the lower grades of officerhood, things, I admit," continued Skobeleff, "are better. The company officers and the heads of regiments are good men, and will compare favourably with officers of the same rank in any European army except the Prussian. By a wholesome law recently decreed the command of a company may be given to a lieutenant if its captain should show himself incapable or negligent. As the actual command of a company carries an addition of 500 roubles to the officer's pay, the lieutenants are very anxious to prove themselves competent to command a company, while the captains who have companies are careful by no neglect of duty to give occasion for being deprived of their command, and so lapsing into the position of being simply 'attached' to the regiment.

"Once the captain becomes a major, however, and receives the command of a battalion, the case becomes different. He has then little to fear and little to hope for but his retirement and his pension. Unless he does something very bad, his battalion cannot be taken from him; and unless he finds some opportunity to really distinguish himself, or unless he has powerful friends, it is difficult for him to get a regiment. The result is that he generally settles down into an apathetic, indifferent officer, who barely does his duty and no more, with nothing better to look forward to. The commanders of regiments are a better class of men, as you may have had occasion to notice. They are either those officers who have distinguished themselves in the lower grades and were promoted for bravery, a brilliant action, marked capacity, superior education and intelligence; or else they are officers from the Guards, men of good family, with position, education, and fortune. I will not go so far as to say that they are often very studious, or very much given to consuming the midnight oil, at least for purposes of study; but they are brave, clever, active, and intelligent, with honour and reputation at stake, and, taken all in all, a creditable body of officers."

In the grey morning dawn Kakrinka seemed rather a worse dog-hole than Poradim. But there was one good house where Skobeleff had his quarters, and MacGahan and myself were his guests. After a few hours' sleep Skobeleff called us to a somewhat late breakfast. There was no hurry, he said — Imeretinsky, who was the commanding officer, had not yet begun his march from Selvi, and pending his chief's arrival Skobeleff was to undertake merely the preliminaries. His force was far from strong. MacGahan remarked to him that if the Turks had any enterprise, they would surely come out and cut him to pieces. "What are the relative strengths?" asked Mac-Gahan. "Oh," replied Skobeleff with a yawn, "I suppose good Mr. Adil Pasha has some 15,000 men in and around Loftcha." "And you?" asked MacGahan. "Well, I don't grumble," answered Skobeleff,— "I have some 3,500 infantry, the Caucasian Cossack cavalry brigade, and two batteries; and I can either stand or run as I think best." I had already seen a good deal of Skobeleff, and he had not seemed to me to be the kind of man who was fond of running.

It was September 1st. About noon Skobeleff left Kakrinka and marched with his little force along the Selvi road in the direction of Loftcha. After a two hours' march, he halted near the foot of a long ridge running north and south. On the ridge, some distance northward of the point where the road crossed it, was a small Turkish

camp without artillery. On this camp Skobeleff opened
fire with his guns, and the Turks very soon retired, skirmishing as they went. Pickets were sent up to hold the
ridge while the force occupied the adjacent village of
Paltijan. This seemed to me not much of a day's work,
and posing in my ingenuousness as an embryo military
critic, I made a remark to MacGahan to that effect. After
a passing allusion to the profound wisdom of young people who addict themselves to the instruction of their
grandmothers in the science of sucking eggs, he suggested
that I should wait until night fell, when I should see what
I should see. In the dusk Skobeleff mustered his detachment and marched up to the ridge, where his pickets were
already. Then the whole force went to work to entrench
the position and to construct epaulements for 24 guns, in
readiness to be placed in which were the eight guns belonging to the detachment. MacGahan had told Skobeleff
of my comment on the idleness of the day. The general
came to where I was and sat down beside me to smoke
a cigar. He had been working with his own hands in
a trench, part of the earth from which he had brought
away on his clothes. "Well, young fellow," said he,
"how do you like night work?" "What I wonder at,"
was my sage reply, "is why you should prefer to work in
the darkness instead of doing yesterday afternoon what
you are doing now." "I am a very humane man," said
Skobeleff — "it is my misfortune and my sorrow that
sometimes I cannot avoid having my men killed; but I do
spare them all I can. We are here within range of the
Turkish cannon on the Red Hill, which you have not yet
seen; had we set about entrenching in daylight they

would have made things very unpleasant. Now that it is comparatively dark, you may have observed that I had forbidden all lights. The Turks keep bad watch, and we are working in safety."

At daybreak of the 2nd Skobeleff opened an enfilading fire on the Turkish battery on the ridge south of the road. The battery soon gave out, but the Turkish infantry who had been in camp behind it were not dislodged until the afternoon. As they reluctantly departed, Skobeleff determined to send a regiment after them to quicken their pace and to force the Turkish infantry which he believed to be behind the Red Hill to deploy and thus show their strength. It was a pretty sight enough, the desultory skirmishing between the Turkish rear and the riflemen in the Russian front. Presently, however, the Russians pushed forward rapidly, and in less time than I had thought possible they were nearing the foot of the Red Hill. Skobeleff, who had not closed an eye all night, was taking forty winks in the lee of an epaulement. MacGahan woke him, and silently pointed towards Loftcha. The Kirghis lad who was his groom had recognised the situation, and was standing close by holding Skobeleff's white Arab stallion and having his master's white coat over his arm. Skobeleff threw off his cloth tunic, scented himself, donned the white coat, mounted the Arab, and with his escort of a dozen Caucasian Cossacks at his back, galloped down the slope and along the road towards the Red Hill. By this time the Russian soldiers had broke into the double, and were running at top speed towards the hill, up which, indeed, some were already dodging by twos and threes under cover of the bushes and the little hollows. At first we thought Skobeleff had the intention to head an assault on the batteries on the hill. But as the Turkish infantry gathered on the flanks of their batteries, MacGahan scouted that idea. "Our fellows," said he, "are out of hand. They have got the fighting madness on them, and Skobeleff is galloping forward to stop them — that is what no other man could do now, and I question whether Skobeleff will succeed!"

We saw him tearing along the road, he and his handful of horse, the Turkish shells falling all about them. The white coat and the white horse formed a splendid target for the sharpshooters on the slopes of the Red Hill. Suddenly he stopped, waving his sword to right and left; then he dismounted and got on another horse; the white Arabian had been wounded — through the glass I could see the blood running down his shoulder. His escort of some twelve Cossacks when he started was now reduced to three, the others we had seen struck down in succession. The fire along the Turkish entrenchments was increasing and the Russians were still pressing forward. Skobeleff gave the spur to his fresh mount, a chestnut, and galloped forward at speed. As he reached the foot of the hill we could discern him gesticulating while his trumpeter kept sounding the "retreat;" and then his soldiers began sullenly to withdraw. Just then we saw him go down, man and horse together; MacGahan gripped me tight by the arm and exclaimed with a gasp: "He has got it this time!" I saw Skobeleff scramble to his feet, but then we lost sight of him, and MacGahan became greatly excited. "It is impossible," said he, "to go on in this way long without getting himself killed. He had two horses killed under him in the Plevna battle!"

Meanwhile the Turkish fire was on the increase. "The bullets must be falling about them like hail," said MacGahan; "it will be a miracle if Skobeleff comes out of it alive!" A cloud of dust and smoke gathered for a moment — the wind swept it away in a few minutes. And lo! there was Skobeleff on a third horse, coming back along the road at an easy trot in evident composure. He had not received a scratch — his white coat had hardly a stain on it. He swung himself out of the saddle, came up to us with a smile, and lit a cigarette. "The old gentleman will swear," he blandly remarked. "This makes the fourth horse I have had shot under me within the month. Poor papa! he little knows how many roubles he will have to fork out when next we meet!" Although Skobeleff did not know, he had lost a fifth horse. As I was going back to the camp, I found his Kirghis lad sitting on the ground weeping bitterly over the carcase of Skobeleff's noble Turcoman horse — the animal on which he had swum the Danube. Lad and horse had come all the way from Khokand. The Kirghis, although himself slightly wounded, had brought the horse back from under fire, and finding that his state was hopeless had killed him, skinned him, cut off his hoofs, and was now sitting by the carcase weeping over it, without paying the slightest attention to his own wound. He had been utterly indifferent when Skobeleff's other horses were killed; but this one, he said, was his countryman and brother — the only thing he had to remind him of his far-away home. The tears were running down the poor fellow's cheeks in a stream. He had two bullets through his clothes, one of which had made a flesh-wound in his arm.

Before starting on the ride which I have tried to describe to you, Skobeleff had ordered one of his regiments to occupy the position which the Turks had just evacuated on the section of ridge south of the road. The second night was spent there in entrenching that position, and in constructing battery emplacements. When Imeretinsky arrived on the evening of the 3rd with the bulk of the force, which, including Skobeleff's detachment, consisted of about 20,000 men and 80 guns, he found Skobeleff in possession of the commanding ridge east of Loftcha, with epaulements prepared for 56 guns — 24 on the ridge north of the road, 32 on the section to its south. During the night the guns were brought up into position by the infantry. General Dobrovolski with the 3rd Rifle Brigade was away to the right in front of the village of Prissiaka, from which he had driven the Turkish pickets.

The line of the Turkish position was along a series of knolls on the eastern bank of the river Osma, the commanding position being at its southern extremity which the Russians called the "Red Hill" of which I have already told you. In strength of men as well as in number of guns the Turks were considerably the weaker; but they had the counter-benefit of a strong defensive position further strengthened by a series of lines of entrenchment. The town of Loftcha is on the western bank, and on an elevation behind the town the Turks had a strong redoubt, several batteries, and several successive lines of entrenchments. All this which I now tell you, we only knew after the place had been carried.

Skobeleff had carefully prepared overnight the scheme of attack. I wish I had a copy of that document to read to you: it would convince you that Skobeleff was not less a skilled and wise scientific officer than a man whose presence in front of his troops carried his men with him like a whirlwind. His scheme enjoined the bombardment of the Red Hill for several hours, and then an assault upon it to be followed by the occupation of the trenches further north. This scheme was somewhat interfered with by an attack made by the Turks from those northern hills on the village of Prissiaka, which after some hard fighting was repulsed by General Dobrovolski, who dislodged the Turks and drove them across the river with considerable loss.

The cannonade lasted for eight hours. It was an unequal strife, for the Russian batteries on the ridge mounted 56 guns against the 12 with which the Turks held the Red Hill. At length about 2 p.m. the latter were crushed, and Skobeleff moved out to the attack at the head of two regiments — about 5,000 men. The bombardment, as we found when we followed Skobeleff on to the Red Hill, had knocked about the Turkish entrenchments very severely. They were full of dead and wounded, and the Russian attack encountered very little resistance. By three o'clock there was not a Turk east of the Osma. Skobeleff hurried up two batteries which he stationed on the Red Hill to fire on the redoubt beyond the town; then he crossed the river, fought his way through the town in spite of a strong resistance on the part of the Turks whom he ultimately drove through and out of it, and then deployed his troops in the gardens on its outskirts in face of the second Turkish position. By this time his force had been increased to a strength of some thirteen battalions — about 9,000 men; two more were lining the river to the north and the Rifle Brigade was working round the Turkish flank. While the infantrymen among the gardens were resting after their exertions, four batteries were maintaining a continuous fire on the Turkish redoubt. At length, at half-past five, Skobeleff gave the word. The cannonade ceased and the whole infantry line sprang forward, Skobeleff himself making a direct assault from the gardens, a detached brigade fording the river lower down and taking the Turks in flank, while the Rifle Brigade on the extreme right held the Plevna road and prevented the Turkish retreat in that direction.

The Turks fought on the defensive with great desperation. They succeeded in carrying off the whole of their artillery, sending it to the south-west by the Mikren road. Their infantry covered the withdrawal with fine constancy, maintaining a hot fire which was very destructive to their Russian adversaries. But the resolute Russians steadily continued their advance; and at length the Turks were driven entirely out of their entrenchments and now held only the main redoubt, which, although surrounded on three sides, kept up its fire to the very last. The Russians hung somewhat around it, for it was a grim and formidable obstacle. Suddenly we heard a great cheer; a broad back in a white coat was seen to rush up the sloping face of the Turkish work. A swarm of dark-clothed men followed their guiding spirit, and the redoubt was carried at dusk in the midst of a hand-to-hand struggle in which perished all its defenders and many of its assailants. At the close of the fight we entered the redoubt to witness a ghastly sight. The bodies of the dead and wounded, Russians and Turks together, lay piled up in a mass six feet deep around the gorge. Skobeleff stood panting in the heart of the slaughter, leaning on his bloody sword. He was unhurt, but there were great smears of blood on the white coat. It was after this success that the Emperor toasted him as " The Hero of Loftcha."

The Turks departed in scattered bands along the road to Mikren. Imeretinsky was under orders to move towards Plevna, but he detached the Caucasian Cossack brigade to follow up the Turkish retreat which soon degenerated into a rout. Pursuers and pursued were co-religionists, but there was no ruth in the hearts of the Cossack Mahomedans for the Ottoman followers of the Prophet. When they rejoined Imeretinsky's command their boast was that they had slain 3,000 Turkish fugitives in the long and fierce pursuit. In the capture of Loftcha the Russians lost 1,500 officers and men. The Turks suffered dreadfully. There were but 15,000 of them all told in Loftcha when the operations began: there were buried in and about Loftcha 2,200; 3,000 fell in the retreat. In effect Adil Pasha's force was cut to pieces: it made no attempt to recover Loftcha, and never showed a front any more.

CHAPTER VIII

THE SEPTEMBER BATTLE OF PLEVNA

MACGAHAN and I returned from Loftcha to the dog hole at Poradim on the evening of September 5th. The filthy village by this time was swarming with correspondents representing some half-score of European nationalities, not to speak of the gentlemen from the other side of the Atlantic. In the Bulgarian school-house of Poradim Prince Charles of Roumania was now in residence. He had been appointed to the chief command of the whole Russo-Roumanian army now before Plevna, with General Zotoff, lately commanding the 4th Russian Army Corps, as his chief of staff. As you know, Prince Charles — he is King Charles now — is of the great house of Hohenzollern, to the older branch of which he belongs. It is the junior branch which gives to Prussia its kings and to Germany its emperors. The prince was a lieutenant in a Prussian dragoon regiment when in 1866 he was chosen to be the ruler of Roumania. I believe that he had to reach Bucharest in the disguise of a courier — some say a footman — because of the opposition his election encountered on the part of unscrupulous malcontents. A quiet but resolute man, the prince made good his footing in Roumania; and in the course of the first ten years of his reign he had created a very respectable army, to which the Russians were much beholden during the crisis of their precarious tenure of Northern Bulgaria, while as yet their much-needed reinforcements were still on the way.

Three fine divisions of the Roumanian army were now before Plevna; the Russian corps which had lost heavily in the earlier fighting about Plevna had been replenished from the reserves at home; two fresh divisions, hurried forward from Russia, were now on the Bulgarian side of the Danube. The whole region east of Plevna swarmed with armed men, and the ground was cumbered by regiments of cavalry and great parks of artillery. We were on the eve of witnessing the third attempt by the Russians to expel Osman Pasha and his Turks from that position which they had occupied so long and so obstinately, and had fortified with so much skill. For myself, in my innocent worship of numbers, I took it as a pure certainty that the Russians this time would accomplish their purpose. The closest estimate of the Turkish strength was based on figures which MacGahan obtained from the headquarter staff;—according to which Osman had about 56,000 infantry, 2,500 cavalry, and 80 guns. He spent the evening in working out the Russian strength from figures in his possession, and his final estimate was that it amounted in round numbers to 75,000 infantry, 10,000 cavalry, 364 field-guns, 54 horse-guns, and 20 siege-guns of 15 centimetres. That seemed to me overwhelming odds in favour of the Russians; but MacGahan to my great surprise prophesied frankly that they would be beaten. "It is an axiom of war," he explained, "that the minimum strength of the assailants of a strong position held by an adequate force of resolute troops must be double that of the defence;

PRINCE CHARLES OF ROUMANIA.

and to ensure success ought to be three times as great. You will observe," he continued, " that the Russian strength is in excess of the Turkish by scarcely one-third. It is true that the Turks are disproportionately weak in artillery; but in this case that is far from being the serious matter you may suppose. The Turkish defences are exclusively earthworks; and I learned to know in our civil war how little avail is artillery against solid mounds of earth. For well on to a year Lee's rebel army in Petersburg held at bay from behind their lines of improvised earthworks all the efforts of Grant's army more than double its strength, and in the end was beaten out of the position neither by artillery-fire nor by assault, but withdrew to escape from being invested. Mark my words, youngster," remarked the shrewd American — " the Russians will be whipped before Plevna this time as before; then they will realise that they cannot scoop Osman out of it by dint of hard blows, and they will do with him as the Germans did with Bazaine in Metz — compel him to surrender by the argument of starvation."

On the afternoon of the 6th we rode out towards the front in the direction of Bogot. The order had been given that the whole army except the reserves should bivouac tonight close up to the forepost line. Everywhere the troops were advancing. The scene was very impressive. Here a long column of cavalry, with dancing pennons on their lances, wound up the gentle green slope of the downs. There a whole infantry regiment stood in dense black square waiting for the command to march. Yonder another, deployed into line, swept briskly forward with bayonets flashing in the sunshine. Battery after battery passed onward, the rattle of the wheels muffled by the grassy carpet. Slowly and with infinite labour the ox-teams lumbered forwards, drawing the great siege-guns and their ammunition on the way to the prepared positions whence to-morrow the huge projectiles would hurtle into the Gravitza redoubt. On our right tramped the men of Krüdener's corps carrying fascines, gabions, and hewn logs, to be used in constructing the platforms for the siege-guns. Ambulance waggons, empty as yet, were going towards the front by the score. The soldiers were in high condition and fine spirits. There was a hearty ring in their shout of answer to the greetings of the generals who rode past them. As the Grand Duke Nicholas dashed by at a striding gallop amidst a hurricane of cheers, "*Morituri te salutant*" murmured the pessimist MacGahan.

We rode back to Poradim for the last regular meal we were to partake of there for a good many days to come. The arrangements for bivouacking were complete. MacGahan's long-lost waggon had at last turned up, and Isaac rejoiced to rejoin his erratic master. Both it and Villiers' waggon had been victualled very fully in Sistova; and if the fighting should last a fortnight without intermission there would still be corn in Egypt so far as we were concerned. A couple of trustworthy couriers had been sent on from Bucharest and had accompanied the waggons. The plan of journalistic campaign was the joint production of MacGahan, Jackson, and Villiers, with an occasional suggestion from myself. The two couriers were to remain at a certain straw-stack on the ridge in front of Zgalevitza, equidistant from each Russian flank. There Mr. Jackson ensconced himself, with a fine commanding view and an excavation in the straw-stack in which he spent his nights. Young Mr. Salusbury was with his friends the Roumanians; Mr. Millett, who had come from the Dobrutscha, took charge along with Villiers of the Russian left centre on the Radischevo ridge, a region not new to the latter; and MacGahan was to be with Skobeleff on the extreme left at the village of Brestovatch. A depôt of supplies was to be left by the waggons at Mr. Jackson's straw-stack as they passed it on the morning of the 7th, dropping the couriers at the same place. Thence Villiers' waggon was to go forward and take post in the village of Radischevo, and MacGahan's to proceed yet further to the left and station itself in Brestovatch. I was primarily to accompany MacGahan, but my duty was to visit the other gentlemen from time to time, take any despatches which they might have ready, and carry those on to the couriers' station at Mr. Jackson's straw-stack. That gentleman despatched a courier every evening from the field. He had only to travel to Simnitza whence to Bucharest another relay of couriers was established, and he was to be back again at the straw-stack within twenty-four hours, so that there was a daily service between the straw-stack on the field of Plevna and the telegraph wire at Bucharest. Villiers, who was a fanciful young man, maintained that the dispositions made were calculated to elevate war-correspondence to the dignity of a Fine Art.

We started for the front so early as 3 a.m. of the 7th, because MacGahan was anxious to see the first shot fired from the siege battery, which he had been told would occur at daybreak. Riding forward in the darkness we struck on the battery soon after four o'clock. Here all was bustle and activity; but it was wonderful how quietly the work was gone about, the anxiety being that the Turks over against us in the Gravitza redoubt should not discover what was being done. They made no sign, whether from ignorance or from indifference it was impossible to know. Had they been at all on the alert, they could not well have missed ascertaining that during the entire night there were two whole Russian regiments in the village of Gravitza down in the intervening hollow only a few hundred yards from the redoubt, pushed out there to cover the construction of the batteries. Both these had been begun about 9 p.m., and were finished soon after midnight, the infantry working under the direction of the sappers. The first battery, containing eight guns, was built on a spur distant from the redoubt 4,300 yards to the south-east; the second, mounting 12 guns, was further back and to the left at a range of about 5,200 yards. The field artillery of Krüdener's corps was massed in the folds of ground behind and on either flank of the two siege-batteries, his infantry partly in the first line in their front, partly on either flank and in rear. As the day dawned, we could discern the positions of the rest of the Russian army. You have yourselves seen and travelled over the ground about Plevna; and you will also remember that, when telling you of the previous battle of Plevna on July 30th, I described the amphitheatre of Plevna as of a horseshoe shape with the town of Plevna about midway between the two heels, and its rim formed by a semicircular sweep of ridge. Krüdener's corps and the siege-batteries now occupied the section of ridge at the toe of the horseshoe. The Roumanians were on the northern upland behind and above the Gravitza redoubt — one division due north of it, another north-east of it, the reserve division in rear at the village of Verbitza. The southern rim of the horseshoe formed by the long Radischevo ridge, was occupied by the 4th Corps, its five batteries on the crest with the infantry in the valley behind. Further westward on the same alignment was Skobeleff, holding the ground on either side of the Loftcha road in front of Brestovatz, having the Turkish redoubts on the Krishin Hill on his left front.

It was clear, as soon as daylight enabled us to scan the scene, that Osman had made full use of the five weeks' interval of non-molestation accorded to him. From the Gravitza redoubt along the northern upland to Bukova on the west, there was now a great continuous shelter-trench studded with redoubts and batteries. On the lower elevation east of the town, the redoubts which Schahofskoy had taken and abandoned on July 30th were greatly enlarged, and on the successive neighbouring knolls were five or six more redoubts forming a regular nest and linked one to the other by lines of entrenchment. There were now defensive works in rear of Plevna itself, and on the Krishin Hill south-west of it, on which the Turks had not so much as a picket on July 30th, was now quite a group of redoubts elaborately constructed and occupying commanding positions. MacGahan studied the scene in front of him through his telescope for many minutes; when he closed it he quietly remarked: "The Gravitza redoubt is no longer the key of the position. It might fall to-day and Osman would be but little the weaker. Yonder, away to the south-west, that Krishin Hill with its redoubts — that is now the key of the position. That is in Skobeleff's country; if he had a couple of army corps instead of a detachment and if he were not killed in the attempt, I believe he could be in Plevna on the second day!"

At six o'clock the first shot was fired from the 8-gun siege-battery at the Gravitza redoubt. The aim was good; the shell fell into the work. The scene was immediately very comical. Before the shot not a Turk had been visible in or about the redoubt; there was not even a sentry. At the sound of it a few men came up on to the parapet, patently rubbing their eyes as we watched them through our glasses. I distinctly saw one man yawn. They stared around in a curiously absent way — it seemed clear that the shot had been the first intimation to them of the proximity of the Russians. It struck me that they were half-thinking of going to bed again when there came a second shot, and that seemed to convince them that business was on hand.

But all the same they took things very leisurely, and their guns did not begin to answer the Russian artillery for quite half an hour. The cannonade lasted all day. Twenty siege-guns and 88 field-guns hammered at the Gravitza redoubt without ceasing. Clouds of dust rose every few minutes from its thick parapet, proving the accuracy of the Russian fire; but little perceptible damage was done, and the eight guns which were the armament of the redoubt answered leisurely throughout the day.

Throughout the 8th the bombardment was steadily maintained and as steadily endured. The damage done by the Russian fire to the Gravitza redoubt had been made good overnight, and in the morning it looked as trim as if never a shot had struck it. The Russian siege-batteries had been brought forward under cover of night, and now overhung the Gravitza village. It was passing strange to look from the battery down into that village in the hollow below where the villagers, with shells interminably whistling over their heads, were actually busy treading out their barley on the primitive threshing-floor of hardened mud, the men tossing the sheaves about, the women driving the ponies in their endless round. I went down into the village on the errand to ascertain how the folks of Gravitza and their Turkish neighbours in the redoubt had been getting along together during the term of Osman's occupation of Plevna. A Russian officer came along with me, who told me he had heard that the village had been the scene of horrible atrocities committed by the Turks. He was undeceived to some purpose. The head-man of the place, who was standing by the threshing-floor in the middle of the village, told us that the Turks had never taken anything from his people without payment on the spot. The Russian officer scarcely liked what the honest farmer added, that " he would be very well pleased if, when the Turks had gone and the Russians come, the Russians were to behave as well as the Turks had done."

The bombardment lasted without abatement for five long days. During the last three days of that time I was mostly with MacGahan in or before Brestovatz in Skobeleff's region; and it was only when I rode from thence to the straw-stack in front of Zgalevitza, that I learned or saw anything of what was going on in the Radischevo and Gravitza sections of the attack. I remember that on my way to the straw-stack in the afternoon of the 9th conveying MacGahan's daily budget — the day was the Sabbath, but there was no Sabbath-keeping before Plevna — I saw a spurt of Roumanian infantry in the direction of the Gravitza redoubt, which was promptly crushed by a most murderous rifle-fire by its defenders. The Gravitza had almost entirely given up even the pretence of replying to the Russian artillery fire, but it could still sting venomously with its small arms. Through the glass I could discern masses of the Turkish infantrymen lying in the hollows of the northern upland, having quitted the shell-scourged redoubt for, as I supposed, the sake of comparative safety.

What I witnessed when with Skobeleff and MacGahan on the left wing during the four days' fighting, I will presently recount to you. Skobeleff's fighting was a thing altogether isolated from the rest of the operations, and I mean to finish the narrative of what I casually saw of the latter before entering on the description of the former. Tuesday the 11th was the Emperor's fête-day, and a general assault had been ordered for three o'clock in the afternoon. The cannonade was to last along the whole line from daybreak until 8 a.m.; then a pause until 11; then a heavy fire until 1 p.m.; then another pause until 2.30 p.m., and then a fierce cannonade until 3 p.m., when the assaults were to begin. Fog interfered with this programme, the intention of which I never knew anybody who understood. During the lulls in the cannonade the Turks jauntily came out from behind the parapets of their works and strolled about the glacis with the coolest indifference. The fog lifted in the late afternoon, just as I was quitting the straw-stack after having given in to Jackson MacGahan's daily letter. Around the Gravitza redoubt a desperate fight was raging. The Roumanians had gone at it in three separate columns and all three had been repulsed; one could see the dead and dying strewing the grassy slopes on two sides of the redoubt. It was now the turn of a Russian brigade which had been occupying the village of Gravitza, and which, by riding to the high ground overhanging the village, I could watch deploying to the west of it and then advancing on the redoubt up the steep and slippery slope from the bank of the Gravitza stream. Averting my eyes from the slaughter which those staunch and gallant men were enduring, I turned my head to witness a spectacle scarcely less thrilling.

I had known, although I had never previously seen him there, that the Emperor Alexander had been present in the field from the first day of this long bitter conflict. The sappers had constructed for him on a little eminence beyond the line of fire a sort of outlook place from which was visible a great sweep of the scene of action. Behind it was a marquee in which was a long table continually spread with food and wine, where the suite supported nature jovially while men were dying hard by. As for the Czar himself, men said that after the first two days he neither ate nor drank; that anxiety visibly devoured him; and that he could not be restrained from leaving the observatory and wandering around among the gunners. I watched him now, on this afternoon of the fifth day of the colossal struggle — it was his fête-day, save the mark! — as he stood there alone on the little balcony of the lookout place in the sullen autumn weather, gazing out with haggard straining eyes at the efforts of the soldiers to storm the Gravitza redoubt yonder. Assault after assault had been made, and had failed; and now the final desperate effort was being made under his eyes, the forlorn hope of the day. The Turkish fire was smiting in their faces his Russians as they battled their way up the steep slope slippery already with Roumanian blood; the pale drawn face on the balcony quivered in agony and the tall figure winced and cowered. As he stood there in solitary anguish, he was a spectacle of majestic misery that I never can forget.

With awful losses the battalions staggered forward and upward. At last one battalion rushed over one of the trenches on the flank of the redoubt. Aided by its fire, another battalion charged the redoubt from the south at the same moment that part of a Roumanian brigade made a desperate attempt on its eastern face. The combined effort was successful, and the redoubt was carried and its garrison slain almost to a man. But it turned out presently that there were now two Gravitza redoubts, and it was only the original and the weaker one that had been stormed. From the second redoubt on the higher ground and from the connecting trenches the Turks maintained an insupportable fire on the conquerors of the first redoubt, and half an hour later they delivered an assault and swept out of it Russians and Roumanians alike. The dusk was gathering, through which one could still discern the confused hand-to-hand fight that was being furiously maintained.

The end darkness prevented me from seeing; but next day I was informed that Russian and Roumanian reinforcements had fought their way up again and that the redoubt was finally lost to the Turks. It was a barren triumph while the second and dominating redoubt remained in possession of the Turks, as it did for three months longer. The trophies of the capture of the Gravitza were five guns and a flag. The interior of the redoubt and its ditch were literally paved with dead bodies. How close and bitter had been the fighting may be gathered from the fact that the Roumanians had more men killed than wounded. Their losses were 56 officers and 2,500 men; the Russian losses were 22 officers and 1,300 men. And after all this slaughter the reduction of Plevna was no nearer than before a shot had been fired!

You will remember that I told you that Skobeleff's position was on the extreme left of the half-circle held by the Russo-Roumanian army. It was in a manner isolated, since the deep ravine of the Tutchenitza brook separated it from the Radischevo ridge held by the 4th Corps. The village of Brestovatz, which was Skobeleff's headquarters, and where MacGahan's waggon was posted from the 7th, lay almost due south of Plevna on the left of the Loftcha road. It was not a very pleasant quarter, for on its left front behind the village of Krishin was a Turkish redoubt, shells from which occasionally fell in and about Brestovatz. Directly in Skobeleff's front and between him and Plevna, there rose a long rounded hill of considerable height studded with trees which were not dense enough to be called a wood. This elevation afterwards came to be called the "Green Hill"—I remember you telling me that when you visited Plevna the other day, you had climbed this hill and had found skulls and skeletons on its slopes lying there still exposed — and you must have observed as you followed the road over it that there were on its summit three successive knolls with intervening depressions. From the top of the knoll nearest Plevna — the "third knoll" it was called by Skobeleff — a wooded slope falls down into a valley in which is a little stream. Beyond this stream there is a steep ascent to the top of a long ridge running westward from the southern environs of Plevna. On this ridge was a long continuous entrenchment in the centre of which was a redoubt; there was another at its eastern extremity, and a third some distance beyond the western termination of the line of entrenchment. "If" — said Skobeleff to MacGahan, as they smoked together on the evening of the 7th — "if I can carry and hold that entrenchment and those redoubts, if reinforcements are sent to me whenever I ask for them, and if our people keep threatening the Turks all round the half-circle and on the day of the assault strike hard at the given points, I believe there is a reasonable chance that this time we may drive Osman out of Plevna. But everything turns on combination and co-operation; and these, as you must know by this time, are not our forte."

On the afternoon of the 8th Skobeleff began to take ground to his front. The advance was led by dragoons in skirmishing order with whom Skobeleff himself rode. Five battalions of infantry followed, which we accompanied, MacGahan on his pony, I on foot. The Turkish pickets among the trees on the first knoll fell back firing and joined the force holding the second knoll. There was some hard fighting before the latter was evacuated; but the Turks abandoned it and also, after a struggle, the third knoll, where Skobeleff was within a short mile of Plevna. He still went forward, sending his men down the wooded slope in loose order. The Turks obstinately hung in the intervening valley, firing steadily and covered by the shell-fire from the redoubts behind; but the Russians pressed on, and from the knoll we could see hundreds of Turkish soldiers retreating up the smooth slope towards the redoubt, other groups going away to their left into Plevna. The Russians, whose skirmish line had reached the bottom of the valley, held on staunchly in the face of a bitter fire of artillery and musketry from the central redoubt and its flanking trenches; but they could not advance and were gradually withdrawn, followed very promptly by the Turks to the second knoll and later to the first, where entrenchments were immediately thrown up by the Russians. The wisdom of this precaution was proved on the following morning, when the Turks attacked twice in great strength; the later attempt came within 60 yards of the trenches and was repulsed by case-shot. They retreated to the second knoll, Skobeleff remaining on the first throughout the 9th, the day of the general assault having been postponed.

As you know, it was finally ordered for the 11th and on the 10th he began his preparations. He had a curious set of men serving him as staff officers. In the rest of the army they went by the name of "the blackguards," and Skobeleff himself owned that they deserved the appellation. But they suited him — he required of them only two things, absolute obedience to his orders and indomitable bravery. Fulfilling these requisites they met his needs; he did not in the least mind that they were ruffians and blackguards. He associated with them scarcely at all except in the field; when he had a quiet hour he spent it with MacGahan. But before Plevna he had very few quiet hours. He was never satisfied until he had seen actually carried out every instruction which he had given. At daylight on the 10th he recovered the second knoll, and stood over his men while they fortified the position by throwing up shelter-trenches with their copper soup-dishes, bayonets, and naked hands — no entrenching tools being available. By the afternoon he had two batteries there with a couple of regiments, and in rear a reserve of two more regiments and two rifle battalions. He posted two batteries eastward of the Tutchenitza brook, whence they could enfilade the crest of the third knoll. Then he came back into Brestovatz and spent the evening talking with MacGahan over Balzac's novels, as much engrossed as if there was no such place as Plevna in the world. I sat in a corner of the hovel, wondering and admiring.

On the morning of the 11th the whole region was enveloped in a dense fog in which objects were invisible at a distance of half-a-dozen yards. It lifted somewhat towards 10 a.m., when Skobeleff began to move his advance forward to the third knoll, since from there his assault on the redoubts in his front could be more promptly begun when the specified hour for the general attack should come. Before the third knoll was in his possession there occurred a sharp skirmish of some duration, during which the fog lifted and showed us a stirring spectacle. About a mile south-east of Plevna, its front directly facing the left section of the Radischevo ridge, the Turks had a very formidable redoubt on the summit of an isolated mamelon with two long entrenchments on either flank. This redoubt, which we afterwards knew as "No. 10," you probably saw when you visited Plevna. Stimulated possibly by the sound of Skobeleff's skirmish although his fire was not in the direction or within range of "No. 10," the Turks in and about that redoubt advanced to attack a Russian regiment on the extreme left of the Radischevo ridge. They were repulsed. But then the Russian regiment, in ignorance or disregard of the general plan of assault and without the order of the division commander, followed up the retreating Turks; and when it became hotly engaged an adjacent regiment went forward in support. The two carried one line of entrenchment, but were dreadfully punished in front and flank from the redoubt and had to fall back into their previous positions. Their adventure cost them dear; one regiment lost one-half of its men and two-thirds of its officers and so was practically out of the fight for the day. We watched with horror the rush from entrenchments and redoubt of the Turkish irregulars hurrying to the butchery of the wounded Russians who lay so thick on the steep bare slopes of the mamelon. Through the glass one could discern the glint of the long knives brandished over prostrate forms and the upraised arms of the wounded appealing in vain for mercy. The fog closed down like a curtain on the scene of slaughter; but it lifted again for a time about noon and then it could be seen at a glance how critical was Skobeleff's position. He had to maintain a front of fire on the crest of the third knoll to prevent the Turks from assailing him, but he was being punished by shell-fire from the redoubts before him; while his troops lying down on the rearward slope, although covered from that fire, were exposed to an enfilading fire from the Krishin redoubt on their left flank.

Special permission was given to Skobeleff at his urgent request, that he might begin his assault so early as 1 p.m.; and he promptly acted. He had at his disposal six line regiments, four rifle battalions, and 24 guns; in all about 17,000 men. His first line, on the third knoll, consisted of two regiments with two rifle battalions in support; between the third and second knoll one regiment; on the second knoll in the fortified position two weak regiments with three batteries; and in reserve one regiment and two rifle battalions.

When his guns had been in action for half an hour he sent his first line forward to the assault, covered by the fire of his artillery. Preceded by a strong line of skirmishers the regiments went down the slope in company columns, with banners flying and bands playing. Skobeleff had ordered all but the skirmishers to hold their fire until near the redoubt, then to fire one volley and storm with the bayonet. The Turks were cleared out of their rifle-pits at the foot of the slope, the little stream was crossed, and the ascent was begun towards the Turkish work. Met by sheer avalanches of lead which only the most devoted among them could face, the soldiers began to lie down and took to firing on the Turkish trenches up yonder above them at a distance of some 200 yards. "The beginning of the end!" MacGahan muttered, as we lay together looking down into the hell of fog and smoke and blood, — "when they begin to hang like that there's not much more

THE ASSAULT ON THE MAMELON REDOUBT.

to be said!" While he spoke, we were trampled upon as we lay by a whole company column. We rose to our feet and became aware that a fresh wave of men, a whole regiment, was pouring down the slope in our front. Skobeleff, his finger on each throb of the pulse of battle, had discerned the symptoms of wavering in his first line. He caught the moment and swept forward to invigorate his front the troops which he had been holding in his hand on the reverse slope. And yonder behind were more supports, hurrying up to wait on the reverse slope the word from the chief who read so clearly the open page of the battle-field. The arrival of supports stimulated to fresh action the men who had been enduring but not progressing, and the loose line drifted some paces up the slope; but the strain of the effort was too great, and the men lay down again and renewed their fire. Clearly this situation could not last. The redoubt must be taken without delay, or the attempt to take it must be forthwith abandoned. The critical moment had come. Skobeleff had already sent forward his two reserve rifle battalions, and now only waited until his reserve line regiment had deployed on the third knoll and was hurrying down the slope beyond. He was wearing a white frock-coat with all his decorations, as was his invariable custom on a day of battle. "Good-bye, MacGahan!" he shouted as he mounted a white charger. — "Wish me good fortune, old friend!" "God bless you, Skobeleff!" was MacGahan's fervent response. The tall white figure on the white horse dashed at speed down the slope, passed the hurrying linesmen who gave their loved chief a great cheer as he sped by them, caught up the riflemen and swept them forward at the double. As the volley of cheering reached the prostrate advance, the men sprang to their feet and rapturously hailed the white-clad leader who dashed to the front blazing like a meteor. He reached the wavering fluctuating mass and imparted to it the inspiration of his own ardour and daring. The enthusiasm reached fever heat, there was a final rush up the slope; the white horse went down, but the rider was up in a moment. A torrent of men, headed ever by the conspicuous figure in white, swept over and into the Turkish entrenchments. There were a few minutes of desperate mêlée; then the Turks gave ground and the Russians, turning to their left, swarmed into the middle redoubt. It was a mass of flame and smoke from out which reached us a blood-curdling medley of shouts, screams, and cries of agony and defiance, that actually rose above the deep-mouthed bellowing of the cannon and the steady awful crash of the deadly rifle-fire.

It was three o'clock. As he lay looking down on the strife MacGahan had been writing hard in pencil, tearing sheet after sheet from his note-book and cramming them into an envelope. "Not a moment to spare, Carnegie!" he exclaimed, more excited than I had ever seen him — "this is the latest intelligence with a vengeance. You'll find my pony down in the hollow. You're a light weight and he can gallop — he is quite fresh. If you are at the straw-stack within an hour, you will catch the courier to Bucharest. Off, my son, and ride h—ll for leather!"

It was a rough road, but the little horse was game. Schnidnikoff's afternoon assault from the western end of the Radischevo ridge on the Turkish redoubt "No. 10" was in full blast as I galloped by, and the Turkish shells were dropping thick and fast on and about the road which I traversed. Passing Radischevo, I shouted to General Zotoff without drawing rein that Skobeleff had carried the Turkish redoubt on the western verge of Plevna. A hurrah from him and his staff followed me; half an hour later I was telling the news to Jackson as he sat in the mouth of his straw cavern, and in five minutes more I saw the courier ride away for Bucharest with MacGahan's matter in his wallet. It was then that I took the liberty of spending a couple of hours in watching the assaults on the Gravitza redoubt of which I have already given you a short account. Jackson gave me some tea, brown bread, and German sausage, and I had a slow ride in the darkness back to the spot where I had left MacGahan at three o'clock in the afternoon. At nine in the evening he was just where I had quitted him.

"Skobeleff has been here," he told me, "and has only just gone back to the second knoll. He hasn't a scratch, although his white coat is both bloody and muddy. His horse — it is his last white one — was shot dead just on the lip of the ditch. He has only got a sword-hilt with a mere stump of blade — a bullet cut away the rest of it just as he reached the parapet. Every man of his staff is either killed or wounded except that truculent war-dog Kuropatkin." I should tell you, perhaps, that Kuropatkin, who in the war-time was Skobeleff's chief of staff, is now a prince, no less. Recently he has been Governor-General of Central Asia, and I think he is now the Russian War Minister. "Skobeleff says," continued MacGahan, "that neither of the two redoubts in this Turkish line of entrenchment — the middle one which was first taken, and the eastern one close to Plevna — is properly speaking a redoubt at all, since both are enclosed only on three sides, the fourth side, that to the rear, being quite open, so that both are exposed to the fire from the trench of the Turkish camp 600 yards rearward. The ground it seems is hard and rocky, and without spades there are no means for closing the rear face of either redoubt. The first attempt from the middle redoubt to carry the eastward one failed, and nearly all the assailants perished. It was finally taken near sundown by some reinforcements which Colonel Shestakoff of Imeretinsky's staff brought up. Kuropatkin has been fighting desperately against a sortie from the redoubt on the Turkish right beyond the entrenchment, and has beaten it back. But Skobeleff recognises how precarious is his position, threatened as it is on both flanks and on both his right and left rear. He is short of troops to keep open his communications, with only four weak battalions protecting the guns in the fortified position on the second knoll. His men are utterly exhausted, he told me, and his ammunition is falling short. He has written to Zotoff explaining his condition, pointing out that it is untenable unless he is strongly reinforced, but adding that he will hold on as long as he can."

We went back for the night into the fortified position on the second knoll, where there was something to eat. Skobeleff was attacked several times during the night. On the morning of the 12th he came back to the second knoll for some guns to be placed in one of the captured redoubts. He told MacGahan that Zotoff had sent him orders to fortify his position and hold out to the last extremity, and that to his request for support the reply was: "We can send you no reinforcements, for we have none." Skobeleff returned to his redoubt just in time to meet another furious attack: it was repulsed; but the men, wearied and discouraged after long and hard fighting, had begun to trickle towards the rear. His position was gradually becoming altogether desperate. Everywhere else quietude reigned, and Osman could thus afford to use very strong forces against Skobeleff, now his only active antagonist. Attempts in great force were made to surround him entirely, the guns in the redoubt had been dismounted and all the gunners and teams killed. An ammunition waggon exploded by a Turkish shell burst in the midst of a mass of men, causing fearful loss and shaking the nerves of those who remained unhurt. Continuous assaults were made and repulsed throughout the day. The Turks were threatening yet another assault when the Russian occupants of the middle redoubt, worn out with continual fighting, began to quit it in an intermittent stream. But the assailants did not find it empty; there still remained as its garrison some 200 men under Major Gortaloff, who fought it out to the bitter end and died to the last man in a fierce hand-to-hand fight.

In the eastern redoubt and the connecting trenches there were still Russian soldiers who stubbornly maintained the fight. But their fate was imminent had they remained, and Skobeleff brought them off, covering the retreat by a regiment which had been sent him from the 4th Corps, the only reinforcement received by him during the two days of fighting and bloodshed. The Turks fired heavily on the retreating Russians, who nevertheless adhered to their close formation; they were reluctant to betake themselves to the extended order. Shoulder to shoulder they came back firmly and resolutely, disdaining to take a panic. But for the blood on hands, faces, and clothes, but for the many wounded in that mass of slowly-moving soldiers who were carried by their comrades on crossed rifles or painfully dragged themselves along leaning for support on their weapons, one might have supposed this to be a body of fresh troops marching quietly along in the ordinary conditions of a campaign. They even kept their distances, those remnants of heroic regiments emerging from a fierce battle of thirty hours' duration. Their strained countenances, their eyes ablaze with feverish brightness, alone betrayed the agitation of those steadfast defenders of the redoubt. Their torn flags drooped over their silent ranks. A few Turkish standards surmounted by gilded crescents unfolded their drapery blazoned with the name of "Allah," and testified eloquently that the soldiers bearing them were bringing back trophies of a defeat as glorious as victory would have been. They had not only preserved their own colours, they had also taken spoil from their enemy. It was a proud yet melancholy sight.

From the third knoll the retirement was continued to the second, but notwithstanding the protection afforded by the guns in the latter position, a stand could not be maintained there, and Skobeleff retired his shattered force to the first knoll, where we met him. For myself I thought for the moment that his mind had given way, so frenzied was his aspect. MacGahan drew a wonderful picture of him in his letter to the *Daily News*. "Late in the afternoon," he wrote, "I met General Skobeleff, for the first time since morning. He was in a fearful state of excitement and fury. His uniform was covered with blood, mud, and filth; his sword broken; his Cross of St. George twisted round over his shoulder; his face black with powder and smoke; his eyes haggard and bloodshot, and his voice quite gone. I never saw such a picture of battle as he presented." MacGahan and I visited him in his tent the same night. By this time he was quite calm and collected. He said in a low quiet voice: "I have done my best; I could do no more. My detachment is half destroyed; my regiments no longer exist; I have no officers left; they sent me no reinforcements; and I have lost three guns!" These were three of the four guns he had brought forward into the middle redoubt soon after taking it, only one of which his retreating troops had been able to carry off. "Why did they refuse you reinforcements?" asked MacGahan — "Who was to blame for that?"

"I blame nobody," replied Skobeleff — "It was the will of God!" he solemnly said as he crossed himself. Ever after that night Skobeleff, it seemed to me, was a changed man. He was much more grave, and made it manifest in many ways that he was conscious of having a greatly increased weight and responsibility. Almost immediately after the fighting before Plevna came to an end, he was promoted by Imperial decree to the rank of Lieutenant-General, and appointed to the command of the 16th Division which had fought under him so gallantly and steadfastly at Loftcha and now at Plevna. Skobeleff's reckless courage, brilliant and magnificent as it was, may be regarded as quixotic and out of place on the part of one who was the commanding officer of a large force engaged in an extremely important undertaking. On the other hand it is certain that the example he delighted in showing to his troops inspired his men with an ardour without which the Turkish positions assailed could neither have been carried nor maintained ; and the legendary stories of Skobeleff's all but fabulous bravery which circulated among the rank and file, especially among the young reservists who kept arriving from Russia to restore the thinned ranks, constituted a positive military factor which had its results in the subsequent enterprises of Skobeleff, such as the assault of the "Green Hill" in November, and the storm of the Shenova redoubts in January, 1878, which compelled the surrender of the whole Turkish army of Schipka.

Except for the unfortunates who fell in the latest fighting in front of the redoubts, Skobeleff had been successful in carrying off nearly all of his wounded; his dead of course he had to leave unburied where they had fallen. His losses, as reckoned on the evening of the 13th when his force had been withdrawn to Bogot, amounted to 160 officers and over 8,000 men, nearly one-half of the whole command. The Russian batteries all round the front maintained a heavy bombardment on Plevna and the Turkish positions during the 13th, 14th, and 15th — a mere waste of powder and shot. The last actual fighting occurred in the late evening of the 14th, when the Turks from the second Gravitza redoubt made a furious assault on the first, which was repulsed by the Russians and Roumanians holding the latter. The Russian losses in this futile and final assault on Plevna were stupendous. From the 7th to the 14th September, both days included, they reached the ghastly total of 18,600. How close and desperate had been the fighting was proved by the abnormal and perhaps indeed unique proportion of the killed, of whom there were more than 7,600, a proportion of one killed to two and a half wounded; the usual average in modern warfare being, I have read, one killed to four wounded. This disproportion of killed to wounded in the Plevna fighting was chiefly owing to the bloodthirsty butchery by the Turks of the Russian wounded whom the stretcher-bearers could not reach, and who were too hard hit to escape from the cruel fate which awaited them as they lay helpless at the hands of the Turkish irregulars.

After the war I read a history of it written from official sources by Captain Greene, the United States military attaché, who made the campaign from beginning to end. His conclusion was "that the Russians were defeated at Plevna, not because the Turkish position was impregnable, nor because they did not have sufficient forces; but because of their ignorance of the enemy's positions, and of their failure to concentrate their efforts on the decisive points." MacGahan was still more terse. "The whole business," according to him, "was one stupid, blind, reckless muddle, relieved only by Skobeleff's skill and daring."

CHAPTER IX

THE SIEGE OF PLEVNA

PLEVNA, from July 20th to September 14th, had cost the Russians well on to 40,000 men, besides having caused the paralysis of their campaign. Osman was stronger than ever; his only loss, that of the Gravitza redoubt, was nullified by the precaution he had taken of constructing a second Gravitza redoubt which commanded the one which the Russians and Roumanians had taken with heavy but bootless sacrifices. "What next?" was the question throughout the Russian army. They are a dogged race, those Russians, and no reverses daunt them. Most of the foreign correspondents made no secret of their belief that the war was now as good as finished, and that the Russians would have recrossed the Danube by the end of the month. But among the Russians themselves, from the private soldier up to the Czar, there was no thought of that nature. It is true that the enthusiasm had temporarily died out, that every one — even Skobeleff himself, to whom war was as the breath of his nostrils — frankly professed to be dead tired of the business, and that, especially, among the soldiers, home-sickness was all but universal. But that was merely a sentiment; there was no falter in the conviction that Plevna had to be taken somehow or other and the war carried through to a successful issue.

From the straw stack which I have often spoken of as the correspondents' rendezvous in the field, we could see no little commotion about the Emperor's observatory a little way on our right, on the afternoons of the 13th and 14th. The Emperor himself and his brother the Grand Duke Nicholas had long talks by themselves, a little way apart; Miliutin the War Minister hung about; Prince Charles of Roumania and General Zotoff, the titular chief of staff to his Highness, rode up together; podgy old Nepokoitschitsky and his ally Levitsky, the *sous chef* of the headquarters staff, arrived in a carriage — no man ever saw either of these two officers on horseback. At a signal all entered the marquee behind the Emperor's gazebo, where long councils were held under the presidency, we heard, of the Emperor himself. The old axiom held good that councils of war never fight; and it presently became known as the policy decided on, that Plevna was to be assaulted no more but was to be invested as soon as sufficient reinforcements for that purpose should arrive; and that General Todleben the famous defender of Sevastopol was to be called into the field to take charge of the investment operations. Meanwhile the Roumanians were to do their best to sap up to the second Gravitza redoubt; and the whole Russian cavalry under General Kriloff was to move westward across the Vid, in order to cut off the communications of the Turks and if possible prevent the entry into Plevna of supplies, munitions, or reinforcements. Elsewhere than about Plevna everything was to remain on the defensive for the time, no provocation being offered to the enemy.

The Emperor moved his quarters forward to Poradim,

where he remained until the fall of Plevna; the Grand Duke Nicholas and his staff occupied the village of Bogot, a couple of miles in rear of the Radischevo ridge.

Villiers I had seen only occasionally during the days of fighting; he had been with the 4th Corps in the Radischevo section of the field, where for a good deal of the time his companion had been Colonel Wellesley. On the morning of the 12th curiosity had led these two to make a very reckless excursion, which some Russian officers who were spectators of it frankly called "sheer madness." They had determined to visit the Gravitza redoubt, which had been taken on the previous evening. "I thought it would make a good sketch," was Villiers' ingenuous explanation of the foolhardy proceeding. With some pressure, for I believe he was ashamed of his folly, I got him to relate his experiences, which I think you will consider worth hearing:—

"From the Russian siege-battery we descended the slope into the valley, crossed it, and made our way into the village of Gravitza just beyond the little stream. Every house in the village was crammed with wounded, and its street was full of ambulance waggons and stretcher-bearers. In rear of the village and also lying down on the slope of the hill, was a line of Roumanian infantry under cover of a continuous shelter-trench; in rear again of which was a reserve of field-batteries. On mounting the plateau above the village we presently found ourselves under cover of a transverse undulation running down from the height into the valley, and sheltered behind it from the fire from the Turkish entrenchments were massed a few Roumanian battalions with a battery or two, the advance of the reserves intended to support an attack on the Turkish entrenched camp.

"We were here told that it would be impossible to ride up to the redoubt, for as soon as we should leave the cover afforded by the hillock we should come on an open space between it and the redoubt, which interval was continually swept by two Turkish guns. Intent on persevering, we observed a short way off a ditch running up the hill in the direction of the redoubt. This we determined to utilise as far as it reached, and leaving our horses with the friendly Roumanians we began to move up along the ditch, which we found filled with Roumanian infantry. After wandering about we presently found that the ditch soon ended in a *cul-de-sac*. Between us and the redoubt, a distance of about 600 yards, there was about half-way a small Roumanian battery, and for this we ran at speed, the ground we traversed literally strewn with dead Roumanians and Russians. The Turkish fire seemed to become heavier as we neared the battery, which, however, we reached in safety. There was nothing for it now but to start running again as soon as we had caught our breath in the little battery. The Roumanian officers squatting in the gorge of the redoubt shouted to us to run in their direction. This we did, and were grateful to them when, as we rushed in among them picking our way through the dead, they pulled us down on the ground and made us squat beside them for protection against the continuous shower of lead.

"We now had time to look about us and examine the exterior of the work. It had a ditch all round it, and the parapets were high and thick. The gorge was a mere narrow opening facing south, by which the Russian battalion fought its way in; the redoubt had been constructed for defence against the north. Presently Colonel Wellesley asked permission for us to enter the redoubt, which was granted with the advice to make a bolt of it as there was a dangerous corner to pass. This we did, and I pray I may be spared ever again witnessing such a sight as now met my eyes.

"The interior of this great work was piled up not only with dead but with wounded, forming one ghastly and tangled huddlement of dead and living bodies, the wounded as little cared for as the dead. The constant fire had hindered the surgeons from coming up to attend the wounded, and the same cause had kept back even the stretcher-bearers. There were not even comrades to moisten the lips of their wretched fellow-soldiers, or give them a word of consolation. There they lay writhing and groaning in their agony. It angered us to think that absolutely nothing had been done — no matter at what risk — to give some succour to these poor wounded fellows; for they were the gallant men who a few hours before had so valiantly and successfully struggled for the conquest of the long uncaptured redoubt, and it was sad now to see them dying by inches without any attempt being made to attend to them.

"Across the captured Gravitza redoubt there runs a kind of traverse which contains a series of caves in the nature of rude casemates, in which no doubt the Turks found protection from the shells which fell into it almost without interruption for days before it was carried. An incessant rain of bullets swept over the work as we made our way over the bodies for which the ground could not be seen. We were interested to know whence came the Turkish fire, and so we crawled up the interior face of the parapet and, taking off our caps, peeped over. To our utter astonishment we saw another Turkish redoubt not more than 250 yards from us to the north-west; and it was from it came the firing. The Roumanians told us that the attempt to take it yesterday had failed; but it was to be attacked that afternoon, since the captured redoubt was rendered all but untenable in consequence of its proximity and command.

"We had to return through a heavier fire than that which had raged as we came up. We rested awhile behind the hillock where the Roumanian reserves were lying. We had scarcely left them when a tremendous shrapnel-fire opened against them, which compelled them to retreat and draw in their skirmish line. We got back safe, and my sketch of the interior of the Gravitza redoubt heaped high with dead and dying, will make a four-page picture for next week's *Graphic*." That seemed to me to be what Villiers chiefly lived for. It was my belief that if a cannon-shot had carried off his right arm, he would have rejoiced in the opportunity of depicting for the *Graphic* with his left the spectacle he would have presented when docked of a limb and rapidly bleeding to death.

By this time MacGahan and I were discredits to our respective nations, because of the tattered condition of our clothing; and he proposed that since matters seemed comparatively quiet we should pay a visit to Bucharest for the purpose of refitting. There went with us Millett, who had recently left old General Zimmermann down on

"Trajan's wall" in the Dobrutscha, covering the Russian communications in Roumania from any attacks from that quarter; and who now purposed attaching himself to the army of the Cesarevich holding the line of the Lom and engaged in occasional fighting with Mehemet Ali's army in the Turkish quadrilateral. Bucharest we found in universal mourning, for the Roumanian army had been decimated before Plevna. But along with the sorrow was a justifiable pride in the conspicuous gallantry of the soldiers who had made light of their own fighting pretensions; and it seemed to me that every man and every woman in Bucharest carried the head higher and trod the Podo Mogosoi more proudly than had been the case two months before. From the first there had been no love lost between the Roumanians and the Russians. The Russians had despised the fighting capacity of the Roumanians, who, for their part, had no scruple in regarding the Russians as but half-civilised, from the grand dukes down to the rank and file. It had been a great day for Roumania when the Russians after their defeat of July 30th had to put their pride in their pocket, and to condescend to beg for the co-operation of that Roumanian army at which they had jeered. It was a prouder day still for Roumania, although in the pride was a great sadness, when it was told in Bucharest how the Roumanian soldiers stormed the high and steep face of the parapet of the Gravitza redoubt, and were inside the work actually in advance of the Russian regiment which entered by the easier way of the gorge.

After the failure before Plevna in September the interest on the part of Europe in the war seemed for a

THE CESAREVICH, 1877.

time to flag, and a great many correspondents left the field and went home. I had now been campaigning for some six months, and being always along with gentlemen who had experience in war and listening closely to their comments on the operations, I had learned a good deal. "Why, Carnegie, you are quite a veteran!" said MacGahan to me one afternoon while we sat in Brofft's garden-restaurant; "by this time you know more of actual warfare than many a man who commanded a brigade in our Civil War." "What little I do know," I replied, "I have mostly picked up from yourself; but the rough smattering I have gathered can be of no use to me for any purpose." "Why should you believe that?" asked MacGahan. "Of all the correspondents whose photographs are in the headquarters album, not one-third ever heard a shot fired in anger before this campaign; yet they write and talk and praise or censure with as much confidence as if they had been engaged in war continuously from their childhood. You could do much better than most of these gentlemen. If you like, I can obtain for you the correspondence for two papers of good-standing — one American, one Scotch — whose representatives are starting for home in a day or two." It was a piece of great audacity for a lad who had not seen his seventeenth birthday to take on himself the duty of a war-correspondent. But MacGahan and Millett gave me great encouragement; I was sure of Villiers' good offices, and I confess to having had some little self-reliance. MacGahan made the arrangements for me with the gentlemen who were departing. It was a proud day for me when I went down to Giurgevo and told my father that I was now an actual war-correspondent, writing a letter a week to the *Philadelphia Budget* and another to the *Glasgow News*, the *honorarium*, as MacGahan called it, for each letter being £3. It was not difficult work, although at first I was very nervous. But I found that the true way to go to work was simply to record what I saw and heard as clearly and plainly as possible, and to try to see and hear as much as I could in order to have matter for my letters.

The day before that on which MacGahan had fixed for returning to Plevna, Skobeleff arrived in Bucharest on the errand of commissioning an adequate equipment for his new rank of lieutenant-general. Notwithstanding his promotion and the great prestige he had gained, Skobeleff was in a state of deep despondency. That in a measure might have been accounted for in the terrible losses of comrades whom he had loved; but as a soldier he was disgusted to the very soul by the follies and blundering that had characterised the recent attempt on Plevna.

"Shall we never learn anything?" he exclaimed. "Can we never bring ourselves to realise that we have responsibilities both to God and man? Are our brave men dirt that we squander their lives as if they were of no account? We don't deserve to have men so devoted, men who die so heroically, men whom no stupidity of ours can force to take a panic, but who fight on steadfastly till they drop. Our dispositions are faulty, our execution is loose, unpunctual, and ineffective — why, the Servians conducted war better than do we, and the Turks simply amuse themselves at our expense! The blood wasted before Plevna had scarcely sunk into the ground when we were committing fresh imbecilities. You know General Kriloff, who took Zotoff's place in command of the 4th Corps while Zotoff was acting chief of staff. Than this Kriloff there is in all Russia no more doddering fool as a soldier, no more sordid knave as a citizen. He is a creature of protection and bribery. Before the war he was Governor of Wilna and at the same time commanded a cavalry division. It is a fact that while at Wilna he never had a charger. When he occasionally had a review of his division he drove to the field, where he mounted a troop-horse chosen for him because of its docility. He pocketed his horse-allowance as a divisional commander. He can ride only at a walk — you never saw him trot; he has forgotten what a canter means.

"Well, this dotard was entrusted on the 18th September with a cavalry force of 52 squadrons and 30 guns, and sent to the west of the Vid to complete a sort of investment of Plevna; with orders also to break up Osman's communications, to reconnoitre along the roads into the Balkans, and above everything to prevent the entry into Plevna of supplies or reinforcements. To send cavalry alone on such an errand was fatuous, since it was certain that any Turkish convoys heading for Plevna would be strongly escorted by infantry; to send any force anywhere under the command of the incompetent Kriloff was mere midsummer madness. Kriloff sent his Cossack brigade to reconnoitre along the Sophia road in the direction of Telis. That place was found occupied by 10,000 Turkish infantry, which next day came on towards Plevna heading a great convoy, at the same time that a Turkish column came out from Plevna to give the hand to the reinforcement. If Kriloff could not have done much with his cavalry, he might at least have broken up and stampeded the convoy with his artillery-fire. But without firing a shot he withdrew to Trestenik, fifteen miles to the north, leaving the road into Plevna quite open, so that the Turkish convoy of 3,000 waggon-loads of supplies and munitions quietly entered the same night along with 12,000 infantry, a regiment of cavalry and two batteries. Two days later a second smaller convoy got into Plevna unmolested. Meanwhile Kriloff rode away on a fool's errand to attempt the bombardment of the fortress of Rahova with his trumpery 4-pounders. During his absence the Sophia road remained open and the Turkish communications and telegraph had been completely restored. On his return to Trestenik he sent a Cossack colonel with a few squadrons to wreck the bridge on the Sophia road near Radomirtza. The detachment broke the bridge and captured a herd of 1,000 cattle and a small train loaded with quinine and salt. It remained for two days skirmishing about Radomirtza with Bashi-Bazouks, but was too weak to be of any account; and on the 5th of this month Chefket Pasha, marching from Orkhanie on Plevna with 5,000 infantry and a swarm of Tcherkesses, brushed the Cossack detachment out of his path, took his troops on to Telis and Gorni-Dubnik, villages on the Sophia road which Osman's troops from Plevna had already begun to fortify, and himself went into Plevna to see Osman. Chefket brought with him a considerable convoy, and as he passed he repaired the bridge at Radomirtza in a few hours. That sluggish beast Kriloff, when I left the front, was still remaining idle at Trestenik with the bulk of his command. He ought to be tried and shot; but he will be let down easy. Gourko is on his way to supersede him, and he will be sent back to Russia into some comfortable, dignified, and lucrative office. By the joint imbecility of the headquarters staff and of Kriloff, I reckon that since the fighting ended and we collapsed Osman has received reinforcements of some 20,000 men, with supplies for his whole army for two months and a great store of munitions." Having thus delivered himself Skobeleff spat viciously — the Russian's invariable sign of disgust.

While we were making our little holiday in Bucharest, General Todleben arrived there along with the few officers forming his modest personal staff. MacGahan told me that when the commands were being arranged previous to the declaration of war, there had been general wonder throughout the army that the great soldier who had defended Sevastopol with such brilliant skill and tenacity, and who had covered the Russian retreat so brilliantly on the day of Inkermann, had not been asked to take the field. It had been expected that he would be appointed to the high position of chief of staff to the Commander-in-Chief, which if he had occupied, it is certain that the follies which Nepokoitschitsky and Levitsky perpetrated and the Grand Duke Nicholas sanctioned would not have occurred. It was the current gossip in the army that Todleben had loyally tendered his services, and that they had been brusquely declined by the Commander-in-Chief. If the reason for this declinature was that which MacGahan had heard on good authority, there was another instance among many how in Russia personal considerations override the obvious fitness of things. It was universally acknowledged that Todleben as chief of staff would be the right man in the right place; but the Grand Duke Nicholas nourished a long-standing grudge against Russia's most eminent soldier. During the siege of Sevastopol Nicholas and one of his brothers paid a short visit to the Crimea, and witnessed from a safe distance the battle of Inkermann. Nicholas had intimated his desire that Todleben should accompany him to the position whence the fighting was to be witnessed. Todleben had respectfully requested that his presence might be dispensed with, since it was probable that the French would take the opportunity to make an assault on Sevastopol, to meet which his presence was requisite. One would think there was nothing in this to give offence, but Nicholas in one of his wayward moods chose to feel himself insulted, and from that day he had nourished ill-will against Todleben. Now, however, he had to swallow his spite, for the Emperor had resolved that the great engineer officer should be entrusted with the conduct of the investment of Plevna. So Nicholas had to accept him, and for the time to become himself a comparative nonentity.

Todleben was a very handsome man, very dignified, and at the same time very affable. At the age of sixty he was still tall, straight, and active, without a grey hair in his head, and he did not look within ten years of his actual age. He had started from Russia so hurriedly that he had brought no horses with him, and Bucharest had been swept so clean of horses that even the street tram-cars had for the time ceased to run. There were ponies, but the general rode at least fifteen stone. I remembered that just before the outbreak of the war my father had bought a powerful grey stallion for my elder brother, your father, who was a big-boned heavy fellow even before he had come to his full growth. When I went to Giurgevo to tell my father that I was now enrolled in the great army of war-correspondents, I asked him whether he still had the grey stallion, and whether he cared to sell him.

"Sell him!" exclaimed the old gentleman — "I should think so, indeed! He will not go in harness; when your brother tries to ride the beast he walks on his hind legs, and shrieks and neighs so loudly that he actually draws the fire of the Rustchuk guns. He is eating his head off here; I have no use for him, and we are all more or less frightened at him. I have tried in vain to sell him to the Russians; but he scared them when they saw him rampant and looking as if he would eat them. One captain offered me 10 roubles for him, but his hide is worth more than that — I paid 100 ducats for him. If you can get half that for him, I shall gladly be quit of him."

"I believe, sir," said I, "that I can get all you paid for him. General Todleben is in Bucharest, hunting everywhere in vain for a charger. His aide-de-camp told me that the general is a splendid horseman, and does not care what he rides so long as the mount is up to his weight. That grey would carry twenty stone even in the Plevna mud, and a couple of days' hard work will knock the nonsense out of him and make him as quiet as a sheep."

The old gentleman fell in with the idea, and the big grey and I started for Bucharest the next morning. We certainly had a very lively time. The grey had no vice, apparently, but he was very much above himself and took a great deal of riding. By road the distance from Giurgevo to Bucharest is about forty miles. There never was such a beast for standing up on his hind legs, and the way he screamed and yelled when we met another horse was a caution. When a railway train passed us he went off at score, right across country. It was all grass with only a ditch here and there, and I let him work his wicked will. After a headlong gallop of about three miles he was not quite so saucy, and I got a pull on him. We were near the half-way house, up to which he pirouetted in a series of modified bucks, but by this time I had him quite in hand although he had not yet settled down to any particular pace. At Kalugareni I lunched and gave the grey a feed of maize; after an hour's rest we took the road again. He was now quite a reformed character, and after a few capers settled down to a good honest trot. He was a bit rough, it was true, and if Todleben had any tendency to liver trouble, the grey was the horse to cure that ailment; but his trot was true and free — a good ten miles an hour, his fore action, as I had expected from the goodness of his shoulders, high without being too high — his hind legs well under him and full of motive power. We reached Bucharest about 4 p.m., the grey quite sobered but not in the least distressed, although he was far from being in condition. I rode him at a trot into the courtyard of Brofft's Hotel, and pulled him up rather sharply so that he might show himself. Todleben and his officers were sitting in the courtyard drinking tea. Before I dismounted I heard the general exclaim softly to his aide-de-camp — " What a fine powerful horse!" Giving the rein to a loafer and telling him to walk the horse up and down the courtyard, I beckoned the aide-de-camp aside and begged that he would present me to his Excellency. Colonel Tutolmin did so, naming me, and mentioning that I was one of the English correspondents. The general rose, shook hands with great cordiality, and observed that he had liked the English ever since the Crimea. I ventured to remark that the English had perhaps "better reason for admiring him than for liking him," an expression which he seemed to regard as a compliment. "Fine horse you have there, Mr. Carnegie," said Todleben; "I suppose there is no chance of your being willing to sell him?" Then I told him that having learned his difficulty as to a charger, I had brought the grey up from Giurgevo for his inspection, and that if he liked the horse he might have him and welcome for the price my father had paid for him in the quiet days before the war. With that I handed him my father's memorandum of the price at which he had bought the horse, dated on the day of purchase.

Todleben threw his arms round me and kissed me on both cheeks. "It is a most kindly action you have done me, young gentleman! I shall never forget it!" "You are most gracious, your Excellency," I replied; "but let me remind you that you have not yet tried the horse — you may not like him. After you have ridden him an hour in the Chaussée you will know him better. He is quiet now after forty miles, but he was a good deal of a rogue for the first twenty." "Oh, I like a horse with some character!" he exclaimed gaily, as he let down the stirrups and swung himself into the saddle. The grey reared and plunged, but he felt the hand of a master, and rider and horse disappeared at a hard canter up the Podo Mogosoi. They were back in the courtyard of the hotel an hour later, evidently on excellent terms with each other. "Perfection, Mr. Carnegie — quite perfection! Fully up to my weight, and merely gay — not an atom of vice. I am everlastingly obliged to you. Do me the favour to settle the little matter with Colonel Tutolmin, and then I shall be much gratified if you and your friend Mr. MacGahan, whom I have already met in St. Petersburg, will give me the pleasure of your company at dinner."

That was for me a most charming dinner party, a night to be marked with a white stone in one's memory. Skobeleff was one of the guests; Todleben was the only Russian soldier whom we reverenced, and, silent himself for the most part, he hung intently on the words of the veteran. Todleben told us that his first soldiering had been against Schamyl in the Caucasus from 1848 to 1851, a series of wild bloody combats of which the mountaineers often had the best. The savagery, he owned, was as conspicuous on the one side as on the other, and on neither was there any thought of quarter. From the Caucasus he had come into the Principalities with Gortschakoff in 1853. "I don't believe," he said, "that there is a man of the Russian army now in the field who knows Wallachia and Moldavia so thoroughly as in 1853-54 I had come to know the Principalities. Those earthworks at Slobosia above Giurgevo which, Skobeleff, as I have read you, armed in the early summer with 'quaker' guns made of straw to impose on the garrison of Rustchuk — that entrenched position with the battery-emplacements along its front I built five-and-twenty years ago, when I was a lieutenant. It used to be a standing piece of intelligence with you youngsters in July — that stereotyped despatch from Haussenkampf, 'All quiet in the vicinity of Oltenitza.' I made the lines of Oltenitza, and was driven out of them by a swarm of mad Turks headed by a madder Englishman. Then Gortschakoff went home with the remains of his army, half of which had died of sickness in Wallachia; and next May I was across the Danube with Paskievitch engaged in the siege of Silistria. We did our honest best, and I believe we should have carried the place but that the Turks found gallant and skilful leaders in a couple of English officers. You spoke, Skobeleff, of that old bridge-head on the Danube above Giurgevo. That was built by Hassan Pasha, after the Englishmen Cannon and Burke had got across the river, taken our brigade in flank, and driven us away. I was wounded in that fight by a gigantic desperado of an Irishman named Burke, who obstinately refused quarter and who killed some half-dozen of us before he was finally put an end to. We were going to give him Christian burial when his servant, a fellow as big as himself, whose head had been cut open, came up leading a horse and demanding the body of his master with oaths and tears. We helped him to lash the body on to the pack-saddle and then offered the fellow some money, for we were touched by his devotion to his master; but he turned on us with fury in every feature, cursed us by all his gods through his tears, and spat on our proffered money which he had thrown on the ground. Certainly we got no change out of the Turks on the Danube under Omar Pasha in 1853-54.

"Men talk of you, Skobeleff," continued his Excellency, "as an instance of exceptionally quick promotion — in three years, I am told, you have risen from colonel to lieutenant-general. You know that with us of the Engineer Corps promotion is mostly much slower than in any other branch of the service. Yet I suppose scarcely any officer in any European army had such a quick run of luck in the way of promotion as happened to me during the siege of Sevastopol. I entered that fortress a captain; in less than a year I had gone through the successive grades to the rank of major-general, had been appointed one of the general adjutants to the Emperor, and had received the second-class of the St. George; and during a considerable part of that short time I was on my back in the Star fort on the North shore with a bad wound in my leg from which I still limp a bit. There were not so many of your profession, gentlemen," said the general addressing MacGahan and myself, "in the allied camp outside Sevastopol as there are to-day in the Russian camp outside Plevna. I remember to have met only one correspondent in the Crimea — Mr. Russell of *The Times*, whom I thought a very amusing man. It was before the fall of Sevastopol, when I met him during one of the truces for removing the wounded and burying the dead. I remember thinking his French accent rather comic. I confess that I thought Mr. Russell's criticisms on my '*Défense de Sevastopol*' pretty severe, and I was more than once tempted to reply to him. But we had met on cordial terms — he came to Moscow to witness the Coronation of the present Emperor and became very popular during his short stay among us. And apart from all that, every man is entitled to his own

GENERAL TODLEBEN.

opinion. I have read of Mr. Russell having been in the Franco-German war of 1870-71."

Next morning all the party who had dined together overnight, with the exception of Skobeleff who remained in Bucharest a few days longer, went down to Giurgevo by train. Todleben's heavy baggage, after being detrained at Giurgevo, was to travel by stages *via* Simnitza to the front. His staff were accommodated in a light vehicle bought in Bucharest and drawn by four screws, the general himself was to ride the grey stallion, MacGahan and I had our ponies at Giurgevo and we mounted there. I had telegraphed to my father to meet us at the Giurgevo railway, and I presented the old gentleman to General Todleben on the platform there. His Excellency was most courteous to your worthy grandfather, praised the grey horse, tried in vain to persuade the old gentleman to accept an addition to the price already paid and gratify him immensely by promising to send him a large photograph of himself, which you see there hanging on the wall above your heads.

We started on the long dreary ride across the plains to Simnitza. The grey horse for the first few miles was decidedly obstreperous. Once he got his forelegs over the back of the vehicle in which Todleben's officers were riding, but the rest of him remained outside along with the general. He, for his part, was greatly amused at the animal's vagaries; but regarded it as rather above a joke when in the middle of the ford across the Vede at Brigadir the beast deliberately lay down and cooled himself and his rider in the swift-flowing stream. At this period of the campaign Simnitza was simply a foul nest of Polish Jews selling all descriptions of impositions from adulterated champagne to sausages whose sole contents were meal and turmeric; of wounded lying rotting and neglected in the canvas marquees which went by the name of hospitals; of thieves, ruffians, and the general scum and dregs of Eastern Europe. When the wind set your way you could smell the sour rancid smell of the pestilential place quite a mile before you reached it. We determined that sooner than spend the night in its atmosphere, we would sleep under the beautiful stars; but MacGahan said he knew of good and sweet quarters in a house on the outskirts of Sistova. So we crossed the Danube by the upper bridge of boats, toiled up the steep slope, and did actually find the accommodation he had described, in the house of a returned Turk whose women had gone across the Balkans.

Next morning we pursued our journey. At Poradim, where the Emperor was now lying in very mean and comfortless quarters, General Todleben left us to pay his homage to his Imperial master and confer with him on the situation. Before parting he told us to come to him whenever we wanted information as to the operations which he was to conduct, and assured us always of a hearty welcome. We were proud to have made the acquaintance of a man so illustrious and so cordial, and congratulated ourselves on the good fortune which gave us the opportunity of knowing him. We rode on through a quietude that was actually startling in contrast with the horrible din of the recent bombardment, past Radischevo now the quarters of General Zotoff who had resumed the command of the 4th Corps, and so on to Tutchenitza, where our waggon was and where was now the headquarter of General Skobeleff although he himself was temporarily out of residence there. In consequence of the retreat which he had been compelled by order to take on the evening of the 13th September, he had surrendered all the ground he had previously won, and the Turks were now not only in the village of Brestovatz but held the " Red Hill " behind it.

While we had been idling in Bucharest the indefatigable Villiers had been hard at work. The Plevna bombardment was no sooner over than he learned that there was mischief in the Schipka Pass. He at once rode thither, reaching the position on the 16th in the midst of a furious cannonade from the Turks, to which the Russians were able to reply but languidly. Radetski was still up there in the clouds; a fixture — in his own words — "Come Turk, or come devil." Well, the Turks did come, and that with great fierceness, before daybreak on the morning after Villiers' arrival. They had bombarded steadily for four days with mortars as well as with guns, and now their infantry came forward to the attack on all sides, their chief efforts, as before, being directed on Mount St. Nicholas. Here in the darkness they stormed up to within a hundred paces of the defences on the summit, forced the Russians out of the advanced trenches, and made good the captured position with the gabions and fascines they had carried up. The actual fighting for the possession of the hill lasted from daybreak until past noon. Radetski was there himself in the thick of the fighting, reinforcing by another the regiment holding the hill which was the key of the Russian position. Again and again the Turks made desperate efforts to sweep the Russians from the summit, but in vain; equally in vain were the Russian attempts to fling the Turks out of the trenches which they had carried and strengthened before daylight. The bayonet was the weapon chiefly plied, and the Russians were the better men with the "white arm." Early in the afternoon a simultaneous rush was made on the Turks, who were finally driven down and out. An independent attack on the Russian right was not pressed so strongly and it withered under the Russian volley-firing at fifty yards. Radetski's loss on this 17th September amounted to 31 officers and over 1,000 men; a heavy cost, but accomplishing the result that the Turks never after made any serious attempt on the Russian position. Radetski estimated their losses at about 3,000 men; the south side of Mount St. Nicholas was piled high and thick with corpses. By the end of the month Suleiman was withdrawn from the army of the Schipka and sent to the Eastern Quadrilateral, and he was succeeded at Schipka by Reouf Pasha, who in his turn was succeeded by Vessil Pasha. Radetski kept his grip on the Schipka without relenting until after the new year, and then quitted it only to advance into Roumelia.

One of the most remarkable things in connection with the Imperial and the Grand Ducal headquarters throughout the Russo-Turkish war was the leakage from both of information regarding matters which one would have imagined to be profound secrets. Probably there was the intention that the secrecy should be maintained, but if so, the intention was more honoured in the breach than in the observance. On the day after we returned to the army before Plevna, MacGahan went to the headquarters of the Grand Duke Nicholas at Bogot on the hunt for information. He came back late with quite a budget of news which he recounted to me. It appeared that during the early part of the interval between the battle of the 30th June and the September fighting around Plevna, the intention was that when the weather should break towards the close of the year, the Russian army should go into winter quarters and undertake a second campaign in the spring of 1878. But a personal intimation from the Queen of England to the Emperor, in direct contradistinction to an official intimation of an entirely different tenor made by the British Foreign Minister to Prince Gortschakoff the Russian Chancellor, had been given to the effect that the war should be finished in a single campaign. The Emperor had accepted this intimation, although with great umbrage; doing so only on the suggestion of which it was said that the Grand Duke Nicholas was the author, that a campaign need have no specified duration and might last indefinitely, providing there was no formal cessation of active operations in the field. The Grand Duke was reported to have added that the injunction from Osborne which in effect made winter campaigning obligatory, would cause heavy mortality from freezing and frostbites among the soldiers, but that the responsibility for this suffering and mortality would not rest on the Russian military authorities who were reluctantly bound by the intimation referred to. The continuation of active operations throughout the winter thus decided on in a manner perforce, there remained to be settled, now that at the beginning of October the Guard was arriving in the vicinity of Plevna and the Grenadier Corps following closely, affording a disposable force of more than 70,000 men, what disposition should be made of these reinforcements. There were already forces around Plevna amply strong enough to cope with Osman, and the army of the Lom had proved its capacity to defend the eastern flank. This being so, it had been urged by the forward party in the Grand Duke's staff that those 70,000 men, reinforced *en route* by Radetski's command to nearly 100,000, should immediately proceed to cross the Balkans by the Schipka Pass, sweeping before them the Turkish forces in their path, and march straight on to Adrianople. The project included the appointment of the Cesarevich to the command of this active army, and so early as September 23rd an order of the day had directed that prince to take command of the Guard as a preliminary measure. The safer men of the headquarter staff had meanwhile been pointing out that there was a Turkish army in the Sophia Balkans which, while the Russian active army was on the march towards Adrianople, might move down on Plevna and join forces with Osman, with results possibly extremely inconvenient to the Russian army investing Plevna. Within the last few days, added MacGahan, the forward plan had been definitely abandoned, the Cesarevich remained in his command of the Lom, the Guards and Grenadiers were to rendezvous about Plevna, and the capture of Plevna was to precede any further far-reaching operations.

That the Turks in Plevna were still in good heart was presently to be manifested. The industrious Roumanians had been steadily sapping up to within a few yards of the ditch of the second Gravitza redoubt. On October 19th several battalions made a rush only to be driven back with great slaughter. The Roumanians tried again just before sundown, and actually got into the ditch. But the Turks sprang on to the parapet and blazed down at arm's length on the Roumanians below them; when the latter strove to ascend the outward face of the parapet the Turks gave them the bayonet and heaved them back. When darkness fell the Roumanians were glad to get back into their own positions with a loss of nearly 1,000 men, and they made no further attempts on the second Gravitza redoubt.

Plevna was still only partially invested. But the whole of the Guard had now arrived, and Todleben set about his preparations for making the investment complete. So far as concerned the actual garrison of Plevna, that task was not arduous; he would only have to close the gap in the environment from the Loftcha road to the Vid, and along the left bank of that stream to the village of Dolni-Etropol, where he would meet the right flank of the Roumanians. But merely to do this would be to leave outside the ring of the investment three more or less strongly fortified and garrisoned places along the Sophia road, within a distance of some 25 miles from Plevna. These places were respectively, in the order of their distance from Plevna, Dolni-Dubnik, Gorni-Dubnik and Telis. The task of driving the Turks from these positions was assigned to General Gourko, who had returned to Bulgaria from Russia at the head of his division of Guard Cavalry. He was now to command an army consisting of nearly 50,000 men, of which in the reduction of the Turkish positions I have named, he was to employ for the most part the Guard Corps, exclusive of its 3rd division, which was to join the investing force. The Guard lay in readiness to move, in and about the village of Cirakova on the right bank of the Vid, about equidistant from Telis and Gorni-Dubnik.

MacGahan's ankle was troubling him again, and since for the time he could neither walk nor ride, on the 21st October I went to the army headquarters at Bogot in quest of information. There I had the good fortune to meet General Gourko, who had been visiting the Grand Duke Nicholas. He beckoned me to him, shook hands very cordially, told me that he had not forgotten the pioneer work in the Hainkioj Pass which I had done with Prince Tzeretleff in the early days of the war, and asked me what I was now doing. I told him that I had only just come back from Bucharest, and asked his permission to accompany the operations which I understood he was about to undertake, adding that I was now commissioned to write war-correspondence for an American and a Scottish newspaper. Just then Prince Tzeretleff, whom I had not seen for a long time, came up and greeted me with great friendliness. He was now, it seemed, one of Gourko's orderly officers. After a little conversation the general gave his consent that I should accompany his expedition, and told me I might join the reconnaissance which he meant to make from Cirakova towards Gorni-Dubnik on the following day. You may be sure that I thanked him very warmly. He and Tzeretleff then rode away, and I returned to Tutchenitza to tell MacGahan of my good fortune. He congratulated me, and added that when I returned I should find Skobeleff no longer here at Tutchenitza, but probably at or about Brestovatz, in the old familiar region which we both knew so well. So we parted, and I rode off in the afternoon for Cirakova, where I shared Prince Tzeretleff's tent for the night.

In the early morning of the 22nd Gourko was in the

GENERAL GOURKO.

saddle, with a few staff officers and a small escort of cavalry. We forded the Vid and rode across the rolling country on its left bank, heading at first towards Telis, the Turkish position most distant from Plevna. That place looked rather formidable, with a strong irregular line of breastwork across the high road on the crest above a bare slope and a large redoubt on the further side of the village. Few Turks were visible, and not more than a dozen rifle-shots were fired at Gourko's little party from the shelter-trenches. We then rode along the high road in the direction of Plevna for some six miles till we approached Gorni-Dubnik. That seemed a position of no great strength. The village was about a mile north of the road and was not fortified at all. But close to the road on a hillock there was one of those tumuli so common in Turkey, and of it the Turks had taken advantage. They had levelled off the top of the mound at a height of about fifteen feet and had on the flat top a battery of four guns. This mound they had surrounded with a hastily thrown-up redoubt of irregular shape, the parapet of which did not appear strong. Close to the road there was a small stone structure, and opposite to it across the road there was an insignificant-looking lunette at which the staff officers sneered—indeed, they made very light of the Gorni-Dubnik position as a whole. Gourko was a silent man; he looked hard and said nothing. You will readily believe that I was not qualified to form any opinion on the subject. Making a circuit to avoid the fire from Gorni-Dubnik we presently returned to the high road, and went on a few miles further until within sight of Dolni-Dubnik, the Turkish position nearest to Plevna. It seemed pretty strong, surrounded as the village was by no fewer than six small redoubts. Whether the village itself was fortified was not to be discerned. There was nothing more to be seen, and we rode back to Cirakova for the night. Before going to sleep Tzeretleff told me that Gourko considered Gorni-Dubnik as, if not the strongest, at all events the most important of the three Turkish positions; and that he intended attacking it on the morrow with the whole of the 2nd Guard Division and the Rifle Brigade, using the 1st Division with most of the cavalry to cover the attack on the Dolni-Dubnik and Telis sides.

That night there was little sleep in the Cirakova camp. Before daylight of the 24th the whole force had crossed the ford and was on march towards Gorni-Dubnik. There was great eagerness and excitement in the massive ranks. The Guards had been full of discontent when line corps after line corps was being sent into the field while they, the picked soldiers of Russia, were detained at home in ignoble passiveness. But that feeling existed no longer; the Guards were marching to their first battle, and they would show the line how victories were to be won. Gourko divided his command into three separate columns: General Ellis went to the right, north-east of the redoubt, with his Rifle Brigade and 16 guns; in the centre were the Moscow and Grenadier regiments with 16 guns under General Zeddeler, on a little eminence south-east of the redoubt; General Rosenbach had the Paul and Finland regiments with 16 guns, on either side of the high road south-west of the redoubt — all at a distance from the redoubt of some 1,800 yards. The Caucasian Cossack brigade sent from General Arnoldi's camp was in position north-west of the redoubt with its six horse-guns. By nine o'clock 56 guns were concentrating an incessant fire on the Turkish redoubt, which could reply but feebly with the four guns which were all it possessed. And now their chronic disregard of simultaneous co-operation was, as ever, to work the Russians cruel losses. The Grenadier regiment of the centre column was the first to advance to the assault. Leaving my horse with a Cossack I went forward with the Grenadiers about half-way, then lay down on a little hillock and intently watched the result. The terrible fire which the Turks poured upon the close Russian line wrought immense havoc, and staggered the advance for a short time; but the men hardened their hearts, and with one strong rush climbed the parapet and carried the lunette on the hither side of the road. There was a few moments' bayonet-fighting inside; then such of the Turks as survived I watched dart across the road and race up the steep slope to the redoubt. A Turkish officer waving his sword as he stood on the parapet was shot down by a Grenadier officer. A charge was then made with great dash upon the redoubt; but it was driven back by a crushing fire, and the men fell back into the lunette and into and behind the little stone house and the ditches on either side of the road, maintaining a hot fire as they lay. General Zeddeler then, but not till then, sent forward the Moscow regiment, the sister regiment of the Grenadiers; but all that it could do was to find shelter in the ditches to right of the latter regiment, having lost severely in its advance. Two batteries had followed it half-way, but so fierce was the Turkish fire that they could not even unlimber, and had to hurry back

to their first position. About the same time the Paul and
Finland regiments constituting the left column, formed,
crossed the hollow, and tried to climb the eminence on
which was the redoubt. But they could not stand the
gusts of fire that smote them, and they recoiled into folds
in the valley where they found some protection. The
Rifle Brigade on the right, having left its batteries to be
protected by the Ismailoff regiment which had joined
from the force watching Dolni-Dubnik, moved down into
a valley along whose slopes it crept until arrested by the
fire of the redoubt. So close up were the prostrate infantrymen that the action of the artillery was greatly
impeded by the danger of hurting friends instead of foes.
For hours the fighting remained stationary, the Turks
never relaxing their fire, the Russians beaten down as
soon as they ventured on efforts to get to closer quarters.

I had got back to the centre where now there were
only a few companies, the two infantry regiments being
forward in the ditches on the roadside. Only the batteries were in the original position, and behind them some
little distance were Count Schouvaloff commanding the
2nd Division of the Guards, his staff and escort. He
was asking me some questions as to what I had seen
when out to the front with the Grenadiers, when Gourko,
who had been with the Ismailoff regiment on the right,
rode up looking very gloomy. Just at that moment an
officer came galloping up from the force on the Telis
flank, and announced to the general that in attempting
to carry the works in front of that place, it had been
badly repulsed and compelled to fall back with heavy
loss. "Then," said Gourko in a strange quiet tone, " I

am to understand that the road is now open to an attack upon us here by Turkish troops coming down from Telis?"
"I fear so, Excellency," replied the officer; "I know we have been pushed back in the direction of Cirakova."

"Then," said the general, "we must strike hard and soon, else we may find ourselves in an awkward position. All the troops are now from within 100 to 400 paces of the Turkish redoubt. A simultaneous attack from all sides will be made at three o'clock." He then gave orders to the staff officers about him to ride to the troops in their respective positions, and inform them that three volleys were to be fired by the batteries on the left; that three volleys should then be fired in succession by the batteries of the centre and right; and that after the last volley fired by the guns of the right, all the infantry should simultaneously rush to the assault. The officers departed; and then Gourko desired to send instructions to be carried to the respective batteries in the terms of which the troops were being informed — the volleys to be commenced by the left batteries, and to be ended by those on the right. It occurred that he found himself short of staff officers, several of whom in the course of the day had been killed or wounded; and turning to me Gourko said in English: "Mr. Carnegie, you will greatly oblige me by riding to the batteries on the right with the instructions you have just heard me give. You will incur no risk; the batteries are well out of rifle-range from the redoubt." It was a trying moment for me, but I had to answer at once. "It is not that consideration, sir, that causes me to beg that you will be so gracious as to excuse me, but because I am a neutral. Bid me under fire to be of service to the wounded, and you will not have to command me twice; but what you now desire of me is quite another thing." Gourko spat from between his teeth, as is the manner of a Russian when angry. "Neutral!" said he with a sneer. " Is it not owing to our hospitable reception of foreigners that you are here? Were you a neutral in the Hainkioj Pass?" "I have long since realised, your Excellency, that I was wrong in doing what I did then. I have to thank you for many courtesies; and you will add another if you will allow me to remain until this battle is decided." "Oh, certainly!" was his reply as he turned away abruptly.

It was a strange thing that the very message which Gourko would have entrusted to me should have either been wrongly communicated or disregarded by whomsoever received it. The volleys which Gourko wished to be delivered last were delivered first. "It was," he said afterwards in his despatch, "with a sinking heart that I realised what was now inevitable: in place of the simultaneous assault at all points which I had intended, there were going to be isolated assaults one after another, of which the success was more than doubtful." His gallopers had returned to him, and he sent them back again at speed to bid the troops wait no longer for the signal, but immediately to support the attack which the right column had already entered upon. The attacks were delivered; but instead of being together they were made one after another, and all failed. The Turkish fire was so murderous that no one body could reach the redoubt. But there was no recoiling; unable to charge home, the several detachments lay down under whatever shelter they could find and maintained a steady fire. The artillery had to cease firing altogether, owing to the proximity to the redoubt of its own troops, some of whom were actually in the ditch of the work. They could not be withdrawn so as to enable the guns to renew the cannonade; the losses would have been immense and a retirement however short would have injured their *morale* and might indeed have caused a panic. There was nothing for it but that the troops should remain where they were until nightfall, when they could either be withdrawn or renew the assault.

This was Gourko's project, but the gallant men whom he commanded took the matter into their own hands of their own intuition, without any suggestion on the part of their officers. They had tried it Gourko's way, and that had failed; but they did not intend to be thwarted, and they set about doing it according to their own way. It was at 4 p.m. that the last of the attacks ordered by Gourko came to an unsuccessful ending. By-and-by a few daring fellows sprang out of the lunette, darted across the road and got shelter in and behind the little stone post-house on the further side. Others found cover behind a straw-stack close by. Presently it became the swagger thing to do in the face of the less courageous for the more adventurous to jump out of the lunette, saunter across the road, and gain the stone house or the lee of the straw-stack. The fellows took to daring each other, the inspiration to get forward caught hold; the occupants of the stone house and the shelterers behind the stackyard quitted their cover, darted forward up the steep slope, and, those of them who were not shot down on the way, jumped down into the ditch of the redoubt and held on there. The lucky ones who had reached the ditch found there to their great surprise that they were perfectly safe, since the Turks could not fire on them, as to do so they would have to mount on to the parapet, and that, owing to the steadily maintained Russian fire all round the environment, was simply sure death to the man who should so expose himself. The men who had attained the ditch kept instigating and beckoning to their fellows to follow them into their unexpected haven of refuge; and the hints were taken so freely that in course of time the ditch of the redoubt was pretty well full of Russians squatting in it right under the weapons of the enemy. The Turks did their best to make things uncomfortable for their undesired neighbours by heaving stones and logs of wood over the parapet into the ditch, to which rough compliments the visitors retaliated with clods and loose pebbles, while others busied themselves in hewing steps in the steep scarp of the ditch by which, when the time should come, they might mount the more easily to the slope of the parapet. The numbers of the occupants of the ditches grew as the dusk set in. I was curious to learn by what signal they at length with one accord all round the work clambered up its face and sprang down into its interior. The simultaneous assault which Gourko was unable to attain unto, the soldier-men by some magnetic freemasonry of their own accomplished with a thoroughness which proved that the Russian soldiers of the Guard, whatever might be the case with those of the line, had no lack of intelligence and were able so to act on their own initiative as to bring off a completely successful combination. General Ellis II., who commanded two battalions of the Ismailoff regiment which he brought forward several hundred paces crawling on hands and knees until within a few paces of the edge of the ditch whence he and they came with a rush, considered that it was that final rush of his which gave the stimulus. But that at the most could only have been partial, since his onslaught was against but one face of the work, whereas the action of the men in the ditch was as if prompted by a simultaneous impulse all round the polygon.

The assailants, once inside, fell upon the Turks and slaughtered them like sheep. Within the narrow enclosed spaces of the redoubt men fought hand-in-hand in one corner, and the Turks waved the white flag in another only to gain time to gather under it for another desperate and treacherous onslaught. The work of slaughter was finished by seven o'clock and the scene of carnage was left to the dead and wounded, of which latter unfortunates many lay neglected all night long, bleeding away their lives for want of the attention which in many instances would have saved them.

When I recounted to MacGahan the story of Gorni-Dubnik, that shrewd and experienced man remarked: "This first battle of the Russian Guard has proved them the best soldiers in the army, because while clinging ever to the determination of carrying the redoubt as their governing motive, they had shrewdness enough to recognise the value of cover as a means of effecting with the least loss the capture of a redoubt which would have held out just as long as its ammunition would have lasted and as long as men should have been hurled against it in masses, for nothing solid could stand against its fire. The Guards have learned in one day what the infantry of the line have failed to find out in all their fighting of the summer and autumn. The regiments which fought at Gorni-Dubnik will never forget the lesson they have learned there. No doubt they had been sedulously trained in the home camp of exercise to deploy in skirmishing order and to take cover while firing; but until the day of Gorni-Dubnik probably nine out of ten had never practically understood what cover really means to the skilled and crafty soldier. The Guards, the picked men of all Russia, have proved themselves better soldiers than the honest stupid soldiers of the line, in that in a single day they have discarded all the woodenness of their parade training and have won an important victory in the only way it was possible to obtain success; and this of their own spontaneous accord, without any previous tuition and even indeed by going counter to the expressed intention of their commanders, who pointed at the great redoubt and with a wave of the hand exclaimed 'Come on and let us get into it!'—meaning all the time to suggest 'Let us take it with a rush!' which was practically impossible. The officers tried this game, for to do them justice, their word is never 'Go!' but always 'Come!' and they suffer accordingly, as the casualties among the officers at Gorni-Dubnik proved. The generals and colonels had their innings and either paid for their failure with their lives or honestly owned to their failure; so the soldiers took the problem into their own hands and solved it in the only way practicable in the circumstances. And this— the spontaneous self-helpful initiative on the part of the soldiers — is the reason why I consider the battle of Gorni-Dubnik as the most interesting piece of fighting in all the war."

The Turks lost in killed and wounded about 1,500 men. There fell into the Russian hands a Pasha, 53 officers and 2,250 unwounded men: a standard, 4 guns and a great quantity of rifles and ammunition. But when the news reached Russia of what the victory had cost, a great wail went up, and Gourko was warned that Russia would not endure such another wholesale massacre of her *corps d'élite*. The best blood of the Empire had soaked into the brown earth around the redoubt of Gorni-Dubnik. Two brigade commanders and four staff officers had been wounded, two commanders of regiments and one battalion commander killed, one regiment commander and three colonels wounded. Of field and company officers, all men of rank and family, 116 were among the gross total of over 3,300 killed and wounded in the capture of one weak although obstinately defended redoubt. "There must be no more of this!" said the Emperor warningly to Gourko, as we heard, to which caution Gourko responded by tendering the resignation of his command. That was not accepted, and he was well advised when he altered his tactics. But to this day, so I have heard, St. Petersburg and Moscow have never forgiven him.

When the fighting ended the headquarters staff returned through the darkness to Cirakova. I had left in Prince Tzeretleff's tent some belongings which I could not easily spare, and I accompanied the cortege, but kept away from the staff and rode in rear of it with the captain commanding the escort. Before we reached the ford Prince Tzeretleff came riding from the front, and I heard him more than once call out my name. I answered and rode forward to meet him, when he said simply: "General Gourko desires to speak with you." I pressed on, certain that I was to be told that I was to be forbidden to enter the camp. Recognising the general in the moonlight, I moved up alongside of him and mentioned Prince Tzeretleff's message. "Ah! yes, Mr. Carnegie," said Gourko in English. "I wish to tell you that I behaved badly this afternoon. I was much disturbed, and at the moment I forgot myself. You were in the right, and I think the better of you that you held your own against me. I desire to apologise to you, and beg you to forget an incident which I sincerely regret." As you may believe, my boys, I was not a little moved and for a few moments could not control my voice; but at length stammered out a few words expressing my sense of the general's graceful and handsome expressions — the more so because he must have had so many things of deep importance with which to concern himself. He gave me his hand, and desired that I should sup with him and Prince Tzeretleff when we should reach the camp. Ever after this little episode General Gourko was kindness itself to me.

The troops which had at length won the position of Gorni-Dubnik spent the night in and about the redoubt, and next morning Gourko's headquarters were moved to the adjacent village. There were enemies on both sides of him, and the general promptly set about fortifying his position and protecting his flanks. The Second Guard Division garrisoned the works which on the previous evening had been captured from the Turks, with a brigade thrown forward on the road towards Telis. During the fighting inside the redoubt we had noticed the sudden outburst of a great volume of flame which illuminated the whole vicinity, but the origin of which was not immediately known. The day after the battle I happened to meet among the Turkish prisoners a Hungarian army-surgeon, who told me that before the actual storm was delivered Achmet Hefzi Pasha, the gallant Albanian commandant of the redoubt, had determined to surrender since the ammunition was exhausted, and that by way of intimating the surrender a white shirt which the Hungarian doctor stripped himself of for the purpose was hoisted on a pole; but that the Russians had taken no notice of this apology for a white flag. He assured me that the Russians continued to fire on the Turks after the works had been carried, and added that the blaze we had seen rose from the Turkish huts built of dry branches which had been fired by the Russians and in which a number of Turkish wounded soldiers were burned to death.

The Russian attack on Telis on the 24th had been badly managed, and the force consisting as it did of only one infantry regiment and twelve guns, was far too weak. After an hour's artillery firing the infantry had advanced, had driven the Turks out of some rifle-pits about 200 yards in front of the main work, and had occupied those. But they were untenable being open to the rear, and it was necessary either to assault or to retreat. The former course was adopted but failed; and the regiment had to fall back with a loss of nearly a thousand men. Gourko moved against Telis on the morning of the 28th. Determined to make a sure thing of it with as little loss as possible, he surrounded the Turkish position on three sides with seventy-two guns supported by an infantry brigade of the Guard, with a whole cavalry division on one flank and the Caucasian Cossack brigade on the other. The guns opened fire with shrapnel at a range of 1,500 paces and maintained a steady cannonade for three hours. Then Gourko sent in a Turkish prisoner with a letter summoning the Pasha to surrender, and intimating his intention to attack on all sides if the required answer was not sent out within half an hour. Ismail Hakki Pasha had had enough of it and promptly surrendered, with 100 officers, 3,000 men, four guns and a vast quantity of small-arms ammunition destined for Plevna.

The slope up which we rode towards the breastwork on the crest was littered with the corpses of the slain in the attempt of the 24th. We counted 300 bodies at a distance of from 200 to 400 paces from the face of the Turkish work. About one-third had received immediately mortal wounds, and those were the fortunate ones; every body had been stripped stark naked and the fatal wounds were easily discernible. Those dead lay otherwise untouched. But it was far otherwise with the other two-thirds, and the spectacle they presented was ghastly beyond words. They had for the most part been shot in the leg and so disabled from getting away; and they had been done to death in cold blood with a barbarous and inhuman ferocity. There lay the mangled corpses, some headless, others deprived of ears and noses, others hacked all over with sword-slashes, and yet others covered with bullet-wounds from firearms held so close that the powder had discoloured the skin. There were other atrocities of which I cannot tell you; and the evidences were cruelly clear of slow torture which American Indians would have hesitated to perpetrate. Gourko's face was pale and stern as he picked his way through the corpses — he sent Tzeretleff back with the order that the troops should not be allowed to come up within sight of their mangled comrades.

Just inside the work Gourko drew rein at the head of his staff, and looked down with stern, cold face on the cringing form of the short and enormously corpulent Hakki Pasha, with his battle-stained, tattered handful of officers at his back. The Russian general would not acknowledge the Turkish Pasha's salaam; he pointed in grim and ominous silence with outstretched arm to the murdered Russian soldiers, some of whom lay stark within 40 paces of the Pasha's hut. There were significant mutterings among the staff and I noticed a young guardsman fumbling with the flap of his revolver-holster. There was a moment when, to my thinking, the Pasha's life was not worth five minutes' purchase. But Gourko kept his self-control; he spat disgustedly on the ground and turned his horse's head away from where Hakki stood ponderously wriggling. Just then a very English-looking man in civilian dress and with the Geneva Cross brassard on his arm, came up to Gourko, and saluting, asked the general in French to give him a party of his men to carry off the wounded Turks. "With great pleasure," replied Gourko politely, and he ordered thirty men to be at the disposal of this gentleman, who thanked the general and joined two young men also wearing the Red Cross brassard. I overheard their short conversation in English and going up to them asked if I could be of any service, at the same time handing my card to the senior of the three whom the other two called "Colonel," telling them that I had gained some experience in bandaging wounds.

"Come along with us, then," replied one of the young men whom I afterwards knew as Vachell. "Douglas and I are going to apply the first dressing to the wounded where they lie, and the colonel has obtained a Russian stretcher-party to carry them to the arabas." We were going towards the entrenchment when I happened to look back and saw the gentleman whom the two young surgeons called "Colonel" rather at sixes and sevens with the Russian party which had been sent him. I went back to him, when he said that he could not make the men understand him, since he knew no Russian and they knew nothing else. Just then Tzeretleff came up, spoke to the colonel in English and ordered the men to yoke bullocks into the empty arabas, go to the trenches, and bring the wounded lying there back to the house to which the English gentleman would lead them. The "Colonel," who now gave his name as Colonel Coope of the Imperial Ottoman Gendarmerie, started off to the hospital with Tzeretleff. I went and helped the two young Englishmen in bandaging, and saw the first instalment of wounded carted away to the khan which, it seemed, had been converted into a hospital. Soon after a few of Gourko's field-gendarmes rode up to where the two young surgeons, whom I now knew as Vachell and Douglas, were dressing the wounded, and took them into custody. I was on my way to inform Colonel Coope of this circumstance when I met him returning with the empty arabas; and presently he too was made a prisoner of by the same detachment. One of the gendarmes, speaking in French, abused the colonel and the nation to which he belonged in the bitterest terms — the fellow clearly knew a good deal about

England and must have had some personal grudge against us. Gourko happened to ride by, when Colonel Coope appealed to him for some information as to what he and his young friends might have to expect. Gourko was rather non-committal, but gave it as his opinion that the three would be sent across the Danube in the course of a few days. I met them again and for the last time on the following morning, when as Prince Tzeretleff's guests they breakfasted in Gorni-Dubnik with the officers of Gourko's staff. By noon they were on their way under escort to Bogot, where the Grand Duke Nicholas was courteous enough to the two surgeons who were presently set free, but he treated Colonel Coope with truculent contumely, stripped him of the Red Cross brassard, and sent him a prisoner of war to Russia where he was prison-bound until after the new year. Colonel Coope was unfortunate in having no papers, even his passport having been lost; and the Grand Duke took advantage of this accident and chose to have him treated with much greater harshness than was the lot of Turkish officers who became prisoners of war. Colonel Wellesley was not permitted to see him.

If Chefket Pasha had not been an unenterprising man, it might have gone hard with Gourko at Telis. He was not aware when he approached that place with a force only some 8,000 strong in infantry that Chefket Pasha was at Radomirtza, not six miles from Telis, with 15,000 men and five batteries. If in the early morning of the 28th Chefket had marched his command down to Telis, Gourko would have found himself opposed by nearly 20,000 men, including the Telis garrison. As it was the Cavalry of the Guard and the Caucasian Cossacks pushed on towards

Radomirtza. About half-way they were met by a large band of Tcherkesses, who were driven back only to disclose an infantry line which the Russian horsemen could not cope with. During the following night Chefket abandoned Radomirtza, the strongest both by nature and by art of all the Turkish positions in the valley between the Vid and the Isker, and retreated into the Balkans.

This same evening the Caucasian Cossack brigade of which I have so often spoken to you, came into bivouac just outside of Telis; and I went to their camp to pay my respects to the colonel of one of its regiments, who although a Russian officer was also by ancestry a countryman of our own. We had previously met at Poradim on the eve of the Plevna battle of 30th July. He had heard that there were a couple of Britons in the camp and he was Briton enough to favour us with a visit. Villiers' servant brought his card into our tent, and this was what was printed on it in Gothic characters:

Lieutenant-Colonel

Lewis-Mackenzie-of-Banar.

A tough little old gentleman in the handsome Caucasian Cossack uniform entered and greeted us affably in Russian, from which he changed into German at Villiers' request. He should have worn a kilt instead of a caftan; with his slightly withered florid complexion, his high cheekbones, huge eyebrows and yellow hair, he was the Scottish

Highlander to the life. He never had learned any English, but there had come down to him from his forbears a few words of genuine Gaelic — he could and did sing to us a little Gaelic song. He was the lineal descendant, he told us, of a Lewis Mackenzie, Laird of Manar in Inverness-shire, who had followed Prince Charlie in the rebellion of 1745, was attainted, lost his estate, and had to fly the country lest worse things should befall him. This ancestor had drifted away into the Caucasus, settled and married there, and ultimately became a disciple of Mahomet. He — our visitor I mean — was the great grandson of this disinherited Inverness-shire laird. His particular Caucasian clan had bowed the knee to the Great White Czar twenty years in advance of the death of the patriot Schamyl; he had received a commission in the first Caucasian Cossack regiment which Russia had constructed of her quondam bitter foes of the mountains, and he had passed through the successive grades until now he was a lieutenant-colonel in command of his regiment. One day, he said, he meant to visit the old place of his ancestors should he survive this war, in which all the riskiest share seemed to be given to the Caucasian brigade. "So much the better," said he blythely; "our fellows hate inaction, and fighting is the very breath of their nostrils. I am afraid they are a little cruel, but what would you have? They are only about half-civilised from the European point of view. You must remember that they are Asiatics — I myself am a Scoto-Asiatic, if such a mixture there can be. I regard myself as a link between barbarism and civilisation. I hope, gentlemen," he added quaintly, "you are not too far gone in civilisation to share with me my pocket-flask of vodka." At the moment we were both all but faint from inanition, and we did not need to be asked twice. Subsequently we met the Scoto-Asiatic colonel quite often; he was ever the same cheery, quaint, genial old gentleman, and that flask of his was a real widow's cruse.

There remained now only the Turkish position at Dolni-Dubnik to be reduced, and for this purpose Gourko intended to use the services of the two divisions of the Grenadier Corps now on march towards Plevna. One brigade of that Corps reached Dolni-Etropol on the night of the 31st, and Gourko meant to assault Dolni-Dubnik on the morning of November 2nd. But at daydawn of the 1st one of its outlying works seemed to be empty, and a reconnaissance disclosed that the whole position had been evacuated; the fag-end of the Turkish column which had been holding the place was seen crossing the bridge over the Vid and withdrawing inside the works around Plevna. Gourko had accomplished his task. His troops closed up and filled the gap in the Russian environment. Tidings were promptly sent to the Commander-in-Chief that the investment of Plevna was complete. Todleben came out and fixed on the contour of redoubts and entrenchments to the westward of the river from Medevan to Dolni-Etropol, and the ground was taken up by the Guards and Grenadiers. Osman could not now any more expect to receive either reinforcements or supplies, nor was it possible for him to break through the strong cordon which encircled him. Henceforth, in Bismarck's phrase, he had to stew in his own juice; it remained to be seen how long he could endure that depleting process. He was a resolute and indeed a stubborn man and he showed no symptoms of giving in. His troops were assiduous in the use of the spade, and their readiness to fight was as keen as it had been at the beginning.

CHAPTER X

SKOBELEFF AND THE GREEN HILL

THE greatest error committed by the Russians before Plevna was to compel Skobeleff's entire withdrawal from the positions on the successive knolls of the Green Hill of which I have spoken so often. When about the 20th October that commander was once again ordered back from Tutchenitza, he found the Turks with their pickets on the Red Hill behind Brestovatz and in possession of that village, as well as holding in strength lines of trenches on the southern slope of the first knoll of the Green Hill. He did not have much trouble in pushing them off the Red Hill and clearing them out of Brestovatz, but that village was within a few hundred paces of the Turkish trenches in front and on both flanks, and was a regular danger trap where the crash of shells and the singing of the Peabody-Martini rifles were all but interminable. MacGahan was there with Skobeleff, and Millett had now joined his brother American in the mud hovel in Brestovatz, in the yard in rear of which was the marquee in which the hospitable general who had a father whom he threatened with arrest if he did not fork out, entertained his staff officers and visitors.

I had been with MacGahan and Millett in Skobeleff's headquarter for a couple of rather dreary days notwithstanding that the Indian summer still survived, when on the evening of the 8th November Skobeleff entered our hovel and announced that he had received instructions from headquarters to drive the Turks from the first knoll of the Green Hill right over against us, entrench the position, and hold it to the last extremity. Orders were issued overnight, four p.m. being specified as the hour for the assembly. The 9th was a busy day. Rifles were cleaned, ammunition was replenished, the batteries were fully supplied and entrenching tools were served out. The men put on their best clothes wherein to go into battle in accordance with the Russian custom. The officers were busy all day among the men preparing them for the night attack, which was an entire novelty to a large proportion of the troops. Skobeleff's force now consisted of his own (the 16th) division, a brigade of the 30th Division, and the 3rd Rifle Brigade, all of which had lost very heavily in the September fighting. Their ranks had been filled up, but with new and green troops who never had been under fire. There was a great deficiency of officers, and those who had newly joined were as yet untried. Skobeleff never ceased to lament those who had fallen at Loftcha and in the assaults on the Plevna redoubts. But he put a good face on the situation, and the troops seemed in good heart. The bands played all day as usual, and the Ouglitski regiment, the vocalists of Skobeleff's force, sent forth their songs into the grey gloomy air from early morning. The fog hid the hostile lines from each other and the batteries were silent. To us waiting for action this silence was strange and weird, scarcely broken as it was by the muffled tramp of men and the occasional words of command, as the troops drifted by into the fog to where the concentration was gathering beyond the Loftcha road.

At four p.m. Skobeleff came out, dressed in full uniform, fresh and scented; he swung himself on to his white horse and led the way through the tortuous alleys of the village, close behind him his mounted Circassian bearing the red-and-yellow banner displaying on one side the white cross of St. George, on the other the letters M.S. (Michael Skobeleff) and the date 1875, the year in which he had made his victorious Khokand campaign. Behind the banner followed a medley of staff officers, Circassians in long surtouts with silver-mounted accoutrements and arms, young gallopers with breasts almost covered with decorations, Cossacks huddled in their greatcoats and hoods, correspondents were muffled in ulsters and capes. Pressing onward and losing our way again and again, we at last reached the rendezvous where the troops were massed. In front were the volunteers — detachments formed of old soldiers who were to rush the Turkish trenches and bayonet their occupants, — very much what I suppose with us in England would be called the "forlorn hope." .Certainly there was nothing of forlornness in their aspect. The faces that looked up at Skobeleff were simple, honest soldier-faces, some of them wearing a good-natured smile, in every eye the wistfulness of trust and fidelity. It was a dramatic and impressive scene, those masses of earnest serious men, every one with his eyes fixed on the face of the general, who rode along their front giving the customary greeting, answered with a will like one voice from each battalion in turn. The background of grey mist which had now settled down so thick that objects could scarcely be discerned the distance of a company-front, brought out the forms of men and horses in strong relief, and imparted a strange picturesqueness to the ranks of expectant soldiers. Skobeleff never harangued his men; his intercourse with them was of a much more familiar kind.

"Well, comrades," said he, in his clear, far-carrying voice, "what do you say? Are we going to beat the Turks to-night?"

"We will try, your Excellency," was the response from out the ranks — the spokesman some old sergeant who had the right to speak for his fellows.

"You won't disgrace yourselves?"

"Why should we, your Excellency? — we are anxious to fight and to win."

"Remember one thing, my men," said the general. "Don't go rushing headlong. We are not going to storm Plevna — not this time; we may later. Our business to-night is merely to turn the Turks out of their trenches and take them ourselves. They really belong to us — we have taken them once before——"

"— And we shall take them again!" interrupted a voice from the ranks.

"Well, remember this is an affair not so much of bravery as of discipline and obedience. When you are ordered to halt, halt you must, though you may want to pitch into those fellows ever so much. As for the Turks, they are nothing to be greatly afraid of."

"We are not afraid of them!" was the response of the ranks; and so Skobeleff moved from one battalion to another, explaining, conversing, heartening; telling his soldiers what he expected of them.

Skobeleff had intended in the first instance to remain with the reserves, so as to bring them up in the nick of time. But now he changed his mind. I heard what he said to Kuropatkin and Makhram, his favourite staff officers, before ordering the advance.

"I confess I am uneasy about the young soldiers," said the general. — "Night! — fog! It is altogether a risky business. Even an old hand, if not used to this sort of thing, might easily lose his head here. I shall not remain with the reserves as I intended. I will lead the troops myself."

The order was passed to "fall in;" and presently the adjutants reported that all was ready for the advance. Skobeleff came out to the front, bared his head, and solemnly crossed himself. The air seemed to rustle as officers and men instantaneously followed his example. A low mutter ran through the ranks as the men prayed, each man in that brief moment looking into his own soul. We foreigners felt the simple solemnity of the rite, and we bared our heads as did the Russians.

The sharp word of command "Close up!" was sent along the lines in a brisk undertone, and the chain of skirmishers went out to the front as the successive lines marched down the slope into the trenches at the foot of the gentle slope, there to halt while the artillery should prepare the onslaught of the infantry. In the dip we found the Vladimir regiment, charged with the duty of digging the trenches as soon as the proper position should be indicated to them. There was now no more entrenching work with soup-dishes, bayonets and naked hands; shovels and pickaxes were in plenty. The Turks kept their usual careless watch and the Russian troops reached their own advanced trenches without detection. Skobeleff was already forward. I followed Kuropatkin as he passed along the front of the volunteers warning them that they should be wanted soon. In such a moment one might have expected to find fire and enthusiasm depicted in the faces of brave men who had volunteered for what was in effect a forlorn hope. But I looked in vain for any such manifestations. There were simply the usual honest, soldierly, well-drilled faces without a trace of unwonted expression. Some looked a little bewildered and careworn, but most seemed but to be stolidly awaiting the word of command, prepared to carry it out as if on parade. There was not a single striking face; one and all looked just as if they were about to march to relieve comrades on sentry-go. There was no indication whatsoever of the motive which might have induced them to be the first to receive the volleys of the enemy and the points of Turkish bayonets against their breasts. Yet they had deliberately volunteered for a service of exceptional hazard.

The Russian front was within 600 paces of the Turkish outposts; yet its vicinity had not been detected. The chain of skirmishers was creeping up, Skobeleff himself with it. After a short suspense there was the report of a single rifle, and presently from the Turkish left there came a rattle of musketry to which for the moment the Russians made no reply.

"Children, follow me!" shouted Skobeleff's powerful

voice from somewhere in the fog. It was drowned in the cheer that followed it, in the beating of the drums, the clamour of the rushing masses and the crashing volleys of the enemy, who had suddenly sprung into full activity. We could see nothing save the flashes through the darkness; but the Turkish bullets were reaching us, singing over our heads, and occasionally striking down a man of the reserves. Millett and I went forward on foot, leaving our ponies with the Cossacks in the trenches. Passing a wounded man slowly dragging himself rearward using his rifle as a crutch, we asked him where was General Skobeleff?

"Where?" was the answer. "He is up in front, leading the skirmishers who are climbing into the Turkish rifle-pits. He is a devil of a man!" And so the wounded soldier limped on.

As we drew closer we could every now and again hear Skobeleff's voice, audible through the fog, cheering, directing, commanding. "I want guns brought up here!" we heard him shout — "I must have guns! Makhram! hurry back, and bring up a battery!" And then Makhram passed us like a flash, galloping at headlong speed, and was lost to sight in the darkness and fog. Now we heard behind us a rush of shouting men — the volunteers hurrying forward to occupy the outpost lodgments from which the Turkish pickets had been driven out by the skirmishers. Their advance was curiously ragged; they came on in loose clumps destitute of any order, the officers in front shouting and brandishing their swords. The bravest men came straight on, reached the lodgments, and went forward towards the advanced trench of the enemy's main work, driving before them the fugitive Turkish pickets. The less enterprising followed with feebler dash in support; getting forward, it was true, but more slowly than the ardent leaders and staggered occasionally by the heavy fire from the Turkish trenches. The rearmost of the volunteers, after passing the lodgments, had not heart to endure the storm of bullet-fire. They hung, and some ran back into the feeble shelter offered by the lodgments in the lee of which we were; most lay down and waited, suffering as they did so, for the hostile bullets, always fired high as was the invariable Turkish custom, spared the advancing Russians, but dropped fast among the prostrate men further back. But the hesitation did not last long. The foremost volunteers sprang over the first Turkish trench and drove out the Turks with lusty cheers. Those who showed fight were bayoneted on the spot; it was not a time for taking prisoners. Then the laggards took heart, jumped to their feet, and rushed forward. Skobeleff came back among them, stormed at them vehemently for their momentary poltroonery, caught them up with a wave of his sword and swept them on at the double. They followed him through the lodgments, then over the first trench, and mingling them with the men in advance he hurled the whole body in strenuous and successful attack against the face of the Turkish main work, which was carried and held at least for a time.

Meanwhile the Vladimirsky regiment came tramping forward and deployed in line just upon the outpost lodgments vacated by the Turks. Officers traced the line on which the Russian trench was to be thrown up; the Vladimirs laid down their rifles and went to work with their spades and shovels. They wrought with desperate energy, toiling vigorously against time. They had a double incentive to be assiduous. They were working amid a rain of Turkish bullets against which they had no protection until they had created that protection for themselves. And they were working, also, to furnish cover for their comrades out to the front who were not strong enough to hold the positions they had carried, now that the Turks had rallied in force and were bearing them slowly back with a furious rifle-fire. If those devoted men out to the front should be unable to maintain themselves there until the busy working-parties should have built up a solid epaulement, then the whole enterprise might fail and Skobeleff undergo a defeat.

Therefore it was that no man put his spade down for a moment. Now and again a soldier would give a groan, drop his hands, and fall wounded or dead. But his place was promptly filled and the work steadily progressed. Towards midnight the enemy's attack became so violent that it seemed a wonder any one could stand up in the hail of fire. But the staunchness and industry of the Vladimirs gradually told. The parapet of the new trench grew so high and so solid that the wearied toilers could rest a while in safety from their labour. Some guns had been brought up and placed into positions in the entrenched line. Its flanks had been made good, the reserves had come up, and the wearied Vladimirs were relieved. Most of the volunteers had come in, but the gallant riflemen still held their ground out to the front, their supply of ammunition maintained by men crawling out to them from the trench. About two a.m. of the 10th great masses of Turks came on with menacing energy. But by this time the protection offered by the trench was fairly complete. The skirmishers were called in; there was now therefore a clear field of fire, and the men stood behind the earthworks and faced and repelled the Turks with sustained volleys.

Skobeleff had come in with the skirmishers. I scarcely recognised him, so begrimed with powder-smoke were his face and coat. When the Turks came on he sprang on to the parapet in full exposure to the enemy's fire, and steadied his men by his own dauntless coolness. The Turks quieted down at dawn, and Skobeleff took occasion of the lull to ride back into Brestovatz in order to send a despatch to General Todleben at Tutchenitza. By this time I was mortally hungry, and in the hope of some breakfast I desired the general to allow me to accompany him to the village. He wrote his despatch, we had some food, and Skobeleff, bidding me waken him if the fighting should rekindle, threw himself on the straw and was asleep in a moment. I should have very much liked to have followed suit, for the excitement of the night had wearied me; but he had set me on watch and I had to keep awake, although with many yawns. An hour had passed when there suddenly came a wild uproar of firing from the front. Our horses were saddled outside; I touched the general's shoulder, and in a couple of minutes we were galloping towards the "Green Hill," or as the Russians called it "Zeleny Gory," I with a haversackful of bread and meat for MacGahan and Millett.

A fierce fire was raging and the shrapnel-bullets came thick and fast as we rode forward. At a glance Skobeleff recognised what was happening. Turkish sharpshooters had worked round his left, and had opened an enfilade-fire on a body of Russian troops covering a working party digging a zigzag covered way from the first trench back to the hollow occupied by the reserves. These troops, who, it seemed, were mere recruits, had taken a scare, thrown down their rifles, and frankly run away. Skobeleff encountered them in their flight and accosted them with grim humour.

"Good health, my brave fellows!" he shouted affably.

The men halted and gave the customary response; but their confusion was amusingly apparent.

"You are noble fellows; perfect heroes — I am proud to command you!" They saw that he was deriding them, and they shambled about in shamefacedness, rubbing elbows awkwardly.

"By the way," said Skobeleff still blandly, "I do not see your rifles!"

The men looked down at their feet but made no answer.

"Where are your rifles, I ask you?"

There was a painful silence which Skobeleff broke in quite another tone. His face changed; his voice was angry; his glance made the fellows cower.

"So you have thrown away your weapons! You are cowards! What, you run from Turks! You disgrace your country! Right about face and follow me!"

Skobeleff marched the runaways up to the spot where they had left their rifles, and ordered them to take them up and follow him. He led them out into the space in front of the trench right in the line of the Turkish fire, and there he put them through the manual exercise, he himself giving the words of command standing out in front of them with his back to the Turks, while the bullets whistled over and around the detachment. And there he drilled them under fire till they went through the different motions with all the smartness and precision of the parade-ground; after which he let them go back to the trenches with the warning that if they ever ran away again, he would have them shot. A couple of them limped back wounded.

The Turks gave no molestation to the newly-taken positions throughout the whole of that day, although they assailed on both flanks. The soldiers worked at the trench until its parapet was made strong enough to resist shell-fire, and banquettes were finished all along its interior. The guns were brought into regular battery-emplacements pierced by embrasures and along the front wire entanglements were laid down. The troops remained on the alert, for it was thought certain that the Turks would not delay their attempts to recover the position from which they had been driven. Skobeleff slept soundly in a hole excavated in the trench and half-filled with straw. The men contrived for themselves little stoves in the trenches and made their soup and tea in their field-cans. After dark dinner was brought up from the village for the general, his staff and friends; and after having eaten we sat round the samovar drinking tea and wondering whether the Turks were sleeping or waking. We had not to wonder long. It was near midnight when a scout came in with the tidings that they were leaving their trenches and forming for action.

"I was sure they would try again to-night," said Skobeleff. "Gentlemen, to your posts!" he added, — "Order up the reserves and let no man go outside the parapet."

Almost immediately the stillness was followed by noise and tumult as the Turks approached, loading and firing as they came on. It was not a dark night, and we could dimly discern the advance of the solid Turkish line. The volleys came closer and closer till the air above us was tortured by the hail of bullets. The Russians remained still and silent, waiting until the Turks were close up. Their first line was now within seventy paces. In the red flash of their volleys we could see the faces of the men plying their rifles, and above the crash of their volleys rose the shouts of "Allah!"

"Battalion, fire!" shouted Skobeleff, and the order was taken up all along the front. The rain of bullets and the simultaneous storm of grape staggered the Moslem line. "Don't give them time to recover!" roared Skobeleff — "fire in platoons!" But the Turks pulled themselves together and came forward with a rush, until they were barely thirty paces from the parapet. Death was making havoc in their ranks, but the brave fellows came on undaunted. Skobeleff leaped up on the parapet the better to conduct the defence. The flashes of the volleys threw a lurid red glare on the dark faces around which the smoke was eddying, and lit up the tall supple figure of the general. It was wonderful how long those brave Moslems held their ground out in the open, destitute of all cover; fired into vehemently by enemies snug behind the protecting parapet. At length they began to waver — one final volley from them, another into them in reply, and then Skobeleff was justified in his exulting exclamation, "We have repulsed them!" All night lights were visible in front of the Russian trenches, and the sentries fired at the lanterns until Skobeleff, who was still on the parapet watching, shouted : "Are you Turks, or are you Christians? Don't you see that they are gathering up their killed and wounded? No matter under what provocation, we must not degrade ourselves to become barbarians."

For several days and nights Skobeleff scarcely ever quitted the trenches. His staff after the first day made efforts to make him comfortable after a fashion. An excavation was made in the inner face of the parapet in which he could lie at full length among furs and rugs. A table and a few stools were brought up from Brestovatz. In the trench was constructed of earth a species of hut covered in by thatch taken from an adjacent cottage; and there was built into the earthen wall a stove round which we used to sit in detachments;—when men got frozen all but stiff out in the open in the still watches of the night, they would crawl into the hut to thaw themselves out. During the short intervals afforded between the Turkish attacks and the superintendence of his own lines of defence, and when he was not gossiping with his friends, Skobeleff was always studying or writing; he was the sort of man who never could be idle. Except in Skobeleff's command I had seldom heard the music of a military band since the crossing of the Danube. He alone cultivated martial music because of its enlivening influence on his men. It was passing strange to listen to vocal and instrumental music in the trenches not a couple of hundred paces from the enemy. The effect it had was wonderful on fatigued and dispirited men, worn by the recoil after long excitement and brooding in the nostalgia to which the Russian soldier is more a victim than the

Swiss peasant. I have heard the Russian Anthem played to the accompaniment of the roar of cannon and the shrill ping of bullets, and when the hymn was over the din of the martial accompaniment drowned by the clamour of the cheering. It was as much the custom in Skobeleff's regiments to bring the "music" into the trenches as it was to bring the company kettles. We were within hearing of the Turks, and there were those among us who averred that when a Russian band began to play our friend the enemy hushed himself to listen to the Muscovite strains. "We have in one sense lost the art of war," Skolebeff used to maintain. "Our forefathers were better military psychologists, and were well aware of the influence of music upon soldiers. Music raises the spirits of an army. Napoleon — the God of War — knew this well, and led his men into battle to the stirring music of a march."

I am no soldier, and what rudimentary knowledge of military affairs I had once casually gathered has long since gone from me. But it was always a wonderment to me why the lives of brave men should have been wasted so lavishly in maintaining this forward position on the first knoll of the "Green Hill." The reason assigned was that the occupation of this position shortened by about a mile the circuit of the Russian investment of Plevna. But what substantial effect was obtained by making this petty contraction at the cost of so much bloodshed, I was always unable to realise. The Turks were quiescent on the knoll — they showed no symptom of intention to push any extended offensive, and if they had done so the lines of Brestovatz would certainly have brought them up. Was not the curtailment of the cincture by one short mile too dearly bought by the loss of several hundred gallant men?

The Turks were very persistent. As if for the mere empty boast of the thing, they strained every nerve to recover that barren position which Skobeleff had clutched so masterfully. On the morning of the 14th November his Russians saw with surprise that during the night the Turks had constructed opposite their left a strong redoubt armed with guns. It enfiladed a considerable section of the Russian position. While daylight lasted the infliction had to be endured; but Skobeleff counted the hours until darkness should fall. Meanwhile he went about among his young soldiers, instructing them as to the method of assailing the Turkish redoubt which had sprung up so suddenly. It was a strange thing to see a general of division sitting in the centre of a ring of non-commissioned officers of the Souzdal regiment, the outer circle formed of private soldiers eagerly catching every word uttered by the chief. His final instructions were simple and to the point:

"You must march up to the redoubt as silently as possible. When you are within twenty paces, then you must 'hurrah' and the drums must beat. Then you must storm the Turkish earthwork, go to work with the bayonet, drive the enemy out, and capture as many rifles as you can; I will give three roubles for every rifle you bring in. When you come back you must not only bring back your wounded, but also your dead: I will not have brave Russians left to be mutilated by those savages."

Nothing could be done until after midnight, when the

moon should have gone down. Meanwhile there was
dead silence in the Russian trenches; the faces of the
young soldiers waiting the command to sally out wore an
expression of wistfulness. Skobeleff himself was restless
and nervous. He gave his final orders that when the
attacking party had gone out over the parapet the men
should form line and march on elbow to elbow — "so,"
in his own words, "that each man may feel his comrade
by his side." From the banquette we strained our eyes
in the effort to discern how it fared with the men out to
the front. Suddenly a cheer rent the stillness of the
night, followed promptly by the roll of the drums and
the crash of musketry-fire. Then there was a headlong
rush back toward us, and fugitives came swarming over
the parapet in a wild panic and huddled down into the
trench behind the cover of the work. Skobeleff called
the supports up to the banquettes, but forbade firing until
he should give the word. It was only the scared cowards
who had come running in; the good men led by Colonel
Kashin were doing their duty, as evidenced by the heavy
firing out to the front. What was actually happening
we could not know, until presently Kashin brought in
what remained of the two companies which he had led
out. One company had stormed the Turkish work, ex-
pelled the Turks at the bayonet point, gathered up all
the rifles found, then quitted the trench and lay down
outside along with the other company. Then the Turks
had come back in great strength, and we had heard above
the firing the triumphant shouts of "Allah!"

Skobeleff had underrated his enemy. He had supposed
that the new Turkish work was held in little force, and he

had acted recklessly from an impulse of anger. Instead of two companies, he owned later that he should have sent two regiments to attack the work. What he had done was merely to provoke the Turks to make fierce reprisals, and we were near enough to recognise that they were massing for an attack in great strength. It seemed as if the question who should possess the first knoll of the "Green Hill" was to be fought out on this dark and sullen morning of November 15th.

The reserves were called forward. The parapet was lined two-deep and the trench behind the banquette was full of men. There was a singular absence of disorder. The very men who twenty minutes before had come running in with every symptom of abject funk, now that they were on the defensive with something solid in front of them by way of protection, stood calm and resolute on the banquette ready to meet the shock of the Turkish assault. That was now imminent. It was not so dark but that we could dimly discern the oncoming masses, and their front was outlined by the flashes of their rolling volleys. With fierce cries and shouts they came pouring on in loose order, their irregular front as defined by their fire extending far to right and left. The air above us seemed absolutely dense with their bullets; it was well for the Russians that the Turks when in motion fired always from the hip, so that they took no aim and always fired high. The Krishin redoubt in front of the Russian left came into action, showering shells into the hollow behind the earthworks, and plying with shrapnel the flank nearest to it.

Skobeleff held his men as if in a vice. One might almost have felt the strained silence in the ranks. No

man drew trigger; the self-command was supreme. A
low whisper ran along the line that the Turks were being
led by Osman Pasha himself. I was close to Skobeleff,
who was less confident than usual. "Who would have
thought," said he, "that half the Turkish army would be
upon us in this sudden manner?" The leading Turks
were within twenty paces when at last the word to fire
was given. The crash of sound was deafening as volley
answered unto volley. A few brave Turks charged forward shouting "Allah!", but the Russian bullets struck
down the gallant fellows. One man did actually climb the
parapet and sent his bayonet into the breast of a Russian
soldier on the banquette; but next moment he fell back
pierced by bullets and bayonet-stabs. From out the darkness in front there came to us cries of pain, moans and
groans. Still the Russians plied their volleys, till at
length we heard the rushing noises and tumult of masses
in retreat.

All breathed more freely. The assault had been repulsed, and since the loss of the Turks must have been
heavy it was hoped they had given up the attempt.
But that hope was soon to be dispelled. We heard again
the noise of the advancing hordes; then it seemed as if
there was a halt.

"Yes," said Skobeleff, as he looked over the parapet,
"they are forming up for a new attempt. They may carry
the work. It may be as well, gentlemen, that you should
have your revolvers in readiness." This hint was taken
by the staff, but I derived no solace from it, since for one
thing I had no revolver, and for another, being a neutral
I was not entitled to use a revolver if I had one.

It took the Turks some time to reorganise. Meanwhile the nervous excitement on the Russian side visibly increased. The strain was wearing men down. It was with feverish impatience that we endeavoured to distinguish what was happening out yonder in the open, but in vain. As we strained our eyes the Turkish bugles sounded, a stunning volley was delivered, and then nearer and nearer came the rushing sound of the swift charge. By this time the dawn was breaking, and we could discern with what fiery nimbleness the lissom Turkish soldiers bounded forward. But now the Russians could aim more accurately than in the darkness, and their steady volleys staggered the Turks in their onslaught. They did not maintain the pace with which they had started and a good deal of tailing-off was perceptible. At length the effort came altogether to a standstill and volley after volley was exchanged. When halted the Turks fired very steadily, taking good aim, and many Russians fell back into the trench from the banquette killed or wounded.

The Turks were reluctantly retiring, covered by a screen of marksmen, when I noticed Skobeleff suddenly clap his hand to his side with a muttered exclamation of pain. "What is the matter, General?" I asked.

"Hush," was his reply, "I am hit!" and it seemed as if he was about to faint.

His officers closed around him in great solicitude, begging him to go into his hut and rest till a surgeon should arrive. But Skobeleff broke away from them, bidding them to take no notice of him; and he led off a cheer at the retirement of the Turks which ran along the whole line. Wincing a good deal he nevertheless tramped from flank to flank, congratulating the soldiers on their staunchness. Then he went into his tent and stripped.

"Why," exclaimed Kuropatkin, "there is no wound!"

"No wound, — what do you mean?" asked Skobeleff, flushing.

"What I say. I congratulate your Excellency on having received a sharp contusion." In ten minutes more he was out among his men again.

CHAPTER XI

IN THE BALKANS WITH GOURKO

IT seemed to me that life with Skobeleff up on the Green Hill — a life of squalor freely relieved by bullets — was becoming rather monotonous. MacGahan was still lame, and he was content to remain for the present at Brestovatz, enjoying snatches of the society of his friend Skobeleff when that restless soldier took occasionally a few hours' respite from battling with his next-door neighbours the Turks. On the afternoon of the 15th I rode up to General Todleben's headquarters at Tutchenitza. It was rather impudent on my part, but he had been so kind to me at Bucharest that I had determined on venturing to ask him when he thought the fall of Plevna was likely to occur. I met him as he rode back from Radischevo on the big grey stallion which I had procured for him. "Ha! Mr. Carnegie," he exclaimed as I saluted, "you see the grey has given up his antics and does not stand any more on his hind legs. Come and have a glass of tea, and tell me where you have been."

As we sat by the samovar General Todleben said that it would not surprise him if Osman should hold out for a month longer. "I am sure," he observed, "that he will not surrender until his provisions are out — he is the kind of man to eat his boots and then to finish with a desperate sortie. Up at the Grand Duke's headquarters the hot-heads have been eager for another assault, but I have argued them out of that folly. Do you know that Mehemet Ali is now in command at Sophia, and that General Gourko is going up into the lower Balkans to make it impossible for him to come down to the relief of Osman?" This was quite new to me, and I asked when General Gourko would probably start. "Why," said Todleben, "he actually marched to-day, I believe. His Cossacks went forward ten days ago. His force consists of the 1st and 2nd Guard Divisions, the Guard Rifle Brigade, the 2nd Guard Cavalry Division, and the Caucasian Cossack Brigade." I said that I was desirous of accompanying this expedition, but beyond everything desired to be on the spot when Plevna should fall. "You will be in good time for that by my reckoning," said the general, "if you are back by the end of the first week of December." I thanked him and rode back to Brestovatz, where I found Millett and gave him the information I had received from General Todleben. Millett, like myself, was dead tired of the investment of Plevna; and we resolved to start on the following morning and overtake Gourko. We had each a good-riding pony. Millett had his servant who rode his pack horse; a pair of capacious saddle-bags served my turn.

Next morning we bade farewell to MacGahan and Skobeleff and rode away across the Vid to Dolni-Dubnik, where we were so fortunate as to find Gourko just in the act of starting. He was very civil and readily gave us permission to accompany him. Telis was dismal, empty, and foul-smelling; but Radomirtza was still a pretty village with many good houses uninjured, whose courtyards were full of grain-stacks and bins piled high with maize. In Lukovitza were many Bulgarian fugitives from the Balkans — they seemed of a very different type from the sordid sullen people of lower Bulgaria. We overtook the army in Jablanitza, quite a civilised village under the shadow of the Dragovitza range, which is reckoned the first portal of the Balkans. The troops were camped around the village among the oak-trees on the hillsides; forage was abundant for the horses and there was no lack of wood for the camp fires. The reconnaissances which the general busied himself in making proved, we were told, that the main road to Sophia by Orkanie and all the tracks leading over and through the Balkans in this section of the great range, had been carefully fortified and were held by the Turks in force. The nearest of the hostile positions was on both sides of the high road near the village of Pravetz, at a point where the road, after passing the village of Osikova and climbing over a high mountain spur, suddenly falls into a narrow gorge the heights on both sides of which were strongly fortified, commanding the gorge and enfilading the road. On a side road a few miles south of the main road was the large village of Etropol, in front of which were several redoubts blocking the thoroughfare.

The Pravetz position was considered too strong to be forced by a direct attack, yet until it was taken no further advance could be made. General Dandeville was ordered to move against Etropol with an infantry brigade and thirty-eight guns. To General Ellis with a regiment, two rifle battalions and fourteen guns was given the duty of advancing against the front of the Pravetz position. General Rauch, whom I had known in the Hainkioj Pass, with about the same strength, was to make a wide circuit to the right and take in reverse the Pravetz position while General Ellis was threatening its front. I suppose you find these details rather technical, my young friends, but unless you give yourselves the trouble to follow them you will find it impossible to understand with what skill and dexterity Gourko out-manœuvred the brave Turks with a minimum of loss to himself. He had quite abandoned the butcherly bull-headed tactics which had cost him so dear at Gorni-Dubnik, and he now made turning movements and cannon-fire serve his purposes instead of the sacrifice of men.

Millett and I parted at Jablanitza for a day or two; he was to accompany General Ellis with the central column; I went with Rauch's turning expedition. The 22nd was the day specified for the operations to begin, and the idea in the headquarters was that Rauch had before him merely a long day's march. From his previous Balkan experiences Rauch did not share that sanguine view, and instead of waiting for the general start on the 22nd he quitted Jablanitza on the afternoon of the 21st. Little Colonel Lewis-of-Manar (he dropped the Mackenzie except on his card) had the advance with 300 of his Caucasian Cossacks; then followed the two rifle battalions with a battery before and behind them, and the mass of the column came last — the four battalions of the Simeonof regiment of the Guard. With one interval of three hours the detachment marched all night, and at Vedrara, which village was reached at eight o'clock in the morning of the 22nd, the impatient Rauch would allow no fires to be lighted, so that no soup or tea could be made and the men had to content themselves with dry biscuit. The road as far as Vedrara although rugged did not consist entirely of precipices, and the horses for the most part were able to haul the guns. But beyond that village there was in effect no road — only mere mountain paths — and the struggle to bring on the guns and ammunition waggons was severe and continuous. Virtually, a road had to be made most of the way. Relays of staunch toilers plied pick and shovel in the advance, and other relays, each a whole company strong, helped the guns and caissons over the worst places. A good deal of the march was actually in the rugged bed of the Little Isker, which wriggled tortuously among the crags and which had to be crossed ten times. Fissures in the ledges of hard rocks dragged the hoofs from the horses' feet, which had to be bound up in rags, and the poor pained animals forced to keep on hauling. At one point it seemed actually impossible to get the ammunition waggons forward, and the men volunteered to carry the powder and shells by hand. But Rauch would not permit this and so the hauling and pulling continued. By hauling on ropes lashed to the guns they were saved from rolling down the precipices, but of the caissons three went over in spite of every effort.

Leaving the ravine of the Little Isker the detachment struck into one of its tributaries, the Praveea brook, which takes its rise near the village of Pravetz. The track up this valley was not quite so rugged, and the relentless Rauch hurried on his wearied men. When the village of

Kalugerovo was reached at sundown we all hoped that there at length we were to find rest. But that did not accord with Rauch's views. There were still for the already all-but-spent men some four hours longer of dogged tramping. It was not until nine o'clock that the village of Lakovitza was reached, and Rauch, himself exhausted, at length gave in. The men were too dead-beaten to cook or even to make fires; they fell in their tracks and slept like stones. More than one man died outright of sheer fatigue. The outpost service was a mockery, although we were almost in face of the enemy. The sentries were found asleep at their posts and the officers found it impossible to keep them on the alert. By daybreak of the 23rd the implacable Rauch had us on the march again, now heading southward. As the morning advanced while we were following a rising valley flanked on the west by heights, the column was brought to a halt by hostile fire from those heights. The rifle battalions, firing as they went, pushed directly up the face of the heights; while the Cossacks who had been in front climbed up on to the flank of the enemy. The Turks did not wait to make a fight of it at close quarters, and they fled after having delayed our advance for nearly two hours, during which a sharp fire was maintained on both sides. The march was promptly resumed and long slow hours were passed in dragging, pushing and hauling the cannon. But Rauch and his tough soldiers were soon to earn the reward of their toils. What Rauch had dreaded was the sheer exhaustion before his men should come in sight of their enemy. The extremity of that exhaustion was very near when the advance attained the summit on the left rear of the Turkish fortified position. The cheer that then rose came rolling back along the column and restored to vigour the men who a moment before were ready to drop. Rauch held his people for a while until he had them somewhat concentrated, and then he let them go. The guns on the summit swept with shrapnel the high plateau in their front, and the flanking slopes. One after another the Turkish redoubts were carried; although their occupants held them stoutly the rush of Rauch's Russians was not to be withstood. The fighting continued till past midnight. Next day I rejoined Millett down at Pravetz in the valley.

A curious thing happened during the night of the 23rd, spent by Rauch's people in bivouac on the steep ridge west of the Pravetz valley. The Turks had mostly gone, and Rauch's soldiers had occupied and were sleeping in the positions which they had abandoned. But in the gloom of the dusk one Turkish redoubt and that, as we later knew, the strongest of the whole series, had been altogether overlooked. In the dead of night, as we lay by the watch-fires, we were awakened by a sudden burst of firing near by, followed immediately by shouts, yells, curses, and the clash of bayonets against bayonets. Then we heard voices in Russian crying: "Let the poor devils go!" and the counter-exclamation: "No, no! Kill them, bayonet them!" mingled with shrieks of pain and prayers for quarter in the Turkish language. The stirring incident passed in the course of a few minutes, and then all was still again. Fatigue was stronger than curiosity and we turned over and straightway fell asleep. In the morning we found that a company of volunteers from the

Moscow regiment had climbed up the steep mountain-side and had suddenly assailed the redoubt still held by the Turks; and that after a short spell of hand-to-hand fighting the Russian volunteers had driven out all of the little garrison who had not been bayoneted in the mêlée.

Because of the difficulties he had encountered Rauch was a day behind his time. Nevertheless he had been beforehand with General Dandeville, whose task it was to force his way into Etropol, a large village on the Little Isker several miles due south of the Pravetz position. Dandeville's attempt to storm the Turkish redoubts in front of Etropol had failed; and he was obliged to drag guns up to the summits flanking the enemy's position. He could not open fire until the afternoon of the 24th, when the Turks left their untenable works and fled through Etropol. Rauch arrived there on the following day, when we learned that part of the fugitive Turks had gone southward to Slatitza, and part had followed an old disused road leading up to the Turkish main position on the long lofty ridge which is the summit of the Etropol Balkans and the watershed of the great range.

Etropol we found a very quaint and interesting place. Its population had been half Turk, half Bulgarian, and the two races lived amicably enough. There were more mosques than churches, but the churches were much handsomer than the mosques. The town is jammed in the ravine of the Little Isker, over whose channels many of the houses were built. It is a labyrinth of narrow crooked alleys in which we found it very easy to lose our way. The Turks of course had all fled, and the Bulgarian inhabitants, a fine handsome manly race quite different from the Bulgarians of the Danubian plains, could not do enough to prove their devotion to the Russians. Gourko, who arrived on the 25th, was welcomed with great effusion. The Turks had carried away with them as hostages most of the rich Bulgarians, and the poorer classes only remained to greet the Russian general and tender him bread, salt and oil. The Bulgarian girls of Etropol were good-looking enough to redeem in some measure the plainness of the race. They wore a simple but becoming costume of a scanty robe with long sleeves and open neck bound at the waist by a broad belt of square links of chased silver, their arms loaded with heavy silver bracelets, their necks encircled by chains of yellow, red and green glass beads, and their heads enveloped in a dark-coloured kerchief falling over the shoulders. Every evening they gathered around the fountain with their water-jugs poised on their heads, and made eyes shyly at the smart Russian hussars, who were by no means backward in reciprocating their glances.

The strain and fatigue which I had endured in accompanying Rauch's march told on me so that I was only once able to go up to the Groete position. Millett spent all his days and most of his nights up there. He was a painter first and a correspondent afterwards, and the result was that when you came to read his letters they read as if they had been written with a paint-brush. I never knew any one who had so great a gift of picturesque descriptive writing. He was a very bright fellow, always sunny and good-tempered, full of quaint American humour, making light of hardships and indeed enjoying them in the fulness of his buoyant spirits. And there never was such an obliging chap. When I was on my back in Etropol and so having nothing to write about, I was a bit down on my luck. "Cheer up, old fellow!" shouted Millett in his noisy, hearty way,—"if you like I will write for you a little sketch of our camps up yonder on the mountain-tops." You may believe that I thanked him heartily; down he sat and painted the following pen-picture, the MS. of which I count among my treasured souvenirs:—

"It is interesting to enter these mountain bivouacs, miles away from a village and from supplies, far up among the clouds which at this season drift along between the peaks, frequently veiling the whole landscape and drawing a dense curtain of mist between the opposing lines. It is a little world in itself, this camp among the trees here. Fires are blazing on every side; the soldiers have rigged up their shelter-tents between the smooth straight beech-trunks and have their garments all hung about to dry. There is a continuous musical ring of axes and sabres cutting fuel, only interrupted occasionally by the infernal whizz and angry crack of Turkish shells. Rifles are stacked in long irregular lines or are clustered about the great trees. Crowds of soldiers are gathered about the open-air kitchens or busied with the details of their simple toilettes. Some of the bivouacs are continuously exposed to rifle-fire; not that they are in actual sight of the Turkish lines, but the bullets that go over the crest of the hill and graze the earthworks come dropping into the bivouac in the rear, chipping the trees and wounding men and horses. The soldiers in these bivouacs dig great holes in the ground, pitch their tents over them, and then pile the earth and sods up on the side towards the enemy, so they have a fairly good shelter at all times. Fires are also built in little earthworks, for no one likes to have a live bullet in his kitchen, and whenever there is a fusillade nearly every man is in cover. The shells and shrapnel come in, but the men take their risks of these projectiles and attempt no defence against them. A thin cloud of blue smoke rises out of the tree-tops, drifting away to leeward and marking exactly where the bivouac is placed, both to the eyes of friends away back in the village down in the valley and to the sharp sight of the enemy near at hand. Thus one may see how closely together lie the two armies on the mountain-tops.

"From below in the valley, all day long and even through the night toils up the rough path a procession of soldiers and Bulgarians bearing powder and shells and a long train of pack-horses laden with provisions and fodder. The Cossack posts by the way are comfortable little camps where hay, although brought on horseback for miles, is stacked in abundance and where cooking seems to be continually going on. When the snow covered the ground the picturesqueness of the mountain bivouacs was perfect. The tree-trunks came out sharply with their deep grey colour against the pure white, and every figure was in distinct silhouette. Now that the snow has temporarily gone the grey overcoats of the soldiers harmonise exactly with the colour of the carpet of dead leaves, and it is difficult to distinguish the men from the ground on which they lie."

I must bother you at this point with some geographical details. The Plevna-Sophia road, after passing through the Pravetz Pass of which you have already heard, goes due west through a plain for about eight miles to the village of Orkanie. Thence it makes a great loop, bending southward, and indeed in places south-eastward, past the village of Vratches through a very mountainous region, until at the pass of Baba-Konak it crosses the main Balkan range, after which it goes almost due west across the plain to Sophia. On the assumption that the Russians in their advance would necessarily be limited to the high road, the Turks had fortified three successive positions, all of which commanded it. The first position was at the Pravetz Pass, which you will remember was turned by Rauch. The second, of great strength, was at Vratches behind Orkanie. The third and most important position was on the Balkan summits right and left of the Baba-Konak Pass, having traversed which the road escapes from the mountainous region and emerges on the plain. From flank to flank this position on the Shandarnik ridge — the main crest of the Balkans — had a length of about 7,000 yards. The defile followed by the road was near its western end, and defile and road were completely commanded from the position, which was in effect the key of the Balkans. Gourko might have done what the Turks evidently expected that he would do. Having made himself master of the Pravetz Pass he might have pushed on through Orkanie, and after the manner of Suleiman in the Schipka Pass he might have wasted the lives of his men by hurling them against the serried trench-lines on the slope in front of Vratches. But Gourko had the warning of Dorni-Dubnik to deter him from reckless sacrifice of his soldiers. A reconnaissance proved to him that from the parallel ridge of Mount Greote he could confront along its whole line the Turkish final position, and that attitude would in itself suffice to render untenable the hostile lines at Vratches.

The event proved how sound was his strategy, but the task of carrying out his design was extremely arduous. To crown the Greote ridge he took advantage of an old cart-track up which to bring his guns. The Bulgarian farmers rallied to him with their teams of cattle, for his horses were useless on the steep gradients. Each piece was dragged by four yoke of oxen, in front of which a hundred men or more hauled on a long rope fitted with breast-straps like the towline of a canal-boat. With those large teams of cattle and the strong relays of willing Bulgarians the guns were slowly dragged up the ascent, a score of stout fellows at each wheel and a dozen flourishing whips and yelling at the oxen. It was a long climb from the valley up to the ridge, and from thirty-six to forty-eight hours were spent in bringing up the sixty guns with which Gourko had resolved to garnish the position. He thus rendered himself greatly superior to the Turks in artillery, for they, it was known, had but twenty guns; but the frequent fogs hindered the full utilisation of that arm, and Plevna had proved how little damage earthworks sustain from cannon-fire, especially when as in this instance the range was long. East of the Baba-Konak defile the Turks had six substantial redoubts, the one furthest east a large and formidable work; and they were now engaged in constructing a seventh redoubt on the isolated height west of the high road where it traverses the defile. General Rauch's section of the Russian position taken up *vis-à-vis* to that of the Turks was furthest to the east; General Dandeville carried on the line to the high-road defile, on the further side of which was for the time the force of General Ellis with a regiment of the Guard and the Guard Rifle Brigade.

This was the situation on December 1st, the last day of my stay on the Balkans. General Dandeville, when he reached Mount Greote on the afternoon of the 28th November, found it occupied by Turkish outposts which he drove away, and indeed part of his force had chased the retreating Turks into the Shandarnik redoubt, but the Turks had rallied and driven the Russians out again. But for the delay which Dandeville had encountered in bringing up his guns on to the Greote position, he would have been in time to intercept the retreat upon the Shandarnik summit by the main road of Shakir Pasha's force which had been holding the Vratches lines behind Orkanie, and which fell back on Shandarnik on the night of the 28th. This retreat was compulsory, since the Turkish position at Vratches was effectually turned by Dandeville's possession of the Greote ridge. In the hurry of evacuation Shakir had to abandon in Orkanie the immense mass of ammunition and stores which had been accumulated there to be sent into Plevna for behoof of Osman's army — enough for the supply of our army of 50,000 men for two months. All this accumulation consisting, apart from munitions, of some two million rations, several thousand bushels of oats and a great quantity of clothing, fell into the hands of the Russians; and very opportune was the windfall in view of the bad weather which had set in, the length of Gourko's communications, — 130 miles from the Danube at Sistova, — and the bad condition of the roads.

Millett would not leave the front. It was his conviction that Gourko would push across the Balkans the moment that he should hear by telegraph of the fall of Plevna. If he went back to Plevna to witness its fall, he would run the risk of losing the spectacle of Gourko's passage of the mountains. MacGahan was at Plevna and would describe the grand finale of Osman's splendid defence. Millett had become very popular with Gourko's people, with whom he had the field all to himself. So we shook hands in the main street of Etropol, and he rode up to his friends on Mount Greote. Before starting for Plevna I paid my respects to General Gourko, who had always been extremely kind to me. He was in great spirits and it was natural that he should be so. By his tactics in demonstrating against the front of formidable positions while he turned their flanks, he had been able within eight days to cause the evacuation by the Turks of all their prepared positions among the lower Balkans, and to force them back, with the loss of immense quantities of supplies, into their final position on the summit of the great range. He had accomplished this with a minimum of loss to himself — his casualties did not amount to 500 killed and wounded. He had avoided actual fighting as much as possible; but his troops had to undergo extraordinary exertions in hard marching, climbing, and dragging guns by hand. Several men had died from sheer exhaustion in hauling the artillery up the mountains, especially from Etropol to the Greote position. The Turkish position opposite thereto Gourko considered so strong that he was reluctant to attempt to carry it by direct assault. It was his policy to remain in observation pending the fall of Plevna, when he might expect to be reinforced in such strength as should enable him to descend into Roumelia and sweep eastward along the great Maritza valley. In the meantime the specific object for which he had been sent forward — to prevent the advance of a relief army moving down with intent to raise the investment of Plevna — had been effectually accomplished.

I told the general that I was going back in the hope of witnessing the fall of Plevna, but that with his permission I should return to his army after that event. "Always glad to see you, Mr. Carnegie!" was Gourko's reply — "but you must not expect that I mean to spend the remainder of my life up here in Etropol. It is my notion that we shall all be able to go home presently, and the sooner the better say I. If you want to cross the Balkans with us, young gentleman, don't hang about Plevna after Osman has surrendered!" I thanked him for the advice and took my departure.

CHAPTER XII

THE FALL OF PLEVNA

STILL stiff and sore, I rode slowly back towards Plevna, spending a night in Lukovitza by the way. Passing from the road to the house in which I intended to sleep, I heard a voice calling to me "Effendi! Effendi!"; and entering the cottage whence came the call I found there a young Turkish farmer whom I had often met on the Danube while voyaging between Rustchuk and Braila. The poor fellow, who wore the Zouave uniform of the Turkish regulars, told me that he had been wounded in the leg in the fighting before Plevna in September and had been sent out of Plevna in one of the convoys of wounded which Osman had despatched while the communication remained open. While passing through Lukovitza he had been recognised by a Bulgarian family who owed him some kindness, and who took him into their house and nursed him with great care. He was now convalescent but was in great trouble as to his future, his chief apprehension being lest he should be taken prisoner by the Russians. He could speak Bulgarian fluently and I suggested that he should make his way across country to his own people about Rasgrad, where he would find no Russians. "But, Effendi!" he replied, "how can I travel through Bulgaria in this uniform?" For a trifle I bought for him a Bulgarian suit from the head of the family who had befriended him so kindly, and gave him a pittance to serve him as marching money. He started next morning by way of Loftcha, reached his home in safety, and came to Rustchuk to thank me soon after the close of the war.

When I reached Brestovatz I found that Skobeleff's headquarters had been removed to the village of Ustendol, about three-quarters of a mile south-west from Brestovatz and better sheltered from the Turkish bullets and shells. I found the general and MacGahan in residence there; both had been ailing, probably on account of their long exposure and excitement of the previous month, but both were now well again. Both were exasperated against General Todleben because he had protested with all the weight of his influence against the project urged by the hot-heads of the Grand Duke's staff that a general assault should be delivered on Osman's works. "I am disgusted with these headquarter people," said MacGahan. "They dared in September to attack Plevna with some 65,000 men. They do not dare to attack it now with 120,000, although Osman must be weaker now than he was then. They are allowing Osman with probably less than 50,000 men to neutralise a force nearly three times that number, while the fine season which has so exceptionally favoured us is rapidly passing away. They were foolishly reckless in September; they are foolishly timid now!"

"Yes," said Skobeleff, "look at Kars! — there was no pottering around it — just a rush and all was over. Osman, if left alone, may hold us here for two months longer. When one reflects on the sufferings of the men in the cold and rain and in the mud of the trenches, is it

OSMAN PASHA.

not certain that we should lose more men by the prolonged sickness and exposure than in an immediate assault which, because of the positions we now occupy and our better knowledge of the ground, could not fail to succeed?"

Although I kept my impressions to myself, it struck me that both Skobeleff and MacGahan in their impatience somewhat begged the question, experienced men as were both. On what evidence was it to be assumed that Osman could hold out for one month longer, let alone two? Next morning I rode up to Tutchenitza to pay my respects to General Todleben. That calm, strong man, whose sagacity was not less manifest than his kindly nature, received me very cordially and asked me to tell him what tidings I brought from the Balkans. That was not a very long story; indeed I made it as short as might be, for I was anxiously hoping that the general would say something concerning the situation before Plevna. He sat silent for a few minutes, sipping his glass of tea. Then he began:—

"I have a great respect for Osman. There was a time when I believed that he had made a fatal mistake in clinging to his Plevna position when he might have evacuated it to the infinite advantage of Turkey. I know better now. I have it on unquestionable authority that when Osman became aware of the approach of our reinforcements with the inevitable consequence of our investment of Plevna, he anxiously begged to be permitted to retreat from Plevna while that movement was still practicable, and his representations were strongly backed up by Mehemet Ali Pasha. But Shevket Pasha reported so decidedly on his ability to keep open the communications with Plevna, that the Seraskierate in Constantinople believed that incapable person and ordered Osman to hold Plevna to extremity. Loyal soldier that he is, Osman made no remonstrance, and there he is to-day down yonder, staunchly holding out. You probably do not know," continued the general, " that since you left this front the Grand Duke Nicholas sent a flag of truce to Osman with a letter summoning him to surrender in order to prevent the further effusion of blood, since it must be evident to him that his capitulation could be only a question of time since he was completely surrounded by superior forces. I think Osman's reply was very fine. It stated that he recognised the humane motives of the Russian Commander-in-Chief, but that as a soldier the Grand Duke would readily understand that his military honour forbade him to surrender his army until all his means of defence were exhausted — which was not the case at present."

I mentioned that General Skobeleff had expressed himself in favour of the policy of a general assault. — "Yes," replied Todleben with a grim smile — "not only he but others who had not so good a right to make themselves heard, were urgent for that recourse. But I was fortunate enough to convince the Grand Duke that although the date of Osman's surrender could not be definitely specified, yet that that event must occur soon; and that against this certainty it would be sheer recklessness to risk an uncertainty of a most hazardous character such as was involved in a general assault. I further argued that although we might lose only some 10,000 men in an unsuccessful assault, we should incur a weakened *morale* throughout the whole army and some time must elapse before the *morale* should be recovered; whereas should we wait patiently till the surrender the troops would be in good condition for immediate further operations.

"We know," continued the general, "that Osman must be near the end of his supplies; his sick and wounded must be very numerous and in sad plight: we know from our own experience that the alternating rain and snow for the last six weeks must have rendered the Turkish trenches almost untenable; and there is the further sure indication that desertion is steadily on the increase. I believe, Carnegie, that the end will come within the next seven days. You may be sure that Osman will not, like Bazaine, tamely surrender in his trenches. No; he will treat us to a wild-cat furious sortie; a sortie that will cut through rank after rank and pile the ground with dead and dying!"

It was ominous of the end that while the watchful Russians did not cease during daylight to maintain a steady although not heavy artillery-fire on the Turkish trenches, there was attempted no reply during those final days. On the 9th about noon the rain merged into snow, which fell heavily until after nightfall. I spent most of that day with General Todleben at Tutchenitza. From all quarters throughout the day reports were arriving to the effect that Osman was making his arrangements for breaking out. Deserters brought out tidings that rations of biscuit and a supply of foot-coverings were being distributed to his troops, their ammunition was being replenished and their arms were being inspected. Much stir was seen west of Plevna on the Sophia road, and great gatherings of soldiers and carts were visible in the camps thereabouts. Todleben pointed out that the construction was being set about of a second bridge across the Vid under cover of the guns on the Opanetz heights. The indications were conclusive that a sortie in full force was impending, which would to all seeming strike the section of investment west of the Vid held by General Ganetsky, the commander of the Grenadier Corps.

The friendship between Todleben and Skobeleff of which I had witnessed the beginning at Bucharest had been interrupted by differences of opinion, for which it was the general opinion that the latter was chiefly to blame. But the rupture nowise prevented Todleben from giving practical expression of his faith in Skobeleff as a fighting chief; and although the section commanded by General Kataley of the Guard intervened between Ganetsky and Skobeleff, he gave the order that at daylight on the 10th Skobeleff with a brigade of his own division and another brigade drawn from General Kataley's command should cross the Vid and take up positions in support of the Grenadier Corps in the probable event of its being assailed. I should mention that the long flat line of front held by that corps was fortified with great strength: the first line garnished thickly with batteries, lunettes, and redoubts, in rear of which on the gentle slope was tier upon tier of strong entrenchments linking together the frequent redoubts. All the works were profusely furnished with artillery — 9-pounders in the first line, 4-pounders in the second.

I left Tutchenitza after dark and rode to Skobeleff's headquarters at Ustendol. I remember Todleben's last words to me: "Plevna will be ours within the week of which I spoke when you were last here!"

Everybody about Skobeleff was on the alert. Skobeleff had organised a most effective spy service. One of his rascals brought in the tidings about 10 p.m. that Osman was concentrating on the plain behind the Vid. From Ustendol Plevna could not be seen; but a telegram came in from the Roumanian section stating that unusually numerous lights were moving about in the town. We slept in our clothes and were frequently roused by fresh pieces of news. In the small hours came in a spy with the tidings that the principal Krishin redoubt was empty and that the works about it were being rapidly evacuated. Skobeleff tested his veracity rather severely. Would he guide the troops into the Krishin redoubts with the certainty of being bayoneted if he was found to be playing false? The man consented with alacrity, and he led the detachment of volunteers whom Skobeleff sent forward with instructions to move cautiously. The spy was honest; the redoubts, as well as the trenches on the Green Hill, were found empty and they were immediately occupied by the troops of the 30th Division. Skobeleff left behind to protect his positions a brigade of his division, and acting on orders he had sent away his Rifle Brigade to the village of Gravitza to strengthen Krüdener. It was recalled while on the march by General Todleben when after daylight he learned that both the Gravitza redoubt and redoubt No. 10 had been evacuated by the Turks and garrisoned by the Russians.

Skobeleff was on the march before daybreak and we were more than half-way towards the Vid when the sullen grey dawn began to open. It was about half-past seven. Suddenly the calm heavy air was pierced by the simultaneous crash of a great mass of artillery, promptly followed by that fierce steady roll of musketry which we had learned to know so well. We were on the heights of Medevan, whence we looked down on Plevna, on the cliffs at whose base flows the Vid, and on the wide plain beyond athwart which ran the line on which were the Russian battery emplacements and redoubts, forming a continuous obstruction. A thin fog hung over the valley which mingling with the cannon-smoke somewhat obscured the scene. But we could distinctly see the flashes from the Turkish cannon in rapid action on the bluffs on the right bank, and could discern less clearly the flashes of the return fire from the Russian batteries on the plain. Skobeleff sent on his two brigades across the river; he himself with his staff remained for a time on the Medevan heights watching through the haze of fog and cannon-smoke the deployment of Osman's attack. The Turkish infantry were deploying with great smartness and skill, taking the full advantage of the cover afforded by the long undulation in the ground just beyond the bridge, in the shelter of which no doubt they had been gathering during the night. The skirmishers were already out in the open, driving before them the Russian outposts.

Skobeleff became greatly excited. "Were there ever more skilful tactics?" he exclaimed. "They are born soldiers — those Turks! Just notice how skilfully they are already half-way towards Ganetsky's front and yet have never shown out of cover — hidden first by the darkness, and now protected in their deployment by the long bank yonder in the lee of which they are forming in almost perfect safety! Beautiful! beautiful!" he exclaimed, — "never was a sortie more skilfully prepared! How I should like to be in command of it!"

Skobeleff then turned his binocular on the Russian defence line. He seldom swore, but now a torrent of oaths came hot from his lips. "Oh, that ass Ganetsky!" he exclaimed, striking his clenched fist on his thigh. "What imbecility! Just look! He has had his orders; he was warned of the intention of the Turks; he might have had any quantity of reinforcements. A corporal would have known that this was a time for cramming the works of the first line of defence with all the men they could contain. And what preparations to meet an assault has Ganetsky made? None! His positions are actually occupied by the usual detail — one regiment from each division; in other words, he is confronting Osman's army with six battalions, when he has at his disposition twenty-four battalions of his own corps, not to speak of my division and other reinforcements. Mark my words!— the Turks will carry our first line with a rush. We shall retrieve it; but to have lost it for ever so short a time will be to our eternal disgrace!" With that Skobeleff spat venomously and rode away to overtake his troops. Mac-Gahan and I remained where we were; no better position could have been anywhere found.

The Turks had finished their deployment and now were ready for the assault. Their skirmish lines were rapidly strengthened and as rapidly they advanced. In rear of the skirmishing lines hurried the artillery, stopping occasionally to fire a shell and then hastening on to overtake the skirmishers. There followed at the double a loose but heavy line of deployed battalions supported by the reserves in columns. The Turkish objective was the section of the Russian front between the Sophia road on the south and the fortified village of Dolni-Etropol on the north — the section held by the 3rd division of the Grenadier Corps. In spite of the rapid artillery-fire from the Russian batteries in front and on both flanks — in spite too of the furious musketry-fire from the infantry holding the Russian entrenchments, the Turks came steadily and swiftly on. The Russian shell-fire ploughed lanes through their ranks; the Russian rifle-fire mowed them down as with a scythe. How cruelly they were being punished was testified by the numbers of fallen who marked the broad track of their advance. But no amount of slaughter gave a moment's pause to Osman's gallant soldiers. Their officers seemed to measure the distance with the eye; we could see their swords high in air as the signal. Then with a wild shout of "Allah!" the Turks sprang forward upon the line of trenches held by the Siberian regiment, swept over their parapets, slaughtered their defenders to the last man in a momentary hand-to-hand struggle, carried with a rush the battery in rear, bayoneted the Russian artillerymen who fought round their guns with heroic constancy, and were in possession of the battery.

The centre of the Russian first line was thus broken and in Turkish occupation. Further to the (Russian) left the gunners held their ground in the work No. 4 a little longer, firing shrapnel into the Turks; but they were all but surrounded and had to abandon their position, leaving some of their guns in the work. For the time a single Russian brigade was bearing the brunt of the assault delivered by the whole Turkish army. The lunettes it held were full of dead and dying. The soldiers were exhausted by their efforts to oppose the Turkish rushes;

a number of Russian guns were in the hands of the enemy, who were in actual occupation of a length of Russian trenches and of two Russian redoubts. The Siberian regiment had been all but annihilated. It was certainly a very critical moment. Skobeleff's criticism had proved but too true; Ganetsky had no reinforcements at hand, and the interval until they should tardily be brought up was extremely disastrous. One regiment after a while did casually turn up, just in time to save the *débris* of the unfortunate Siberian regiment. It threw itself valiantly against the Turkish advance towards the second line and at least delayed that movement, but its losses were immense. I heard afterwards that in less than five minutes all three of its battalion-commanders and half of its company-chiefs were either killed or wounded.

It was not until 10 a.m. that reinforcements began to come up; but not until half an hour later was it that a fresh brigade of Grenadiers, brought up by General Stroukoff of the Emperor's suite, charged with a " hurrah!" the Turks who were in possession of the Russian trenches. A hand-to-hand struggle ensued, which lasted for some time owing to the curious obstinacy with which the Turks clung to the guns they had captured. Ultimately they were dislodged with the bayonet, and the Astrachan Grenadiers gained possession of seven Turkish guns and one standard, the only trophies of the action. Gradually the Russian troops succeeded, but not without hard fighting, in re-occupying their whole system of defence. It was not, however, until nearly noon when the Turkish retirement reluctantly began, covered by a heavy fire. The Russian guns were brought up into the infantry line and volleys of shrapnel were poured into the retreating Turks, which converted their retreat into a rout. Some took shelter behind the carts which lined the roadside, but the greater number sought refuge under the bank of the Vid where they found shelter from the Russian fire.

After having halted for a time in their lines the Russian troops moved forward along their whole front, covered by a heavy artillery-fire. The Turkish guns replied but with little energy. In about half an hour the firing slackened on both sides and then stopped entirely. The rolling crash of the rifle-fire and the deep-toned bellowing of the artillery were heard no more. The smoke gradually lifted from the field of the final strife, and there was silence — a silence that will probably not be broken around the quiet Bulgarian town for many a long year, never again, perhaps, by the din of battle. Osman's fierce sortie had failed after a heroic effort to achieve success.

Skobeleff, as I have told you, had left us to follow the two brigades the command of which had been given to him in the orders disseminated by General Todleben. After an altercation which he had with the general commanding one of his brigades, to which I need not allude, we encountered him again some distance from the bridge across the Vid. The battle had ended, but nobody seemed to know what was going to happen. At length there was seen to be waving from the cliffs a white flag. Then there arose from the Russian army a great shout of triumph and gladness. The shout swept over the plain and its echoes came back to us from the cliffs over against us. The Russians had at last been rewarded for all their toil and hopes. Plevna had fallen, and to judge from the expression on the faces of the soldiers, they expected that the homeward march would begin on the morrow. Many a morrow was to pass over the heads of the homesick men before they were to see Russia again — how many would never see Russia more! Meanwhile, at all events, the white flag was an actual fact. A Turkish officer carrying it rode over the bridge, and crossed the plain to where General Ganetsky sat on horseback in front of his division. At the time we could not understand why this officer went back so quickly; but we learned later that Ganetsky had refused to recognise him because of his inferior rank, and had bidden him send out an officer of rank to negotiate regarding the conditions of capitulation. Skobeleff headed a detachment of officers who rode along the Sophia road to within about fifty paces of the bridge, within point-blank range of the masses of Turks on the other side of the stream. Skobeleff and Kuropatkin waved white handkerchiefs, a signal of amity reciprocated by the display of a once white clout on a stick. Then two horsemen came over the bridge, approached, and saluted Skobeleff. His interpreter was not at hand, and I was called up to communicate between Skobeleff and the Turkish officers. Their statement was that Osman Pasha was about to come out, but they did not speak as from any authority. However, they rode back, and Skobeleff announced that Osman was coming out. The Russian officers had a fine spirit of chivalry; they expressed the highest admiration for the Turkish Commander, and it was agreed that they should salute him with great respect and that the soldiers should present arms.

We stood here, while we waited, among the dead and dying of the battle whose embers were not yet cold. The wounded Turks lay all about us, bearing the agony of their hurts with a calm stolid fortitude. The road on which we were gathered was cumbered with dead and wounded men, oxen, horses, and shattered arabas. A few hundred yards beyond was the ground over which Osman Pasha's sallying column had made its heroic charge — ground now literally covered with dead and dying. Russian surgeons were busying themselves with administering the first dressing to the wounded Turks — far other treatment than that which throughout the campaign wounded Russians received at the hands of the Turks.

There was a sudden shout "He is coming! There he is!" and we drew nearer to the bridge. Two horsemen were approaching, the man in advance carrying the white flag, a Turkish cavalryman in dingy and dilapidated clothing. There followed him an officer wearing a smart blue surtout and a bright red fez; clean and fresh, with a pair of white kid gloves — a regular swell, in point of fact. He was quite a young man, clean shaven, with a round rosy face, light moustache, straight nose, and blue eyes. He was not Osman. He handed Skobeleff his card on which he was thus designated:

> Tefik Beg.
>
> Chef de l'état Major
>
> de l'armée de Widdin.

Skobeleff saluted the Turkish officer and informed his companions of his name and rank. There was a general movement of astonishment. Could this young man with the boyish face be Osman's second self, who must have had so great a responsibility in the organisation and maintenance of the great defence? It seemed strange, but it was true. MacGahan remarked to me in an undertone: "The Turks have the merit at least of not being afraid of young men!" Tefik seemed curiously embarrassed. He spoke with great deliberation.

"Osman Pasha," he said, "is wounded."

"Not severely, we all earnestly hope!" exclaimed Skobeleff.

"I do not know."

"Where is his Excellency?"

"There," answered Tefik, pointing to a small house on the roadside just beyond the bridge.

It was clear that Tefik, whether constitutionally or because of emotion which he had difficulty in suppressing, was resolutely taciturn.

"General Ganetsky," said Skobeleff, "is in command here. He will be here immediately; perhaps you would care to speak with him." Tefik made a silent bow. The situation was becoming very embarrassing when General Stroukoff presently arrived. He announced that he had powers to treat, and he asked the Turkish officer whether he was authorised by Osman Pasha to enter into negotiations. What passed I did not gather, but understood that Tefik had replied in the negative. He made a comprehensive bow and galloped away back across the bridge.

General Ganetsky came up after a short delay, and

then we crossed the bridge and were in the midst of the Turkish army. We were in the centre of a thick crowd of men with arms in their hands, who two hours previously had been engaged in mortal strife with the men whom they now surrounded. When we were abreast of the little house our group halted and Generals Ganetsky and Stroukoff entered. Their conference with Osman lasted only a few minutes. Osman agreed at once to an unconditional surrender — he had no alternative. His whole defence had come down by the run. At Opanetz the Roumanians had captured over 2,000 prisoners after a trivial resistance. In the redoubts west of Krishin Kataley's soldiers, after a short fight, had received the surrender of a Pasha, 120 officers and nearly 4,000 men. There remained the troops which had made the sortie of the morning, and them Osman himself verbally surrendered. The army of Plevna, which on December 10th laid down its arms after a gallant and obstinate defence, consisted of 10 Pashas, 130 field-officers, 2,000 company-officers, 40,000 infantrymen and gunners, and 1,200 cavalrymen. The Russians became possessed by the capitulation of 77 guns and immense quantities of ammunition. In the sortie of the morning of December 10th the Turkish loss was 6,000 men in round numbers. The Russians must have lost before Plevna from first to last well on to 50,000 men if the Roumanian losses be included. Of this number about 40,000 were killed or wounded, the remaining 10,000 died of sickness. In the battle of this morning, I afterwards learned, the Russians lost 1,732 men killed and wounded among whom were one general and 10 field-officers.

The conference with Osman had occurred about 2 p.m. He entered a carriage and drove away towards Plevna. We all returned over the bridge to where the Grenadier Corps still remained in position on the battle-field. The Grand Duke Nicholas, of whom it used to be said that he had a great liking for appearing on the battle-field after the fighting was over, now illustrated the aptness of that disparaging remark. He made his appearance with his staff fully two hours after the last shot had been fired. As he rode along the front he was received with vociferous cheers, for he was the brother of the Czar. Halting in front of the centre he spoke some words to the Grenadiers which were received with the wildest acclamation. I was not certain whether MacGahan spoke seriously or in irony when he remarked that the Grand Duke had one of the attributes of a great commander — "the soldierly quality of knowing how to speak to soldiers."

The Grand Duke after the review expressed his intention of going into Plevna and paying his respects to Osman Pasha. We all followed him across the bridge. An hour had wrought a remarkable change among the Turkish soldiers. When we had left them every man had his arms in his hand. The order to lay down arms had been obeyed to the letter. Each man had laid down his rifle where he stood, and we rode over the Peabody-Martinis with which the road was littered. A little further down we found ourselves in the midst of a confused huddle of bullock-carts and arabas composing the train which was to have followed the army if the sortie had been successful. Among them was a number of vehicles apparently belonging to Turkish families, for they were full of women and children sitting about on household effects. This supplementary exodus, although it failed, seemed to me a strong argument in favour of the hypothesis that Osman's effort was no mere bravado for the sake of a punctilio of military honour and in order to impart eclat to his capitulation, but that it was undertaken in the full hope that it would be successful. It was reasonable to suppose that he knew of Gourko's departure towards the Balkans with the Guard which had been holding the section of investment west of the Vid, and he may not have known that the Grenadiers had taken up the positions which Gourko and the Guard had vacated. As for the aspersion that Osman had fallen short of holding Plevna to the last extremity, seeing that his supplies were not utterly exhausted at the time of his surrender, it may be rejoined that if he had succeeded in breaking out as he obviously had intended, his troops marching through an exhausted region on the way to Widdin, for which fortress he certainly would have headed, would have needed a certain amount of provisionment during the march which could be furnished only from the supplies still remaining in Plevna.

It seemed that Osman had heard that the Grand Duke Nicholas had the purpose to visit him, and to forestall the latter in courtesy had turned back to meet the Russian Commander-in-Chief. There was a halt, and then shouts of "Osman! Osman!" It was an interesting moment when Osman drove up surrounded by a Cossack escort — in the nature, I suppose, of a guard of honour — and followed on little bits of ponies by a score or so of young officers who, we learned, constituted his staff. Nicholas rode up to the halted carriage and for a full minute the

two men, Russ and Turk, gazed silently into each other's face. Then they gripped hands heartily, and the Russian Commander said:—

"General, I honour you for your noble defence of Plevna. It has been among the most splendid examples of skill and heroism in modern history!" Osman's face moved slightly — a twitch of pain crossed it as in spite of his wound he stood up and saluted, uttering a few broken words in a low tone. The Russian officers saluted with great demonstrations of respect, and there were shouts of "Bravo!" Prince Charles of Roumania at the moment rode up, paid Osman some warm compliments and shook hands. Courteous to the last, notwithstanding the pain he was plainly suffering, Osman rose and bowed his acknowledgments of Prince Charles' compliments. But now his face was hard and set and his bow was made in grim and stern silence. For Prince Charles of Roumania was a vassal of the Porte, and Osman clearly regarded him as having broken faith with his Suzerain.

The officers on the staff of the Grand Duke Nicholas professed themselves struck with the power, energy and determination disclosed in the features of Osman. "It is a grand face; it more than fulfils my ideal of the man!" was the comment of Colonel Gaillard, the French military attaché. Skobeleff was not less enthusiastic. "It is the face," he exclaimed, "of a great soldier!" They may have been right. For my part, in Osman's lowering brow and heavy jowl I could discern no other expression than that of stolid dogged resolution. To me there was no evidence of high intellect in the coarse sullen features. It is true that there was a certain pathos in the dark liquid eye, but as a whole I saw nothing distinctive in Osman's aspect. He was simply a Turk of the old unregenerate stamp — brave, merciless, and brutal, the type familiar to any one who knows the Turkish race. He was a large-framed, thick-set man, apparently of middle age — there was no streak of grey in the short thick black beard which covered the lower part of his face and but partly hid the thick sensual lips. No doubt he was a fine soldier. But it was quite a mistake that, as I heard one critic remark, he did not command a regular army — "technically speaking," to quote the critic's words — "not an army at all, but a mob of armed men, with scarce any organisation, with no discipline save the natural and passive obedience of the Turkish peasant, and only such military education and experience as were gained around Plevna in the trenches and on the battle-field." Osman's troops consisted almost entirely of "Nizams" — of regular troops, and they were veterans with whom on the Timok in 1876 Osman had fought and won several battles against the Servians officered by Russian volunteers. No man ever accused Osman of being a sybarite. Throughout the whole period of the investment he lived in a common green tent although there was no lack of good houses in the town of Plevna. His tent had now been struck and his last night in Plevna was the first he spent under a roof.

After the short interview between Osman and the Grand Duke the latter rode on into Plevna. In the sullen twilight the town presented an aspect of utter squalor. It had suffered scarcely at all from the Russian shell-fire. But its narrow crooked streets knee-deep in foul mud through which thousands of stragglers wandered aimlessly; the gaunt cowed Bulgarian inhabitants who hung about their doorsteps and saluted timidly as the staff passed by, with a furtive side-glance lest they should be giving offence to the Turks; the houses in which were seen neither lights nor fires but were cold, comfortless and deserted — all combined to make up a scene which in the gathering darkness of a bleak December evening was dreary and depressing in the extreme. On the outskirts of the town we — that is to say Skobeleff's party, while on the way to Ustendol met Tefik Bey, Osman's chief of staff, who had lost sight of his chief and was wandering about in the mud in a pathetically helpless way. Skobeleff promptly asked him to be his guest for the night and Tefik after some hesitation consented. Skobeleff I knew had already another guest in Colonel Gaillard; and I knew also that the accommodation in his quarters was extremely limited. I said good-night to MacGahan and rode back into Plevna in the hope of finding there some food and a sleeping place. But the quest seemed in vain. The Bulgarians of Plevna were in no mood to take in casual strangers, and they averred themselves to be in a state of chronic hunger. I determined to try one of the Turkish hospitals — but which, for the town seemed almost one great hospital? On the steps of a church which had been pointed out to me as the chief hospital I dimly saw a man smoking a short briar-root pipe, and on the chance I addressed him in English. He replied in the same language. In ten minutes later I was in a bare but clean room in which was a good fire, and I was sitting on the floor eating ravenously.

My kind and hospitable entertainer was Dr. Charles

Ryan, a native-born Australian whose guest I have since been in his own home in Collins Street, Melbourne. He had just taken his degree and was about returning to Australia to embark in practice, when the Russo-Turkish war began. Ryan postponed his return to Melbourne, and instead betook himself to Widdin where Osman Pasha accepted him as one of his army-surgeons. He had marched with Osman's army down the right bank of the Danube from Widdin, and then inland to Plevna. The diversion to that place was quite an after-thought. Osman's original intention, said Ryan, had been to occupy Nicopolis. But finding that fortress already in Russian possession, he wheeled to his right and sat down in Plevna to await the arrival of a reinforcement of some 12,000 men coming from Sophia. Before its arrival Osman had but 40,000 men, but they were the best troops in Turkey — the veterans who had crushed the Servians in the summer of 1876. The Sophia reinforcements raised him to a strength of 50,000 before the battle of 30th July. Ryan told me that he was the only English surgeon with Osman; all the others were Levantines. Osman, he said, was not very solicitous in regard to his wounded. After the September fighting and while as yet Plevna had not been invested, a number of English surgeons had accompanied the reinforcements which Shevket Pasha brought into Plevna. Osman had 5,000 severely wounded in the September fighting, whom he had determined to relieve himself of by sending them away to Sophia while the communications were yet open, in the carts which had brought in the supplies. I told Ryan that I read in an English newspaper that when in the middle of October the English surgeons entered Plevna, Osman abruptly refused to receive them and commanded their immediate withdrawal. "That is quite untrue," replied Ryan. "He was perfectly courteous to the English surgeons. This was what happened. Dr. Bond Moore, of the Stafford House organisation, waited on Osman to volunteer the services of his staff of surgeons for work in the Plevna hospitals. Osman explained to him most courteously that he was very much obliged to England for sending him doctors and stores, but that the former were not needed in Plevna, and he would be glad if Moore would take his staff back to Sophia. The surgeons again waited on him to beg him to reconsider his decision. His answer, which I perfectly remember, having heard it myself, was: 'If you wish to see any fighting or to visit my positions, you are welcome to remain here as long as you like; but if you want to help my wounded, go with them to Sophia and attend to them there.' From the military point of view," continued Ryan, "I think Osman was perfectly justified in evacuating his wounded. He had before him the virtual certainty of a close investment, and it was therefore his imperative duty to reduce as far as possible the number of mouths to be fed. Besides, there was the great probability of an epidemic breaking out among the wounded, which might easily extend beyond the hospitals and seriously diminish the number of his fighting men. And I hold also with Osman as to the sanitary point of view in relation to the condition of the wounded themselves. You must consider the impossibility of providing proper food and surgical appliances, and the unhealthy overcrowded state of the hospitals, impregnated as they were with septic germs, making it extremely probable that some serious epidemic would break out if the wounded had remained in Plevna. I know," added Ryan, "that the evacuation, owing to the rude means of transport at Osman's disposal, unquestionably entailed an immense amount of human suffering, and caused many deaths among the more severe cases. But great allowance must be made for the hurry and confusion which necessarily attended this evacuation — those responsible for its execution being in hourly expectation of their retreat being cut off. On the part of the Turkish surgeons, believe me, there was no feeling of jealousy in regard to the Englishmen. On the contrary, Mr. MacKellar's services were so highly appreciated by them that they invited him to consult on many of the most important cases, and they paid him the highest compliment which a surgeon could desire, in requesting him to operate on any cases he might select as presenting special difficulty. As a matter of fact MacKellar performed several capital operations in presence of the principal members of the Turkish medical staff. I must tell you also that not more than 200 wounded remained in Plevna after the general evacuation; Osman Pasha had therefore good reason for desiring that Moore and his comrades should follow the great masses of wounded evacuated on Sophia. But he so far acceded to Moore's representations as to order the wounded to be taken as far as Orkanie only, instead of being carried on to Sophia as Osman had originally intended. And this, remember, was after the very truculent letter which Moore thought proper to address Osman Pasha, protesting vehemently against the decision of the Marshal to evacuate his wounded. Moore did not take into consideration that Osman's first duty as a soldier was to care for the well-being of his fighting men. There was a story — I don't know who invented it but I am sure it is a lie — that Osman was heard to say 'When one has to fight, there is no time for physic. Sick and wounded are a useless burden; they are of no use to the Sultan or to Turkey. It is better that they should die quickly. We have quite enough to do without attending upon them.' If such expressions had been attributed to Suleiman I should not have been surprised; but Osman is not a barbarian. Moore's letter was too strong. 'It has been my painful duty,' he wrote, 'to see among those 5,000 wounded men, fever, famine and gangrene feasting side by side with smallpox in your Excellency's crippled soldiers.' He went on to say that Osman Pasha's resolution to transport to Sophia all his wounded in their deplorable condition 'would result only in sowing the Orkanie Pass with corpses.'" Osman, said Ryan, did not reply to this protest nor did he thank Moore for the great mass of medical comforts, medicines, bandages, &c., which he had brought in and which, since Osman would not permit any English surgeon to administer their distribution, Moore had given over to the principal Turkish surgeon. Ryan said that Plevna was now again one mass of sick and wounded and that it was a matter of surprise to him that a pestilence had not long since broken out.

The Russians are not by nature cruel — they are merely indifferent to human suffering. If after Plevna they horribly neglected the prisoners which the fortune of war threw upon their hands, it may be said of them that they impartially neglected their own sick and wounded. On the morning of the 11th December the Turkish prisoners

of war were divided into two unequal parts, one of which,
numbering about 30,000 men, remained where the poor fellows
stood in mud and snow and filth among their dead
comrades; the other, some 10,000 strong, fell to the Roumanians,
who immediately marched their allotment of prisoners
to the Roumanian headquarters at Verbitza, where
they were as well treated as circumstances permitted, and
were soon set on march across the Danube and through
the Principalities on their way to their Russian captivity.
For their prisoners the Russians did nothing at all; they
simply ignored them. The nominal charge of them was
given to General Skobeleff, senior. At this time, owing
to the breaking of the bridge across the Danube at Nicopolis,
the Russians themselves were reduced temporarily
to short commons and the Turks for three or four days
simply got nothing at all. They were herded out in the
open by Russian sentries, and there they stood in dirt and
mire day after day in the utmost extremity of misery.
They died in great numbers, and as they dropped they
were trodden down into the slush in which the living stood.
When the ground became too utterly abominable, they
were moved from it to another piece of ground as muddy
but not quite so filthy as that which had been abandoned.
But the full measure of their misery was not complete until
the great snowfall which began about the 18th and by the
20th was more than a foot deep. Before this time several
relays of prisoners had been sent away towards the Danube;
but the great mass still remained on the plain by the
Vid, gaunt, foul, faint with famine, frost-bitten in every
limb, living corpses rather than men. I believe that quite
one-fourth of the brave army which Osman Pasha sur-

rendered on December 10th perished in the mud of Plevna before Christmas-day.

The Emperor had been watching the fighting of the 10th from a redoubt on the western height of Radischevo, but he did not enter Plevna until the 13th, when he drove through the town on his way to review the allied army on the battle-field beyond the Vid. The taint from the Turkish prisoners huddled among their filth not far from the road by which his Majesty passed to the field, must have reached his nostrils; and a large body of them, shepherded by Russian bayonets, were near the parade-ground on which the troops were ranked. The muster interested me greatly. The morning fog lifted as I found myself near a regiment of the Russian Guards. Bigger men, better dressed, finer in bearing, I suppose no army in Europe could furnish. In their long greatcoats, every man stepping in exact time, they passed their general in quarter-column; and as they defiled he gave them the customary Russian greeting, which was answered by a short, sharp, fierce shout, quite startling in the suddenness with which it began and ended. A brigade of Roumanian regular infantry came up into position headed by the 2nd Chasseurs, a mere skeleton of a regiment; two-thirds of it lay dead but unburied on the slopes around the Gravitza redoubts. The marching style of the Roumanians differed considerably from that of the Russians, who moved in a slow, firm, dogged way that conveyed an indefinite sense of great power. The Roumanians were smaller and slighter men; they moved with a quick, brisk, supple action, and carried themselves quite jauntily. Behind the Roumanian regulars came some battalions of the " Dorobantz," the Roumanian

Territorial force — something like the English militia, I fancy. They did not march so smartly as did the regulars, but in enduring privation and hardship they were reported to have proved themselves the better men. The parade was being formed up while I was riding with an English correspondent who was with the Roumanians of General Carnot's staff. We chanced upon four or five Turks who had been wounded in the fighting of the 10th, and who although they had lain on the field ever since, were still alive. During four days and nights, without food, without water, and exposed to bitter cold in thin clothing, had these poor fellows kept life in their wounded bodies. They were immediately carried on stretchers to one of the Russian field-hospitals. A staff officer made a very true observation. "If we," said he, "in merely crossing the field four days after the fighting, stumble on wounded man after wounded man, how many more unfortunates may there not be whom nobody has found!"

The parade was very imposing — a gala-day in the midst of the stern reality of war. The troops were formed in two great lines with intervals between the regiments; the second line about fifty paces in rear of the first. The Emperor for once was radiant — a very different man from the bent and anxious figure I had seen in the Gorni-Studen house. He called up and embraced Generals Ganetsky and Daniloff, the former commanding the corps against which Osman's onslaught was made, the latter the officer who brought up the reserves. "All is well that ends well," I mused as I looked on at this performance; had it gone the other way Ganetsky would have been justly charged for having his front too weak, and Daniloff would have been censured for being more than an hour too late in bringing up the reserves. The parade was a mere ceremony, consisting simply of an inspection by the Emperor, who, accompanied by the Grand Duke Nicholas and Prince Charles of Roumania and followed by a large and brilliant staff, passed along the face of both lines in succession. His reception was most enthusiastic, each regiment cheering as soon as the white flag with the bordered cross that denoted the Imperial presence came abreast, and nothing could be more impressive than the enormous volume of sound produced by the excited shouts of 60,000 men.

The fall of Plevna was the signal for many departures from the army. The Emperor and his suite quitted Poradim on the 15th, and thankfully went home to St. Petersburg in the full flush of triumph. I had no opportunity of presenting Mr. Villiers to his Majesty in accordance with the wish which he had deigned to express when I had the honour of standing in his presence while on my way from the Schipka Pass. But he had been so gracious as to hand to Colonel Wellesley the order of St. Stanislaus, to be given by him to Mr. Villiers as a souvenir of the information which his notes from the Schipka had afforded his Majesty. And now that the Emperor was leaving the army Colonel Wellesley himself was also to go, since he had made the campaign in the headquarter of his Majesty and not in that of the Commander-in-Chief. Prince Charles of Roumania, who throughout the siege had been the titular commander of the army before Plevna, also departed for Bucharest and his gallant Roumanians were now free to recross the Danube. Osman Pasha had been the guest on parole

of the Grand Duke at the Bogot headquarters since the
surrender, but he too now was sent away to Russia as
a prisoner of war, accompanied by a Russian officer and
a sergeant. General Todleben told me that while Osman
was at Bogot he had paid the Russian chief a visit, when
they had a long conversation on the events of the siege.

"I put the question direct to Osman," said Todleben,
"why he did not retreat to Radomirtza in October, when
he knew that the guard was concentrating on his line
of communication and obviously threatening to close him
in? Osman's answer was that, for two reasons, he was
resolved against retreating: for one thing because he felt
sure, and that up to the very end, that we would renew
our assaults, and that he was confident in his ability to
defeat them with heavy loss to us; and for another, that
up to the middle of October he was receiving relays of
reinforcements and supplies, and in those circumstances
he could not think of quitting his hold on Plevna."

Todleben added that in his opinion there was another
reason which Osman did not care to mention, but which
was probably more binding than were those reasons which
he actually stated — that reason being that the Seraskierate in Constantinople had sent Osman positive orders
not to withdraw from Plevna on any account.

In the early days after the capitulation Plevna was one
great charnel-house, the horrors of which were sickening.
The mosques and churches were full of dead and dying,
and the houses in the main street were mostly occupied
in the same manner. Corpses lay about on the pavements
and in the gutters, the passers-by stepping over them
unconcernedly. Ryan was the only surgeon who was

doing his duty; his Levantine comrades of the Turkish medical service seemed to regard themselves as having no longer any responsibility. They stood in their doorways, smoking cigarettes, dressed quite smartly and wearing the badge of the Red Crescent, with a healthy aspect quite unlike what one might have expected that hardworking devoted carers for their patients would have presented in a fever-stricken long-besieged place. There were now simply no hospital attendants on duty in Plevna. Those fellows had anticipated that Osman's attempt to break out would prove successful, and they had abandoned their posts to follow the fortune of the sortie. Many of them, no doubt, had been killed or wounded; it was certain that very few of them came back to their duty of attending on the sick and wounded. Day after day passed during which the sufferers lay entirely neglected. They died in hundreds; and before the end of the third day after the capitulation there were probably as many dead as living in the noisome, gloomy rooms which indeed protected the patients from cold and wet, but where they lay in a tainted atmosphere of putridity and death.

General Skobeleff the younger had been appointed governor of Plevna; but he was too much engrossed in military affairs to give much attention to the sick and wounded, at all events for the moment. He concerned himself in the first instance with establishing order. The Roumanian troops had broken loose from restraint and were plundering right and left. Skobeleff summoned the Roumanian officers and told them that their men were sacking the town. Their reply was that they understood the conquerors had the right to make free with the property of the vanquished. Skobeleff met that sort of argument right in the face. "In the first place," said he, "we are not at war with the peaceable inhabitants of Plevna and consequently we cannot consider them as having been conquered by us; and secondly, you will have the goodness to inform your men that I shall have conquerors of that sort shot. Every man caught marauding shall be shot like a dog; please understand that. And there is another thing. Your men are insulting women. This is disgraceful. Let me tell you that every complaint of this nature shall be promptly investigated, and that every case of outrage will be punished with the utmost rigour."

On the evening of the third day after the capitulation Millett arrived from the Balkans. He had become impatient of the pause in events there, and learning that it would continue for some little time, he had hurried down to Plevna in case MacGahan should not have been on the spot to describe the scenes at and after the surrender. Millett was a very tender-hearted man; he was also a man of strenuous energy. The horrors of Plevna and the neglect of any measures to relieve the great mass of human suffering, shocked and angered him. He went straight to young Skobeleff and protested that the state of Plevna was a disgrace to civilisation. Skobeleff gave him full powers to amend the situation, and Millett went to work with a will. Ryan rallied to his standard; I needed no pressure to join the service; some Russian surgeons volunteered their assistance; Skobeleff put forty soldiers at Millett's disposition; and with drawn revolver and whip in hand he forcibly requisitioned three Bulgarian ox-carts for the removal of the dead. Ryan led the way to one of the so-called hospitals. The stench of undressed wounds met us as we entered the courtyard across which we had to pick our way among the corpses. Huddled in one great room were about ninety Turkish soldiers, of whom nearly one-half were already dead and many others in their last extremity. It was difficult to discriminate between dead and living in the clotted noisome mass of putrefying mortality. Groans came from rigid lips, and beseeching wails for water; some of the strongest begged for a morsel of bread, raising themselves painfully and fixing from their sunken eyes a glassy stare on those who had come to relieve them from their contact with their dead comrades. There was a smaller inner room where the atmosphere was beyond description abominable, reeking from the huddled forms of miserable wretches rotting as they lay in the semi-darkness. Living and dead lay commingled in a mass. Most of the forms were motionless, and we knew what that indicated. From other forms came scarcely audible groans as bony hands were raised to lips in token of craving for food. From yet others who were beyond hungering for food, one heard faint whispers of "Water! Water!" All that could be done for the moment was to drag the dead out from among the still living, to let in light and air, and to give water and food in the hope of saving some of those in whom there yet remained life. As the bread and water were being distributed, it was horrible to see the feeble wretches struggling faintly with each other in their extremity of greed. Some slowly munched the bread with stiffening jaws until a greenish pallor came over the hollow face and the dim eyes became fixed in death. Then the living clutched at the crust in the dead man's hand and fought for it with the remnants of their waning strength, cursing each other and wrangling over the scrap of spoil perhaps to sink dead in the actual process of mastication.

One instance may serve as a type of all. As I tell you of the abominations, the nausea which hung in my throat and nostrils during those horrible days seems to come back to me and sicken me. I think the mosques were the worst — their pavements covered with the crouching ghost-like forms crawling about among the stark dead, whose faces came out in ghastly relief with a fixed expression of awful agony. After a day or two the soldiers begged to be relieved from a work which they loathed, and Millett compelled some of the loafing Bulgarians to serve in their stead. They performed the hated task with an ostentatious brutality horrible to witness. They dragged the bodies out by the legs, the heads bumping from step to step with sickening thuds, then hauled the corpses out into the court through the filthy mud, where they slung them into the carts with heads or limbs hanging over the side, and so piled up the load with a score of half-naked bodies. It turned one's blood to hear the conversation of the men at this work. A form was brought out in which there seemed still a flicker of life. "Oh, devil take him!" was the comment — "He is at his last kick anyhow — in with him!" When the carts had their complement they were driven through the streets to the trenches outside the towns. The horrible load jolted and quivered as it rolled along; now and again a body would fall out into the mud and be heaved in again. This procession of corpses passed through the streets several times a day, wending its way through the crowds of natives, soldiers, sick and wounded, and it became such a thing of course that no man cared to turn his head to glance at it. In the first three days a thousand dead were thus carted away, yet the mortality in the hospitals gave no sign of diminution. Russian surgeons were now working in them and some of the Turkish surgeons languidly helped, but the patients were legion and the doctors were few. Devoted service was being given by some Russian Sisters of Charity who moved about quietly busy from dawn till dark bringing comfort to hundreds, whose wounds they dressed and whose pains they alleviated by their tender and humane ministrations.

Millett had not seen the battle-field of the 10th, and on the 16th I rode out with him to point out to him its features. Before we reached the Vid a heavy snowstorm set in which of course restricted the view. As we crossed the river there came from the battle-field a foul and sickening stench. "Your battle-field still smells pretty powerfully!" exclaimed Millett, with handkerchief at nose — "are they never going to bury the dead of it?" I knew the stench — there was a whiff in it of the battle-field, it was true; but it had another and fouler origin. "The battle-field," said I, "is on our right front; it is not from it whence this sickening effluvium comes. Look due to your right through the snowflakes, and tell me what you see!" Millett drew rein and peered through the snow. "Why!" he exclaimed, "it is a mass of men yonder, but they are not on parade nor are they armed. They are cowering in a sort of heap. My God!" he cried, "it is Osman's army — now I can discern the uniforms. And it is from it comes that abominable stench, which smells like nothing I ever smelt in my life before!" Yes, it was the gallant army of Plevna, filthy and long unwashed, huddled together in the snow-slush, fireless, all but foodless, herded rigorously in disregard of hygienic necessities -- it was from this mass of living uncleanness that emanated the stench which was new to Millett.

We rode to windward of the human herd, as near as the sentries would permit. The miserables were separated, it seemed, in great companies of several hundreds. It was a piteous and a solemn sight. It seemed impossible that human beings could remain alive under such conditions. Their manhood was gradually departing from them; it was evident that their privations were making them bestial. They were wrangling, fighting, and snarling among themselves like so many wolves, for the scanty loaves which had been tossed in among them as food is thrown to the lower animals. They huddled together and wrapped tightly round their lean bodies their thin ragged clothing on which the snow was settling, and as they shook it off, trod it into the foul mire with the constant motion of their numbed feet. It was a ghastly spectacle, a flagrant disgrace to the army of a nation claiming to be civilised, a horror that I shall never cease to remember without a shudder. Convoys of these prisoners of war were on the march to Russia across the snow-covered plains of Wallachia and Moldavia. I have often wondered what percentage died on the journey. Villiers met one body of those brave patient unfortunates near the village of Putinein on the road from Bucharest to Alexandria, and it was an awful pen-picture which he drew. Listen! I read from the cutting I made from his newspaper: —

"Before us was one vast plain of snow, broken only by the black telegraph-poles and the heavy wing-flapping of the carrion crows. Soon these foul birds increased in numbers, making almost black the leaden sky. Then afar off, breaking the horizon, a long dark line came slowly onward, moving in caterpillar fashion towards us along the road. It was a column of men on the march — not Russian soldiers or Roumanian, else we now should have heard some cheerful song borne over the snow. It must be a convoy of Turkish prisoners; for in front waver the bayonets of the Roumanian military guards as they plod slowly forward under the weight of their miscellaneous kit. Following them are a few Turkish officers, some on ponies, some on foot. Behind them tramp through the snow the men who so long kept at bay the flower of the Russian army around Plevna. How spiritless and broken they look as they trudge drearily along the road to their captivity! Half-starved, almost dead with fatigue and the bitter cold, many with fever burning in their eyes, — mere stalking bones and foul rags, — come the brave troops who made the fame of Osman Pasha. We get well to windward of those poor creatures, for typhus and small-pox linger round the sorry columns on the frosty air. Several are even now falling out of the ranks to lie down and die. One poor fellow has thrown himself on the snow by the roadside; he can go no further. A comrade, loth to leave him, follows and tries to persuade him to struggle once more to join the lines. There is no response. He has swooned or is dead. A soldier of the rear-guard comes up and roughly pushes the living man back into the ranks. Then he kicks with his foot the bundle of rags lying on the face of the snow. There is no sign. With the butt-end of his gun he turns the head over from out of the snow. The eyes glare at him with a cold fixed stare. The Turk is dead. The soldier brutally pushes the body deeper into the snow, shoulders his rifle, and rejoins his guard.

"Thousands of birds of prey whirl round and settle in front and in rear, always following the grim and squalid procession like sharks round a doomed ship. A few yards further on lies, half covered with snow, the nude body of another Turk, stripped to the skin by his companions for the sake of the little warmth afforded by the rags he had worn. A carrion crow has just settled on the dead man's clenched hand, and the dogs are slinking around their victim. A few paces further brings us to another miserable, lying as he had died with upturned face, staring up to heaven through the fast-falling snow. We are now near a village, and we have just been the witnesses of a skirmish between the swine and the dogs belonging to it, to decide which shall be first to reach the scarcely-cold carcase. It is the village of Putinein, almost lost in the snow and ice. How different the place looks from what it was when I first passed it in the early summer, when searching for Dragomiroff to know where was to be made the great crossing of the Danube! Then we were suffering from mosquitoes, intense heat and blinding dust; now we are shivering in our furs with cold."

MacGahan had gone to Bucharest to be within touch of the telegraph wire. Before he went he gave me the particulars of the little dinner-party at which Tefik Bey, Osman's chief of staff, was entertained by Skobeleff on the evening of the day of the surrender of Plevna. "A warm fire," said MacGahan, "burned brightly in Skobeleff's mud-hut, a glass of vodka and some hot soup soon thawed out our benumbed hands and feet, and we were presently enjoying a hot dinner with the appetites of men who had been in the saddle since daylight without a morsel to eat. Tefik Bey seemed much depressed. He spoke little, and was at first almost as taciturn as he had been on the bridge. He brightened up, however, as dinner progressed, drank a glass of red wine, a glass of sherry, and a couple of glasses of champagne when Skobeleff proposed the health of Osman Ghazi and drank to the brave defenders of Plevna. A merry smile broke over his face when Skobeleff asked him who had commanded the Turks on the Green Hill; and I think it must have occurred to him now for the first time that his entertainer was Skobeleff, with whom he had exchanged so many hard blows on the Loftcha road and the Green Hill. Nobody had mentioned Skobeleff's name in his presence, nor had Skobeleff told him who he was; but the fact that we had ridden out by the Loftcha road, together with Skobeleff's question about the Green Hill, was quite enough to enlighten Tefik. So he said with a smile:

"'Ah! then it was you who gave us such tough work on the Green Hill all this time! You are General Skobeleff?'

"Skobeleff laughed, and simply said 'Yes.'

"'That was a very good attack of yours that evening in the fog and darkness. Very well done. But you did not get all the hill!'

"'No,' said Skobeleff, 'I did not want it all.'

"Then they both laughed. But after this momentary flicker of sunshine, Tefik soon elapsed into gloom and melancholy. Probably it was partly owing to the sadness and despondency under the circumstances, partly the reaction from the extreme excitement and strain of nerves during the last few days when preparing for the sortie, and partly from extreme lassitude and fatigue. We had hardly finished our coffee when Skobeleff, taking pity on him, turned us all out, gave up his bed to Tefik, had another hastily made up for Colonel Gaillard, and then himself retired and passed the night in a hut of one of his officers."

During the last two or three days of my stay in Plevna I lived in the house of a Bulgarian who was a man of considerable intelligence. He was, or rather he had been, an agent of the American Bible Society. He was one of the few politicians whom I found in Bulgaria. He had been a sort of village Hampden in his time, and had indeed served a term of imprisonment for active disaffection but had regained his liberty by bribery. He had been the head-centre of the insurrectionary organisation in and around Plevna in 1875-6, and he was good enough to show me the lists of memberships and subscriptions — the latter not very reckless in their liberality. Everything had been beautifully prearranged, he said, but when the time came there was not even a "cabbage-garden" rising. The conspirators realised that the theory and practice of insurrection were not quite synonymous, and they remained content with the former luxury. The "head-centre" himself had thought it prudent to leave Plevna and to sequester himself temporarily in Poradim, where he made a friend of the local moullah through the medium of presents of poultry.

Knowing how well-to-do had been the Bulgarian population north of the Balkans before the war, and how trivial was the so-called oppression of the Turks who dwelt among them, I asked my host what were the incentives to insurrection on the part of the former.

"Well," said he, "to tell you the real truth, the insurrections were quietly got up by our friends who came in here the other day. Their emissaries swarmed all over the regions on this side the Balkans, telling us that they were ashamed to find their Bulgarian brethren in the condition of serfs, and pointing out to us how the Servians had thrown off the Turkish yoke. The time, they said, was favourable to our emancipation. A good many Bulgarians had indeed already worked out their own emancipation by emigrating; and wherever they found themselves, in Bucharest, in Galatz, up among the hills at Cronstadt or down on the flat in Crajova or Turn Severin, there they sedulously plotted against the Turkish rule over the Bulgaria from which they were exiles. Our people who stayed at home began really to believe that the Turks were oppressing them. They received every encouragement in a furtive way from Russian sources in Constantinople, and they listened to the voices of their exiled countrymen goading them on to insurrection. The outbreak was no doubt a miscarriage. We were not ready and most of us were only half-hearted. But it was nonsense to say, as some said, that it was merely a petty and local affair. I could show you abundant evidence in writing of the widespread ramifications of the organisations for revolt. It was the Russian emissaries who stirred up the actual outbreak, not because they expected it to succeed, — they knew better than that, and indeed would have been a good deal surprised and disgusted if it had, — but because its failure and the reprisals which were certain to follow would afford them the pretext which Russia wanted. I saw through the snare in time, and warned most of the circles north of the Balkans that they would act wisely in remaining quiet and not giving the Turks a handle for suspecting them.

"How much of the conspiracy the Turks actually came to know I have never heard. Where there are three Bulgarians there is sure to be one informer — you see I have not a high opinion of my countrymen. At all events, the Turks knew something, and no doubt they suspected more. They had their hands full enough already, what with insurrection in Montenegro and the Herzegovine, and Servia getting together an army — not to speak of mischief in other regions. This rising was right in the hollow of the Turks' hand, and you know how they stamped it out. The 'atrocities' with which all Europe rang gave Russia the opportunity which she had been cunningly making for herself. I fancy by this time she is pretty sorry that she ever took hold of the job — she did not expect to meet with the obstructions which have cost her so dear. I have been shut up in Plevna for months and know little of what is happening outside; but I reckon by this time the Russian and the Bulgarian are not so fond of each other as they were in the early days of hugging and kissing. The 'Bratoushkas' don't love each other as they once did."

I had chanced on a Bulgarian cynic with a vengeance. He had liberated his mind as to his own race; what were his notions in regard to the Turks among whom he had been living during the investment?

"Well," said he, as he rolled a cigarette—"all Turks are more or less stupid, but Osman Pasha is the most stupid Turk I have ever known. Here in Plevna there have been throughout the investment some two thousand Bulgarians. From the first we have constantly pleaded poverty. Now that it is all over I may tell you that we have food enough to last us during the winter. But we have been rationed by Osman as if we had not a single loaf of our own. Now and then he has called us out to work on the defences, but never under fire. Mostly we have been lounging about doing nothing. Why he did not turn every one of us out of his lines has been a standing puzzle to me. It was only in the daytime that we yawned about. At night every man of us became a spy in the service of the Russians. They know me quite well up yonder at Bogot and Tutchenitza, and I know the feel of their dirty rouble notes. And let me tell you, a good many of us were double spies. If you were with the Russians during the siege you must have noticed that the Turks never were taken by surprise. Osman, however, was a shabby paymaster." Whereupon this outspoken person desired that I should excuse him, since in talking to me he was losing the opportunity for a little quiet looting.

General Todleben was the kindest man I have ever

known. One day he sent me a message that he desired to see me. I immediately rode out to Tutchenitza, where I found the general sitting over a glass of tea. "Come along, young Carnegie!" he said. "Where have you been all these days?" He did not wait for an answer, but continued: "There is a gentleman in the next room whom I think perhaps you may like to see — shall I call him in?" With that he rose and opened a door; and there entered — my good old father! This was indeed a pleasant surprise, and we cordially embraced. The old gentleman was in great feather, and it was clear that the general and he were on very friendly terms. Todleben, it seemed, had never forgotten the transaction of the grey stallion, and he had quietly put a good many commissions in the way of the firm which, said my father, were giving a fine profit and would continue to do so. This was a good hearing, for I knew that the house had not earned a ducat during the first six months of the war, and that the old gentleman had been not a little anxious in regard to ways and means. "Do you know what I am going to do now, youngster?" asked the general. "No, Excellency," I replied, "but I know that you are always doing kind and gracious things." "Well," said he, "do you think it a kind and gracious thing to turn an elderly gentleman out of house and home?"

I glanced at your good grandfather and saw that he was smiling. "Is this the unfortunate," I asked, "who in his old age is to be cast out to the mercy of a stony-hearted world, sir?" "Yes," replied Todleben, with a broad smile, "that is the houseless one. Takes it pretty lightly, don't he? Now let us talk sense! The army is breaking up from around this loathsome Plevna, and I am going eastward to undertake the reduction of the fortress of Rustchuk. Your father tells me that I can find no comfortable quarters in the vicinity of Rustchuk on the Turkish bank, and he has offered me his own house in Giurgevo. We have come to terms, and we shall travel eastward together in a day or two. Now tell me what you mean to do, and whether I can be of any service to you."

I told him that I purposed rejoining Gourko up in the Etropol Balkans and following his fortunes; but that before setting out I was very anxious to know what were to be the general dispositions.

"Well," said the general, "I believe I can give you the information you desire, only I beg that you will keep it to yourself. This time the hot-heads have won the day. I suppose that I am an old fogy now-a-days, and have no enterprise any more. The view I took was that the Turks from all quarters would now rally about Adrianople, and probably make another Plevna of that position which Blum Pasha, as we know, has fortified artistically. Suppose that we should have effected the passage of the Balkans, I argued that we should arrive before Adrianople with a mountain chain in our rear and a line of communication impossible to keep open. Therefore my advice was that the army should go into winter quarters in the villages among the foot-hills north of the Balkans, concentrating a considerable force around Rustchuk and undertaking the regular siege of that fortress. Then in the spring when the troops had been refitted, the army, with a railway at its back, should march on Adrianople by way of Varna. I believe that the majority of the generals are of my way of thinking; but I now know that the two thrusting commanders, Gourko and Skobeleff, have influenced the Grand Duke Nicholas to push across the Balkans as soon as possible, in spite of the difficulties of ground, of season, of bad roads and uncertainty of supplies. Well, be it so! I am a soldier — I am neither a diplomatist nor a politician. I know that there is a secret reason pressing that the war be ended within the limits of a single campaign; and I quite realise that if active operations were postponed until the spring the Turks would thus gain time to reorganise and strengthen their forces, and complications might occur with other powers.

"Anyhow," continued the general, "the resolution has been taken and the dispositions are already in progress. I suppose you know that reinforcements to Gourko are already on the march. The 3rd Guard Division started on the 14th, and the 9th Corps yesterday. When these join him his army will consist of about 65,000 infantry, 6,000 cavalry, and 280 guns. Radetski's strength at the Schipka will be made up to 56,000 infantry, 2,000 cavalry, and 250 guns. Skobeleff and Mirski will belong to his command, and the Grenadier Corps will be in reserve in the Gabrovo-Drenova valley. The Cesarevich will stand fast on the left flank with over 70,000 men. Altogether, for the winter campaign Russia will have close on 300,000 men in the field.

"There, my lad, is a mass of figures for you! If I were you I should give up that note-book and use your memory. Believe me, the use of a note-book simply debauches the memory. But that is your affair. You start the day after to-morrow, you say. Well, stay here and dine with your father and myself, and you will have all to-morrow to make your preparations."

It was a happy night for me, listening to the wisdom and reminiscences of the grand old soldier to whose kindness I owed so much, and with the honest sterling face of my dear old father opposite to me. War, which to so many brings misery and suffering, had to me brought only interest, excitement, intercourse with men of fine character and high position, and something of self-reliance. I was but a stripling yet I felt myself almost a man, and that like "Hal o' the Wynd" I could fight for my own hand if need were.

I spent my last day in foul and loathsome Plevna in making a circuit around the Turkish positions and the localities where had been the heaviest fighting. I rode out over the successive knolls in the centre of the horseshoe, where the ground was pitted all over by the craters of burst shells but where there were comparatively few unburied corpses; and thence up the valley of the Gravitza brook towards the redoubts, the second of which was the scene of the repulse of the Roumanians on October 19th. The interior of the first Gravitza redoubt, which was full of corpses when visited by Colonel Wellesley and Villiers on the day after its capture, had been cleared out, I assumed by the Roumanians, and the bodies had been buried in the long trench below the redoubt which you no doubt noticed when you made the round of the Plevna positions the other day. But all over that slope outside the redoubts and in the very ditches surrounding them, lay thickly-strewn corpses slowly decomposing. I went down into the village and saw there the head-man with whom I had a short conversation during the September bombardment. I suggested to him that now that there was to be no more fighting in his vicinity, he might consider it an act of common decency to clear the village fields of the dead which still disfigured their surface. The head-man said that as soon as the Russians had gone away and the valley and its slopes had been restored to their wonted quietude, there would be a wholesale interment; but that his people were expecting — they were to expect in vain — that the conquering Russians would make some payment to the burial parties.

Riding through the battery whence the siege-guns hurled their huge projectiles against the Gravitza, I went aside a little way to look closely at the observatory from the balcony of which the Emperor watched the fighting in those dread days of September. It was slowly sinking into ruin, and where the marquee in its rear was in which the Imperial suite quaffed champagne while their master winced and cowered as the Turkish fire smote his gallant men, there were now only crushed cans and broken bottles. The straw-stack was still to the fore in the heart of which Jackson had his lair during the nights of the September fighting, and outside of which he was wont to sit all day and watch the scene when he was not despatching couriers. I scarcely recognised again the Radischevo ridge, on the leafy crest of which Schahofskoy, Villiers, and myself sat on July 30th as we gazed down on the carnage on the maize slopes leading up to the Turkish first redoubt. Yonder was the spring around which huddled the wounded begging for the love of God for a mouthful of the scanty water. But the trees had long been cut down on the Radischevo ridge, and in place of them was the grim row of empty Russian redoubts around which still hung the sour unpleasant smell that the Russian soldier seems to carry about with him as a possession. To my right as I descended into the Tutchenitza ravine, lowered the conical mamelon crowned by Redoubt "No. 10," on whose slopes lay thick the decaying corpses of the Russians whom I had watched the Turks hack and mangle on September 11th. And now I was in Brestovatz, wrecked and silent, not tenanted even by a solitary cat. I looked into Skobeleff's quarters on the floor of which still lay some of the many newspapers which he used to receive, and I read the pencil-signature in the door lintel of "J. A. MacGahan." The owner of those initials was curiously secretive in regard to them, and very few knew for what they stood. It was by a mere chance that I made the discovery. He was signing a transfer of some stock and he requisitioned me as a witness. His full name appeared in the body of the transfer, and that full name was — "Januarius Aloysius MacGahan."

In and about the redoubts on that first knoll of the "Green Hill" for which the foes fought with so bitter persistency, lay many still unburied bodies; the successive ridges of the mountain and the intervening depressions, as well as on the steep slope beyond, on the crest of which were the two redoubts with connecting entrenchment which were taken by Skobeleff on September 11th with fearful loss and held by him with even heavier loss until the afternoon of the following day, were thickly strewn with the corpses of Russians and Turks who died so freely on those bloody days. A few of the bodies — for the most part of

Turks — had been sprinkled over with a few spadesful of earth, but most of the dead lay just as they fell, except that they had been stripped and that the carrion dogs had torn limbs away and the vultures had been busy with the eyes. In the shallow water-puddles soaked half-decomposed bodies; pale withered hands and feet stuck out of the shallow soil, and awful faces stared up from each little hollow and from out every clump of scrub. A little nearer to the town there were some traces of burial-parties having been at work recently, but the interment was a mere sham which the first heavy fall of rain would betray; and it is no exaggeration to say that the whole region of which Plevna is the centre was strewn thickly with the ghastliest mementos of the longer and bitter struggle. Plevna may be called the modern Golgotha. I remember you telling me that when you visited the place sixteen years after the last soldier fell around Plevna, you found skulls and other bones.

Around the redoubts the ground was lacerated with the furrows of thousands of shells, and tons of fragments covered the earth. Most of the shells seemed to have fallen and burst just in front of the redoubts; apparently few entered. The whole surface of slopes and plain was scooped into huge craters and all about lay great shells unexploded. Far away back in the crannies of the hollows where the soldiers had their huts, bullets, scraps of clothing, and abandoned equipments littered the ground. One was constantly finding in the least-expected places long-unburied bodies, or sodden in the path the limbs of fellow-creatures who had fallen and lain till the passing footsteps of the living trod hard the thin layer of earth over the remains.

CHAPTER XIII

GOURKO'S PASSAGE OF THE BALKANS

IT was on the morning of the 18th December, in the midst of a heavy snowstorm, that Millett and I rode out of Plevna on our way to join General Gourko's headquarters. The Sophia road was cumbered with much traffic on the Plevna side of the bridge, and our progress was very slow; but we looked forward to being able to travel faster when once we had crossed the Vid. We held our nostrils as we pushed our horses through the abominable stench that came to us from where the Turkish prisoners still stood huddled in the driving storm among the mud and filth. As far as Dolni-Dubnik the road was pretty clear, but before we reached Gorni-Dubnik we found ourselves jammed in the fag-end of Krüdener's train of waggons and baggage guard. The road was full of impedimenta from ditch to ditch, and, as if it were any consolation to us, the sergeant who commanded a handful of men whom he called the rear guard told us that the head of the column was two days' march ahead, and that the road was full all the way forward as far as Jablanitza. This was a cheerful prospect. There is nothing more trying to the temper of a man on horseback than the constant wearing struggle to get forward along a road cumbered with the miscellaneous belongings of troops on the march. Millett was in despair at the prospect of having to bring up the rear of those miles of slow-moving vehicles interspersed with dreary convoys of Bulgarian families on their way from Plevna towards their villages, toiling along the road in painful procession through the mud, laden with great burdens of kitchen utensils and bedding and scarcely moving half-a-mile an hour. "Where does that road lead to?" he asked of a Bulgarian, pointing to a road branching from Gorni-Dubnik away to the left front. Of course the surly Bulgar did not know or would not tell. But just at the moment I remembered that it was by this road Gourko had marched from his camp at Cirakova to the attack on Gorni-Dubnik on the morning of October 24th. We consulted our maps, and found that from Cirakova there was a good road up the valley of the Vid on the left of and parallel with the main chaussée as far as Tetevan. From this road we could either cross to Jablanitza, or we might go on by it to Tetevan and thence follow the track to Etropol which was taken by the 12th Regiment to join Gourko on the 22nd November.

We promptly made up our minds to travel by this road, on which, as far as the eye could reach, there was not a sign of traffic. Further on in the mountains there was the chance of encountering brigands, but we had our revolvers, and as Millett placidly observed, we "took our risks." We made no halt in Cirakova, but rode steadily on until we reached the village of Aglen a few miles further up the valley. The Cossacks had been in Aglen in November but they had not done any serious damage, and we found comfortable quarters, food for ourselves and plenty of hay and oats for our horses. The Bulgarians of Aglen were very eager to be told some particulars about the fall of Plevna, and they crowded our room for news. More snow had fallen during the night, and we congratulated ourselves on the escape which we had from trudging in eighteen inches of snow-slush behind Krüdener's waggons. We had, it was true, the eighteen inches of snow on our road, but our horses plodded gallantly through it at a brisk sustained walk. We made our midday halt at the snug village of Toros situated very picturesquely under a precipice almost overhanging the Vid, where plenty abounded and where the villagers seemed of quite a different race from the sordid Bulgars of the Danubian plain country. They became comically angry when we made an allusion to brigands — persons of that profession, it appeared, were not well seen in the upper valley of the Vid; but methought the villagers did protest too much. We took a very friendly farewell of our Toros hosts, who may indeed have been brigands but who were so un-Bylgarian-like that they were unwilling to accept the trifle we offered them, and although at length they took payment for what our horses had eaten they resolutely refused to make any charge for our own food. In the afternoon we jogged on comfortably to a wayside khan under the shoulder of Mount Isvor, where we spent the night in a good room on a divan the cushions of which, wonderful to relate, harboured no vermin.

Next morning we discussed our future course. Should we cross over to Jablanitza, there rejoin the high road and follow it through Osikovo to Orkanie where, as Millett believed, the headquarters of Gourko now were? Or should we continue on our present road as far as Tetevan

and thence make for Etropol, where we were sure of
good quarters for the night and from which on the following morning a few hours' riding by way of Pravetz and
Lazan would bring us into Orkanie by noon of the 21st?
Tetevan, I had heard, was an interesting hill town, but
at present we were not travelling for pleasure; and the
landlord of the khan told us that if we were bound for
Etropol we ought to turn off to the right some distance
on the hither side of Tetevan. It was to be a long day's
ride, and we started early. After three hours' riding we
duly found the turning-off point, and struck the hill track
by Brusen and Luren which was to conduct us to Etropol.
It was very rugged in places, and we wondered a good
deal how the 12th Regiment marching from Tetevan in
November could have brought along its battery. But
it was mostly the case that where an ox-waggon could
go, guns could go; and deep as was the snow we found
ox-waggons here and there, bringing loads of firewood
from the forests into the villages. One of the surprises
of the Balkans is the number of villages which everywhere
nestle in the folds of the mountain-sides. The tillage
climbs up the slopes almost to the crests; where the field
is too steep for the plough the spade comes into use. We
made a half-way halt at Brusen in the clean and pretty
cottage of the head-man, who was so liberal-minded that
he professed to have no ill-will against the Turks; and
that his sentiments were genuine was proved by the fact
that several Turkish families were living unmolested in
Brusen.

As we rode into Etropol Millett was received with great
effusion by the nymphs of the fountain, who gathered

around him begging for sugar. He was popular; I found myself neglected by the naiads of the Etropol fountain and rode on disconsolately to the Konak, where I took unquestioned possession of the room in which I had lain ailing when previously in the little town. Millett, despoiled of part of his sugar, soon joined me; but before we dined he had to hold quite a levée of his Bulgarian friends of Etropol, and the "Bratoushkas" insisted on embracing him. At last he cleared them out in his masterfully good-humoured way, and we ate in comfort and contentment. Millett had already gathered some news. The Balkans had already been surmounted on both flanks; General Brock with a brigade of the Guard was due south of us at Slatitza, and for quite a while the Cossacks had been over the great divide west of the Baba-Konak Pass and were in full occupation of the village of Curiak and its vicinity. Gourko's advance was to begin on the night of the 24th, so we had arrived just in the nick of time. General Dandeville had quitted the Greote ridge and was now down here in Etropol; Millett had met him in the street and had been asked to go and drink tea with him in the evening. The Turkish main position on the Shandarnik ridge was now confronted from Greote only by Prince Oldenburg's brigade, rather a weak body to oppose the Turkish main army but for the twenty-eight guns which garnished his front; and Count Schouvaloff with twelve battalions of the Guard and twenty-four guns was holding the mountain heights west of the pass through which went the chaussée, and threatening the left flank of the Turkish position which had been strengthened by an important redoubt and formidable lines of entrenchment.

I wonder how long it would have taken me to amass all that amount of information which Millett, in his easy lighthearted way, had gathered in the few minutes between his badinage with the maidens of the fountain and his appearance in our room in the Konak.

Still, in return for his budget of intelligence, I was able to impart to him a piece of information which immediately arrested his interest, and which I had been quietly keeping to myself ever since we two had left Plevna. It was because of my possession of this news that I had led up strategically to our coming on here to Etropol, instead of crossing over from the Isvorski khan to the main chaussée at Jablanitza. On the evening before our departure from Plevna my father had sent me down from Tutchenitza a *Daily News* of December 5th, which contained a telegram from Sophia stating that several English officers, Colonels Allix, Baker, and Maitland, Captains Fife and James, and other English officers were now with Mehemet Ali's army in the Kamarli position; that Valentine Baker Pasha and Captain Fred Burnaby of Khiva renown had recently arrived, and that the former had taken command of Mehemet Ali's left wing on either side of the Baba-Konak Pass. It had occurred to me as I read this telegram that it would be a pleasant thing for me, although circumstances had placed me on the side where there were no fellow-countrymen in arms, to see British officers well out to the front as they were sure to be. Millett was an American, and could not be expected to feel as I did in this matter. But he was a fellow who was always ready for an adventure; and he said in his humorous way that he was specially anxious to see Burnaby because when the war was over he had an idea of going into the showman business, and would be glad to ascertain whether the biggest man in the British army would suit him as his "boss" giant.

My scheme was that in the morning we should ride up on to Mont Greote, follow that ridge, cross the chaussée and join Count Schouvaloff's command to the west of it; that we should then go out to the foreposts and spend some time there with our glasses. If we had the luck to see some of the English officers so much the better; if we failed no harm was done, and we should ride on down the chaussée into Orkanie. Millett cheerfully assented; and at dawn of the 21st we were climbing up the steep rugged road that led up to the heights. I had seen an old map in Tirnova dated before the present circuitous Sophia-Plevna high road was made, on which was indicated as the earlier main road this very track on which we were now riding. It left the present chaussée at Osikovo and followed up the valley of the Little Isker, where the stone slabs that paved it were still to be seen in places. After climbing on to the heights the old road had traversed the hollow between the Shandarnik and Greote ridges, and come out into the Kamarli plain over the Baba-Konak crest. Long disused, this road had been all but bushed over and had needed in November to be cleared with the axe to make it passable, yet here and there I noticed one of the great hewn stones which once had paved it. Old men in Etropol believed that it was originally made by the Romans.

Prince Oldenburg's people on the Greote ridge were chiefly engaged in shivering, notwithstanding the great fires they kept. It had been evident for some time that

Gourko would either have to abandon his upland positions about the Baba-Konak region or else cross the range at any cost, for the severity of the weather had made it all but impossible to bring up supplies and ammunition, and life in the encampments, or rather bivouacs, on the mountain had become daily more and more arduous. Scarcely a night had passed but frozen hands and feet were counted by hundreds. Thirty soldiers had been frozen to death during four days of the storm, and the number of sick from exposure amounted to more than 2,000. The thin shelter-tents, torn by the wind and with difficulty kept pegged to the ground during the gales, had now been to some extent exchanged for rude huts covered with logs and turf, and for holes dug in the steep banks among the trees. We rode along the ridge where once whistled the Turkish bullets; but now the Turks were too chilled by cold to take pot-shots at a couple of men on horseback. We were fired at not more than twice or thrice during the ride along the ridge; as we came down into the pass, however, where the cold was not intense, we were treated with less indifference from the two great Turkish redoubts on either side of the ravine. We rode across the chaussée, where the Turks wasted a shell on us, scrambled through the rocky bed of the Dermente, and in ten minutes more were in the headquarter of Count Schouvaloff. That was in a sheltered hollow; but his batteries on the crest in front were right on the Turkish flank, and the Russian fire enfiladed their redoubts on both sides of the defile. I asked Count Schouvaloff whether any English officers had been recognised on the Turkish side.

"Yes, indeed," he exclaimed — "quite a number of

them! You can see them for yourself if you care to go up yonder. Two of them are old friends of mine, and I should like nothing better than to ask them to come over and dine with me. You are too young to have been in the Aldershot autumn manœuvres in 1871, else you might remember the officer of the Russian Guards who rode with the Prince of Wales and Valentine Baker at the head of the 10th Hussars. I was that officer; and poor Baker was the finest light-cavalry officer I ever saw. Had he belonged to us, do you think we should have lost him to the service he adorned because of a piece of wretched private folly? Pshaw! what a square-toed prudish folk you English are! If Valentine Baker would only forsake those tatterdemalion Turks and come over the trenches to us, I'll engage the Czar would make him a full general within a month! Burnaby! yes, you may see that huge droll fellow as like as not, if you care to go up into the entrenchments. He is quite mad of course — always was, and he hates us. But he was my guest at the mess of the Garde du Corps when he was last in St. Petersburg, and our crack giant, old Protassoff-Bakmetieff, was not in it with Burnaby either in stature or in strength. By George!" exclaimed Schouvaloff, "I'll give you a flag of truce, and if you can persuade Baker and Burnaby to come back with you and dine with us, I shall be delighted beyond measure!"

Just then there broke out the rattle of a sharp musketry-fire. "Oh, that is nothing!" exclaimed Schouvaloff; but Millett and I ran up the steep ascent, passed through the quiescent batteries, and scudded out into the advanced entrenchment. Schouvaloff's orderly officer came with us, and pointed out how easily the Russians could work down into the valley below without using the Baba-Konak Pass at all. There were not 150 paces between the Russian and Turkish entrenchments. The firing was pretty sharp, and we were not at all ashamed to accept the cover the breastwork afforded. " Look!" exclaimed Schouvaloff's orderly — "You see these two men on the top of the Turkish parapet? The big man standing up and showing us his full front is Burnaby; the other one in the fez, sitting down with his legs dangling over the entrenchment, is Baker!" Yes, there they were, calm and unconcerned in the Russian fire! My heart swelled, and the water came into my eyes. The Russians are brave men; but in all the Russian host I had seen but one man so daring — that was Skobeleff, and he only when urgent occasion demanded. And there were my two countrymen, quietly and undramatically exposing themselves as a matter of course, to hearten their wretched " Mustafiz " — I knew by the uniform that their men were not " Nizams."

My boys, wouldn't you have been glad and proud to witness that little piece of quiet unostentatious heroism? I know I was, yet my heart ached, for the chances were all against our gallant countrymen. Millett too was moved, for as he said, quoting the words of old Commodore Tatnall, "blood is thicker than water." We went back into the valley, drank a glass of tea with Count Schouvaloff, and then rode away down the deep valley of the Dermente into Orkanie. About half-way between Baba-Konak and Orkanie, a tributary rivulet comes in from the Etropol Balkans west of the chaussée to join the Dermente. There were evidences of rough road-making along the ravine formed by this tributary, which had cut for itself a ravine among the lower hills under the huge mountainous mass forming the divide of the range. "What do you imagine is going on there?" I asked of Millett. "I don't know," was his reply, "but I guess it is the beginning of the 'Sappers' road' which they had begun to talk of in Gourko's headquarters before I left Orkanie. Stay, here is a picket; let us ask the corporal." But the corporal was either a dull man or a secretive man; we could extract nothing from that worthy but stolid Muscovite. Three days more, and we were to make a personal acquaintance with the "Sappers' road" of an extremely rough and unpleasant character.

Three miles nearer to Orkanie we reached the northern entrance to the pass at the village of Vratches. It was well for the Russians that Gourko's life-sparing strategy had nullified the Turkish position on the slopes behind this village by seizing the Greote position in its rear. Line upon line of entrenchments rose one above another on the rise behind Vratches, constructed with a skill and care that put to shame the most elaborate of the Russian fortifications about Plevna and proved for the hundredth time the great superiority of the Turkish engineers alike in designing and finishing their works. If the task had become essential for the Russians to assail those lines, the issue would have been extremely doubtful for the men whom the comparatively petty obstacle of the Gravitza redoubt so long kept at bay.

As we rode into Orkanie Millett told me of what he called the "sugar famine" in Etropol, and afterwards for

a day or two when the headquarters had been moved
to Orkanie. He mentioned what I was not aware of, that
the Russian officer has a very sweet tooth and suffers
greatly when he is deprived of his luxury. "Fortunately," said Millett, "a sutler arrived presently with an
immense train of waggons laden with every kind of
groceries, delicacies, and small wares, and began to unpack
his goods in an empty shop opposite the general's headquarters. The news of this arrival spread more quickly
than even the report of the fall of Plevna, if one could
judge by the crowd of officers of every rank that be-
sieged the entrances to the shop long before the pro-
prietor was at all in readiness for the opening of his
establishment. The covers were off some of the cases
disclosing sugar, preserves, bottles, and stationery, and
the attraction was too great to be resisted, so the crowd
entered the shop in a fuss of good-natured hustling and
shouldering, and began to pile up the commodities which
each man most wanted with a recklessness that would
have driven to insanity a methodical shopkeeper. This
enterprising Roumanian Jew was at their mercy, and he
gave the masterful customers their will perforce. They
dived into the great cases, fishing out with shouts of
delight all kinds of bon-bons and candies, jams, and
jellies, which they laid hold of with the eagerness of
children and began to devour on the spot. The sutler
and his assistants could do nothing but make spasmodic
efforts to regulate the distribution of the stores, attempts
which only made the confusion worse confounded; and
the happy crowd elbowed and pushed and continued to
help themselves in fullest freedom. As each officer gath-

ered the stock which he had annexed he was as impatient to pay for it as he had been to get hold of it, and although the sutler calmly took four times the price at which he had bought his goods at Bucharest his tariff was never called in question. Bright new gold-pieces jingled into his canvas bag in a steady stream, making music that would have delighted the ears of a miser. No doubt the glitter of the gold blinded his eyes to the scene of indescribable confusion which his shop presented when at length his customers had carried away with them their purchases."

I had not been an hour in Orkanie before I recognised that Millett was a power in Gourko's army. Every second officer we met as we rode along towards his house accosted the American war correspondent with great cordiality. When the headquarter came into Orkanie early in December, he had ridden on ahead and had found unoccupied a snug little isolated house in the main street with four good rooms and a large courtyard. He found a character given to it in advance. It had been occupied by the English surgeons with the Turkish army, and when the time came for them to depart one of them had written on the whitewashed wall an advice to any fellow-countryman who should enter with Gourko in the following words: "Requisition this house; it is the best in the place." Millett was not an Englishman, but he considered that his being of Anglo-Saxon descent entitled him to take possession, which he accordingly did. He occupied it without dispute until he left for Plevna on the news of its fall, leaving in possession a couple of his servants in charge of as many horses. But he was no dog in the manger. He had located

in it a couple of sub-tenants in Prince Tzeretleff and
another officer of Gourko's staff, who volunteered to quit
now that he had come back to "enjoy his ain again."
But this Millett would not suffer. There was room enough
in the little house not only for Millett and the two staff
officers but also for myself, a favour for which I was very
thankful. For I came soon to know what hardships not
only men but officers were enduring in the bitter winter
cold — how bitter you may conceive when I tell you that
the Reaumur thermometer marked seventeen degrees of
cold. General officers were quartered in fireless rooms
and in mud huts. Officers kept arriving at all hours of
the day and night, many having travelled on foot all the
way from Osikovo, unable to get forward on horseback
because the road was blocked by artillery and trams,
exhausted almost to inanition, and searching everywhere
in vain for shelter even of the meanest kind. There was a
temporary dearth of almost all supplies. The salt gave
out, and even bread was at ransom price. Tzeretleff
assured us that one day he had paid fifteen francs for a
loaf that he could have eaten at one meal. Fuel was
almost an unattainable luxury notwithstanding that there
were almost boundless forests close round the town; but
all the carts were employed in bringing in wood for the
hospitals and the baking ovens. There were many cases
of frozen hands and feet in the town itself among the poor
patient soldiers trying to shelter themselves in the lee of
banks of snow or cowering in close groups round meagre
fires. The hedges and hurdle fences had long ago been
used up, and many of the houses had been gutted for the
sake of their timbers. Very few of the soldiers had any

more clothing than that which they had brought from Russia, and they could not afford to buy sheepskin coats from the Bulgarians. Before we left Plevna Skobeleff had been doing this for his men from his own resources, or rather from those of " Papa," in anticipation of the cold on the Schipka, and he thus preserved many lives. Gourko did not concern himself with such matters and the soldiers suffered in their worn and tattered greatcoats. Most of them had in good preservation the spare pair of boots which they had carried from Russia; but I noticed that a good many of them were wearing foot-coverings and leggings of raw hide instead of worn-out boots.

The morning after our arrival Millett and myself waited on General Gourko. He was busy writing, but he laid his pen aside, called for tea, gave us a friendly welcome, and asked for the news from Plevna. Millett told him about the cruel ruin of Osman's soldiers in their mud bivouacs on the plain. I gave him a short account of the sortie of the Turkish army on the morning of the 10th. "Ah," said Gourko, — " I wish I had seen that affair, and had the opportunity of shaking hands with Osman! Was his wound a severe one?" I could give him no details except that the wound was in the leg, but said that I inferred it could not have been dangerous since Osman had been able to set out on his journey towards Bucharest.

"You wish, I suppose," said the general, " to know something about our intended dispositions? You will find General Naglovski in the next room, and he will give you full information. No man can do that better, for the details of the whole scheme have been drawn up by him. I need not introduce you; — both of you know him."

Naglovski was a smart and dapper little man; he belonged to the Engineer branch of the service and was understood to be an officer of exceptional skill. He was cordial enough; his manner was a good deal that of a professor teaching a class, only that he was more informal.

"First," said he as he unfolded his maps, "I ought to tell you what we believe to be the strength of the enemy in our front. In all we take them to be about 35,000 infantry, some 2,000 regular cavalry, swarms of Tcherkesses and Bashi-Bazouks, and about 40 guns. We believe that there are of this number 25,000 men with 20 guns in the Shandarnik and Baba-Konak positions on the summit right and left of the defile traversed by the chaussée. Up at Lutikova, some miles north-west of us in Orkanie here, are about 5,000 men with four guns; there are about the same number about Slatitza on the road to Karlovo and Schipka; and at Sophia there is a reserve of perhaps twelve or fifteen thousand men with about twenty guns. So much for the Turks," said Naglovski.

"We," he continued, "have the good fortune to be about double their strength now that the reinforcements from Plevna have nearly all arrived. We have 65,000 infantry, 6,000 cavalry, and, all told, about 280 guns. We have 81 battalions available besides the three which are standing fast at Vraca, away to the northward beyond the Isker. Our plan, in a word, is to maintain a curtain of troops opposite to each of the Turkish positions in order to detain the enemy from withdrawing; to send a strong column over the Balkan summit to turn the left flank of the main Turkish position and debouch on the Sophia plain, and to pass smaller columns over the Balkans on our own extreme right and left flanks. That is what we tacticians call the 'General Idea'; the 'Special Idea' I will now explain. Old Grandfather Krüdener will have the command of what I call the four 'waiting' detachments, consisting in all of 34 battalions. One of these detachments General Schilder-Schuldner takes towards Lutikova, Prince Oldenburg with another remains on the Greote ridge, Count Schouvaloff stands opposite to the Turks west of Baba-Konak, and General Brock is at Slatitza. These detachments are to remain in position, bombard the Turkish positions, and attack promptly on any sign of retreat.

"The main turning column will cross the Balkan summit by what we call the 'Sappers' road,' and descend into the Sophia valley by Curiak. General Rauch is to have the advance consisting of 13 battalions with 16 guns and 11 sotnias of Cossacks. We expect him to start from here before daybreak on Christmas morning; he ought to be at Curiak that same evening, and on the morning of the 26th, coming down into the valley, he is to take up a position on the Sophia road about Malinne. The main column will consist of the 3rd Guard Division (18 battalions and 24 guns) commanded by General Kataley; following the advance over the Balkan summit it will occupy on the 26th the villages of Rasdanie and Stolnik near the chaussée to the left of Rauch and so nearer Sophia. General Wilhelminoff with a brigade of infantry, 16 squadrons and two batteries, will cross the mountains further west and debouch on the 26th at Zilava, west of the main column; and General Dandeville starting from

Etropol with a brigade, a battery, and some cavalry, will demonstrate on the right and rear of the Turkish main position, and come down into the Kamarli plain on the 26th. By the evening of that day," said Naglovski, "we hope to have at least 30,000 men on the other side of the Balkans. And," he continued, "we hope to accomplish this without encountering any opposition. General Gourko would fain effect the crossing without the loss of a man. The commander of the Sapper battalion of the Guard has reported that the road will be practicable for artillery by the 25th. I have myself been over it and down into Curiak, where the Cossacks have been for the last three weeks. I confess I thought the Sapper colonel rather sanguine, for once out of the ravine the best parts of the track had a slope of one in six, and in the worst of one in three. So I have turned on the Preobrazhensky regiment to improve the grades, widen the path throughout its whole extent, and cut steps in the ice in the steepest places up to the summit. General Gourko himself passed over it yesterday and has pronounced it practicable."

We thanked Naglovski and took our departure to visit the Red Cross Ambulance bearing the name and under the protection of the Grand Duchess Alexandra Petrovna the wife of the Commander-in-Chief, which had made its way right up to the front and established an hospital in Orkanie. I had already known of its devoted services to the great mass of wounded at Gorni-Dubnik, and I had seen its surgeons at work in the fighting line before Plevna in September, after which the Emperor visited its hospital in Bogot and personally thanked the Sisters for their devoted ministrations to his wounded soldiers. In its hospital up here in Orkanie we found 120 patients in the midst of comfort and cleanliness. Its directors had the humanity to establish a number of food stations between the front and Plevna, where warm and nourishing sustenance was supplied to the sick and wounded travelling in the transport trains towards the rear. It was said at the time that English solicitude for the victims of war was wholly confined to the Turks. That this was not so there was convincing proof in the provision-room of the Russian hospital in Orkanie, where I found a number of cases which bore the label that they had been sent by Colonel Loyd Lindsay in the name of the British Society for the Aid of the Sick and Wounded in War. I was told that already there had been distributed tea, sugar, canned provisions and spirits to many Russian hospitals in Bulgaria — part of the supplies which English philanthropists had sent to alleviate the sufferings of the sick and wounded Russian soldiers.

Orkanie had a very dismal aspect on Christmas morning in a thick black fog that was clammy till it froze. Rauch and his command had started long before the grey dawn; I remember turning round for a final sleep after I had heard the réveille sound. Millett's head-man was an admirable caterer and our final breakfast in Orkanie was quite his masterpiece. Flasks were replenished and haversacks were filled, sheepskin coats and fur boots were drawn on, and Millett distributed loose silver among a bevy of children and a batch of crones to whom the kindhearted fellow had been good during his term of residence in the snug little house which we were all loath to leave; and then we mounted and joined the group of Gourko's staff in front of the Konak. A photographer ought to have been on the spot. Some of the officers wore voluminous greatcoats of dressed skins, the hair inside, the leather outside — ornamented with fantastic embroidery and silver clasps. Others were wrapped in Circassian cloaks of several thicknesses of padding and material, their heads enveloped in bashliks and capuchons. The general alone wore no wrap. As he rode in front of the cortége, that iron man was visible to us in strictly correct military attire — the dark-coloured frogged surtout which an officer told me was the undress uniform of the Guard Cavalry, buckskin gloves and cavalry boots. He rode along apparently unconscious that the hoar-frost was whitening his beard and covering him and his horse with frozen crystals. I wondered beyond measure that the cruel cold did not strike him to the bone. But he did not seem to feel it in the least. My teeth were chattering already and I could not have written my name, so numbed and dead were my fingers, if the simple signature would have made me a millionaire. But Gourko's teeth did not chatter; and more than once I saw him pull off his right glove and sign an order with the pencil which he always carried stuck between the buttons of his frock-coat.

The fog remained pretty dense until we had passed Vratches, when it gradually thinned and the white mountain-tops whose sunny sides the sun was illuminating shone through the haze as if hung in the air, their lower shoulders still shrouded in mist. Presently we emerged altogether from out the bank of fog and there came in our faces a warm wind from the south, wafted to us, as I supposed, from the Sophia plain through the Baba-Konak Pass, which melted the frost and thawed the ice on the chaussée. Millett had been right in his conjecture of the 21st. The narrow and tangled glen down which came to the Dermente its tributary from the Etropol Balkans, was to be traversed by the 30,000 men with whom Gourko was to essay the passage of the mountains. As the crow flies, from Orkanie on one side of the Balkans to the Sophia plain at Rasdanie on the other was not more than fifteen miles, and by the track taken by the column was probably not more than twenty miles — a long but not very exceptional march over a reasonably favourable country. In what strange sanguine hallucination Gourko and Naglovski could have allowed themselves to imagine that in the Balkan mid-winter an army 30,000 strong could traverse the distance I have specified, climb and descend the mountains at almost their highest elevation by a track which even as improved could not be called a road, yet over which the army had to haul its guns and caissons and debouch on the confines of the Sophia plain within a period of twenty-four hours, of which only eight were in daylight, was to me, lad as I was, simply incomprehensible; but I kept my sentiments to myself. Millett was not so reticent. "This is going to be a long job, young man!" he remarked. "I shall be greatly surprised if Gourko be in Sophia by New Year's day!"

We were told that the Preobrazhensky regiment had crossed the summit during the previous night, and was already in Curiak. The ravine as we looked into it seemed full of men, but there was no progression to speak of — the column did not move forward at the rate of a rod an hour. There seemed a lack of system, and there certainly was a lack of enthusiasm. Before we had reached Vratches I had observed men falling out and lying down by the wayside although they had marched only a couple of miles. The kibitkas of the Red Cross established where the "Sappers' road" left the chaussée were already full of men who had given out or had injured themselves by falling on the ice. In the afternoon Millett and I, tired of inaction, moved forward up the track in the ravine. We could get along but slowly, for the way was all but completely blocked by guns and infantry. Idleness everywhere prevailed; nowhere was there any zeal or energy. The men had made fires all along the path and were cooking their suppers or lying asleep in the warmth. I remarked to Millett how great was the contrast between the lassitude we were now witnessing, and the energy and endurance the same men had shown in the rougher work of Rauch's expedition which I had accompanied in November. "In one sense," replied Millett, "it is true that they are the same men; in another they are very different men. Their systems have been run down by cold and exposure; the starch is temporarily out of them. They are soft and flaccid from long inaction in the positions. They will rally by-and-by, but Naglovski will find himself quite out in the estimate he gave us of the time that the passage of the mountains would take. I expect when we go up we shall find Rauch jumping mad."

We scrambled out of the ravine and went up the face of the steep ascent. It was not very difficult at first, but presently we came to a bad place where a half-battery with its caissons was being hauled up by hand, the pitch being over-steep for the horse-teams. The ropes were too short, affording room for only about sixty men to haul on each piece. The men on this service were not the stalwart soldiers of the Guard, but young undersized linesmen from the recent reinforcements who had suffered from the long march from Plevna through the snowstorms, and who, having no heart for the work, went about the business with exasperating slowness and stupidity. Rauch was at this point in a white-heat of energy, encouraging, abusing, appealing to the officers to exert themselves and make their men do the same, stamping, swearing, even catching hold of a rope-end himself; but all to no purpose — the men were listless and apathetic. We left that sorely-tried chief and went on, to find the distances between the cannon longer and longer. Now there was not even the pretence of exertion. It mattered not that the essence of the enterprise, if Naglovski's scheme were to be carried out on his lines, was that the army and its guns should have made the passage of the mountain before daylight next morning. The Preobrazhenskys were isolated down in Curiak and the Turks, if they had any energy, might snatch the opportunity to assail them. Nevertheless as we approached the summit we found the men placidly resting everywhere. The officers lay down and slept. The men snuggled together round their fires or scooped holes in the snow in which they peacefully slumbered. In vain Rauch stormed back and forth striving in vain to stimulate the fellows into action. Now and then he succeeded in rousing an officer who made a foray among the sleep-

ing soldiers and forced them to their feet. Then
what happened? The soldiers did not grumble, but
simply walked away a few paces, dropped in their tracks,
and went to sleep as they fell. The officer, himself a
practical philosopher, followed the example of the soldiers.

Chafing at the delay and impatient to exert himself in
dealing with it, Gourko himself, along with his staff, came
up towards the summit about midnight. He had travelled
along a lane fringed by soldiers who were either asleep or
whom no stimulus could stir into exertion. The general
had to realise that for the time there was no help for a
situation which was so utterly unexpected. We were supping from the contents of our wallets beside a Cossack
fire close to the summit when the general and his staff
arrived. "Let us go to sleep!" said he, "we can do nothing for the present!" The Cossacks gave up their fire to
the general and his staff and made another for themselves;
they piled up a bank of snow behind the chief to fend
from him the icy wind blowing across the range, and presently Gourko was snoring with vigour. As I finished my
pipe before lying down alongside of Millett, it struck me
how easily a single Turkish company might capture the
Russian general and his staff. There was a picket on the
actual summit, and where there is a picket there should be
at least one sentry. I had the curiosity to saunter up to
the summit. The picket to a man was dead asleep. As
I walked around it I trod on the sentry. He grunted as
I stumbled over him, but did not awake.

As we woke the bright morning sun was shining on a
spectacle of striking picturesqueness and illuminating a
landscape of serene and varied beauty. Near us generals

and staff officers, some rolled snugly in shubas and bourkas, some in their overcoats only, lay in the snow around the fires which the soldiers had replenished. Cossacks and dragoons were already busy with their cooking, and hundreds of horses made fast to the trees surrounding the mountain-bivouac stamped impatiently on the snow. Below us to the southward as we stood on the skyline spread the wide plain of Sophia, its white surface broken only by the little dark spots which marked where the villages were. Beyond, with the clouds hanging fitfully on their slopes, were the mountains of the Lüntin range further south, and away in the direction of Samakova was the huge mountainous mass which is crowned by the lofty peak of Vitos. Looking eastward through the tree-trunks we could clearly see the great Shandarnik summit and the line of Turkish redoubts and entrenchments on the lofty ridge above Kamarli. That was Curiak down yonder at the foot of the short steep descent from the summit on which we stood full 2,000 feet above it, and a couple of miles nearer the plain was Potop and beyond were Eleznitza and Stolnik among the trees close to the chaussée crossing the plain to Sophia away yonder behind its redoubts. As we stood looking down on the scene Gourko came up with Naglovski and surveyed the wide prospect with great intentness. You see that telescope hanging there on the wall? There never was a better glass. Your father made me a present of it when I went down to Giurgevo with Skobeleff before the crossing of the Danube. Gourko and Naglovski had only binoculars. These are very convenient especially if made of aluminium, and they are useful enough for short distances; but for long range-work they cannot hold a candle to the telescope. MacGahan always swore by it, and I have been told that Dr. Russell the famous English war-correspondent never faltered in his allegiance to the telescope. Gourko had accosted us in his usual courteous manner, and I made bold to offer him my telescope. He thanked me, focussed it, and brought it to bear on Sophia. He broke out into an exclamation of surprise — " What a wonderful glass ! " he exclaimed — " I can discern the clock-face on a church-spire in Sophia ! "

Just then Rauch came up in a better frame of mind than we had seen him overnight. He had got the soldiers to work before daybreak ; now he wanted some breakfast, and then he would be glad if his Excellency would accompany him down the mountain to hasten forward the movements. Gourko was good enough to invite us to breakfast, a proffer which was very opportune. Before the generals went off tidings came in from Wilhelminoff on our right to the effect that there was no practicable track towards Zilava, and that he would be compelled to bend eastward towards Curiak or Potop. There was no intelligence from Dandeville on the left, and I may as well tell you that he came to great grief, having been overwhelmed by a terrible storm that piled the snow up in fathomless drifts in which part of his artillery was buried and had to be abandoned. So intense was the cold that about fifty of his men were actually frozen to death and more than 800 were permanently disabled by being frost-bitten. He had to return to Etropol, but later was able to cross the range and come down into the valley about Bunovo.

We would fain have gone down the descent into Curiak, but the road thither from the summit being within view from the Turkish positions was closed by patrols, and we had to possess our souls in patience until nightfall. All about us just behind the summit soldiers were gathering in the bivouacs in groups as they came up. After resting a while they set about cooking their rations of which they carried in their haversacks hard bread for six days; beef and mutton accompanied them on the hoof to last for the same time. Had we known that the Caucasian Cossack Brigade had crossed during the previous night when we were asleep, we should have been in Curiak before now. As it was we had to wait until twilight of the 26th, when in the company of a number of officers we slid down the deep descent from the summit leading our horses over the ice, and before midnight were once again under a roof in the village of Curiak. Next morning the Preobrazhensky regiment marched eastward to the ridge stretching north and south between the hill villages of Nyagesovo and Hajedanie, and entrenched itself in full view of the little plain of Tashkessen and the steep and rocky crest behind the village of that name. The Caucasian brigade that same day raided on to the Sophia high road, cut the telegraph wires, and after a skirmish captured a convoy of two hundred waggons on its way to Araba-Konak.

There was no longer any object in attempting to conceal the turning movement; the moment had passed when the Turks, if they had any enterprise, might have interfered to some purpose with Gourko's dispositions while in the throes of the crossing of the summit. Two more days had to be spent in bringing over the guns, while the infantry were in bivouac all over the slopes. Wilhelminoff's detachment had to abandon its prescribed route, and came into

Curiak worn out with hunger and fatigue. News came in that the Turks had abandoned their position up at Lutikova and had gone through the mountains to Sophia. On the morning of the last day of the old year Gourko was ready to march eastward and take in reverse the Turkish army. "We may make another Sedan of the business!" remarked Naglovski as he rubbed his hands — "We have already cut the Turks off from Sophia; if we can get before them to Dolni-Kamarli and take a firm grip of the Petricevo road, we may bag the whole crowd!" On the face of things this did not seem an extravagant consummation; only, as it happened, the worthy but sanguine Naglovski did not take Valentine Baker into account.

Reconnaissances had proved that the village of Tashkessen, behind which was a high rocky ridge penetrated or rather surmounted by the high road, was held by a Turkish force estimated to be about 5,000 strong with ten guns. Its actual strength, as we afterwards learned, was 3,000 men, of whom at least 1,000 were of little account. There were only five trustworthy battalions, with five fieldguns and two weak squadrons of cavalry. Gourko was clearly determined that he would not fail for lack of numbers. He employed thirty-five battalions, two cavalry brigades, and thirty-six guns. Rauch had the left with ten battalions and eight guns. Kataley with twelve battalions and twenty guns was in the centre across the high road. Kourloff with ten battalions and eight guns was on the right, with orders to make a turning movement to his right through Cekansevo and push his cavalry brigades forward to Makatch and Dolni-Kamarli to block there the Turkish line of retreat. About 1,800 paces in front of Tashkessen,

there rose out of the plain a long low rocky ridge lying
north and south behind which Rauch deployed, having
first driven from the ridge the handful of Turkish cavalry
which had been holding it, got up on to it a battery, and
opened a lively shrapnel-fire. Climbing on to this little
ridge I lay down between two of Rauch's guns and swept
with my telescope the lower crest behind the village of
Tashkessen. On this crest there were three rocky hillocks
north of the road connected by a rough entrenchment
which also extended some considerable distance south of
the road. The position seemed too extended for the slender strength holding it, but there were no signs of wavering, and the few guns the defenders possessed were in
smart action against Kourloff's detachment moving towards
Cekansevo. On the central rocky hillock I could easily
discern through my glass Valentine Baker and Burnaby
with several other officers about them who seemed to be
Englishmen. From Rauch's left I saw as I looked back
the Preobrazhensky regiment moving out into the plain
round the northern end of the ridge opposite Tashkessen
on which I lay, and wading slowly through the deep snow
in the direction of the village of Danskioj. Its guns had
come into action against the Turkish right, but the infantry
were not yet engaged, and indeed the battalions were advancing less energetically than might have been expected
of the crack regiment of the Russian Guard. Meanwhile
Kourloff's division had reached and passed Cekansevo,
and was now moving over the plateau in the direction of
Makatch, whence it might either go on to Dolni-Kamarli
or take in reverse the Turkish position on the Tashkessen
ridge. Baker had clearly been extending his left to hinder

a procedure so ominous of danger to him, and Kourloff's flank as he neared Makatch was being smartly galled by the Turkish rifle-fire. All at once Kourloff's whole force halted, and changing front to the left, took the new direction which would bring it on Baker's flank. "Now he's done for!" I muttered with a sinking of the heart — "Kourloff will roll him up, and the Preobrazhenskys there on his right front will strike in and finish the business!"

My heart was beating hard as I lay on the snow watching the critical scene. Presently Kourloff's leading battalions broke into loose order and dashed forward with shouts the clamour of which rang from valley to hill. I heard faintly the sound of Baker's bugles, and then with a ringing cry of "Allah!" his gallant Turks dashed themselves against the face of the great Muscovite wave surging up the rocky slopes. The din of the rifle-fire was deafening. But the Turks could not maintain their offensive against odds so heavy. They fought every inch of ground, reluctantly abandoning peak after peak. Stimulated by the example set by the Russian right Rauch's division now abandoned its halting and hesitating attitude. Its leading brigade advanced up the sloping spur near the village of Danskioj, and struck at once on flank and front the knoll held by the two battalions which constituted Baker's right. The odds were immense — eight battalions against two, but the Turks were staunch, they had the higher ground, and they fought from behind cover. The Russians made a sturdy fight of it but the Turkish fire was too strong for them, and they fell back around the rocky roots of the spur. They had suffered severely, and some time elapsed before they pulled themselves together again before resuming the advance.

By this time it was afternoon, and the Turks were still dauntlessly holding their own. But the position which Baker had been maintaining since daylight was obviously now seriously compromised. Both his flanks were threatened, and Kataley was now moving forward along the chaussée with the seeming object of assailing his front. It seemed to me that Baker had already done a good day's work, and that the time had now surely come when he was amply justified in retiring from the unequal struggle. But it soon appeared that this was not at all Valentine Baker's view of the situation. It was truly beautiful, the quiet cool deliberation with which he withdrew his little command up on to the main upper crest of the ridge, into a position which I could easily discern was infinitely stronger than the one which he had previously been holding. He had befooled the Russians to some purpose in letting them imagine that they were outflanking him on both right and left, whereas they had been doing this as regarded only his initial position; and now they must go right at the front of his new and stronger position, or recommence from the beginning a fresh series of outflanking movements. I could scarcely contain myself from cheering as the skilful tactics gradually dawned on me; and how I wished that I had a fellow-Briton by my side with whom to take pride in the brilliant military genius of our brave unfortunate countryman!

"*Sapristi!*" shouted the Russian major commanding the battery — "Here is that enterprising countryman of yours coming down on to the plain with a regiment of cavalry! Well, we shall see how he relishes our shrapnel!" The major spoke true. Baker himself was not leading the horsemen, but that their chief was an Englishman I recognised at once by his seat in the saddle. "Oh, I see!" said the major — "It is merely a demonstration to cover your friend's retirement to the main crest. Very neat dexterous business I call it. I wish your Baker Pasha belonged to us, then one day our cavalry might do something that men would talk about. Well, we've emptied a few Turkish saddles; and that long-legged Englishman, having arrested events for half an hour or so, is shouting 'Threes about!' and going up the hill again. I will make it hot for him as he goes!" And sure enough the Russian major let drive viciously till the Turkish squadrons were out of range.

At the khan where the road crossed the crest Baker's guns were in position firing shrapnel on the Russian skirmishers advancing on the Turkish left front. The khan itself, a large building with many windows, was full of infantry who swept all the approaches with their fire from the windows. It staggered the heavy Russian columns and even caused their skirmishers to desist from advancing — the Peabody-Martinis had the advantage of the Russian Berdans. We heard heavy artillery-fire up in the mountains about the Shandarnik; and I asked the Russian major what that meant? "Oh!" he replied, "that is only Prince Oldenburg's fire to keep the Turks where they are up yonder, while Gourko is smashing Baker and getting into position to cut off the Turkish retreat." It seemed to me that Baker was not being perceptibly smashed, but on the contrary that he was gallantly holding his own. Kourloff was gradually crowding in on his left, and the Preobrazhenskys were trying to approach his centre and right but were catching it heavily from Baker's shrapnel and rifle-fire. The afternoon became hazy but there was no actual fog. As the dusk set in the Russians gathered themselves together for a final desperate effort. They brought up fresh troops and came tramping up over the snow, in the face of the withering fire from the rocks around the khan and from the khan itself. As the converging attack neared the crest the Turks sprang to their feet and rushed forward with the bayonet. Indistinctly I saw through the telescope a brief but wild mêlée, and then the Russians gave back pursued by their fierce adversaries. Baker had not been "smashed," and his skill and resolution had thwarted Gourko's intention to intercept the Turkish retreat. I afterwards learned that of the 2,000 men composing the five trustworthy battalions with which Baker really made his protracted and successful defence, 800 had fallen, a loss of nearly one-half. But it was the constancy of Valentine Baker and his staunch 2,000 which alone covered and made possible the retreat of the Turkish army. The losses of the Russians amounted to 1,000, including a general commanding a brigade and thirty-two other officers. The losses incurred by Gourko in his passage of the Balkans, in action and because of the cruel cold, were altogether something over 2,000. At that sacrifice he might have forced the Baba-Konak Pass, and saved a good deal of time.

The Russian troops bivouacked where they found them-

selves when the fighting ended. We found quarters of
a kind in the village of Tashkessen, many of the houses
in which were filled with dead, sick, and wounded. Soon
after daybreak on the morning of New Year's day tidings
came in that the Turkish army was nowhere to be found.
The Russians had missed their expected prey, thanks to
the cool fortitude of Valentine Baker, who held the Tashkessen Pass all day long and on until the evening while
Shakir Pasha was withdrawing his troops from their positions on the Shandarnik heights. It was the only occasion on which I ever saw Gourko's composure greatly
disturbed. He threw himself on his horse and galloped
up to the crest behind the khan, where he drew rein and
looked down with knitted brows upon the empty plain of
Kamarli on which he had expected to find the Turkish
army. All that was to be seen were a few belated Turkish stragglers whom the Cossacks were chasing through
the deep snow. On the long steep ascent behind the
village of Dolni-Kamarli up which wound the road to
Petricevo, was visible against the snow the dark column
of Turks slowly marching away out of cannon-range.
We counted some half-dozen battalions, but the main force
must have been already well forward on its retreating
march to Petricevo. The advance of Kataley's column
presently approached Dolni-Kamarli, but the Turks had
left there a rear guard of a few hundred men who maintained a stout and prolonged defence from the fences and
houses of the village; and when at length the little band
abandoned the place, it gave further pause to Kataley by
throwing up some hasty entrenchments on the summit
of the hill, which were held until the Russian guns com-

pelled an ultimate retirement. Gourko's dispositions for the previous day, in spite of Baker's heroic stand behind Tashkessen, would probably have afforded him the consummation of "bagging," to use Naglovski's phrase, at least part of the Turkish army, but for the errors committed by his own people. The cavalry division which he had ordered to take and hold Dolni-Kamarli, on approaching that village had fallen back before a few shots and then had remained doing absolutely nothing during the day; and Kourloff had been enticed into taking part in the fighting, thus leaving open to the Turks a line of retreat through the unoccupied Dolni-Kamarli.

Well, there was no help for the Russian misadventure, in which I own I secretly gloried. Gourko ordered a detachment of cavalry to move up the chaussée towards the Baba-Konak Pass, where it met the head of Krüdener's corps marching down from the northward. On the further side of the Kamarli plain the Red Crescent flag was flying from a large marquee close to the village of Strigli. I rode across and found in the village among about 1,000 Turkish wounded several English surgeons hard at work, along with Mr. Bell, the artist-correspondent of the *Illustrated London News*. The senior surgeon was Dr. Leslie, who went to the general to ask for a temporary guard, as the Turks had deserted the village and the Russians had not occupied it. The Turkish surgeons had all gone with the troops. I also found in Strigli Colonel Baker of the Turkish Gendarmerie, who was too ill of dysentery to be able to leave along with the army. The surgeons were good enough to ask me to spend the night with them, an invitation which I was only too glad to accept, for my new friends seemed to be living in clover. I rode back to where General Gourko still was at the cross-roads, just in time, as Krüdener's people were seen descending the pass, to hear him address the staff with great earnestness in the words: "Now, gentlemen, we can say in all conscience that we have completely accomplished the crossing of the Balkans!" There was a ripple of cheering as the chief shook hands heartily with all around him, and then served us out with the little bits of chocolate which seemed to be the only penchant of this iron and stoical man.

We followed the general up the road past Araba-Konak to pay a visit to the abandoned positions on the Shandarnik ridge. The Turkish redoubts were admirably constructed and they were as neat and trim as a well-kept garden. The Turks had left seven fine Krupp guns, on account, the Russian officers held, of the exposure to which they would have been subjected in being dragged under fire along the whole length of the position, which had no other line of retreat than the high road. Rather than leave them to the enemy, it struck me that they might have been thrown over the steep declivity in rear of the position, where probably they would have remained undetected in the brushwood at the foot. It was a delightful evening I spent with the English surgeons in their snug common-room in the best house in Strigli. For the first time since leaving Todleben's table at Tutchenitza did I partake of what I believe has now come to be called a "square meal." My friends were gentlemen of education and knowledge of the world far beyond what I could aspire to, and I felt it was fitting that I should be more of a listener than a talker. But they were very hungry for information about the events of the war on the Russian side, and I had to describe the fighting around Plevna and its ultimate fall. They were very curious to know what had happened in the case of the two young dressers (it seems they were not surgeons) Vachell and Douglas who had fallen into the Russian hands at Telis. I was able to inform them that the Grand Duke Nicholas had been very courteous to them and that they had not been long in his headquarter before he gave them their liberty and, I had heard, had furnished them with funds to take them home. This pleased them greatly, as bearing probably on their own future. In reply to Colonel Baker I had to state that Colonel Coope had been treated as a Turkish officer and that I understood he had been sent to Russia as a prisoner of war. "Bad look-out for me!" remarked the colonel dolefully. Sure enough, when next day Prince Oldenburg came down from the mountain-tops into Strigli, he sent an officer of his staff to inform Colonel Baker that he was a prisoner of war and to demand his parole. What finally befell this officer I never heard, but what happend to the Strigli surgeons I became aware of later to my great indignation. I recollect that just as I was leaving Strigli on the forenoon of January 2nd, there arrived Prince Tzeretleff and Mr. Millett, who had been sent back to ascertain the truth or the reverse of a statement that Baker Pasha was lying wounded and a prisoner here at Strigli. The misconception was soon cleared up, and after a charming luncheon with the cheery and hospitable surgeons we three started off for Gorni-Bugaroff, where the headquarters were for the night. We had a long ride before us, for Gorni-Bugaroff was more than half-way to

Sophia and the road was too slippery to allow us to make any pace. As we neared Bugaroff after nightfall the road and the numerous dead bodies lying across it and in the ditches on either side were lit up by the glare from the huge bivouac-fires. We rode into the village to meet a line of soldiers carrying out a number of corpses for interment in the fields hard by. I had not heard of any fighting in this direction, but Prince Tzeretleff informed me that on the previous day Wilhelminoff's column, some 3,500 strong, a little way beyond Bugaroff had defeated with heavy loss a sortie from Sophia made by 5,000 Turks. The latter were some time in sight as they approached and the Russians had time to throw up a line of shelter-trenches. Lying down in those they waited patiently until the Turks were within a hundred yards, when they poured in steady volleys and then sprang up and charged with the bayonet. The Turks, staggered by the fierceness and suddenness of this attack, broke and ran, leaving 800 of their number dead on the ground and carrying off twice as many wounded. Wilhelminoff's entire loss was only 250 men. Before tumbling into a cellar half full of hay which we were glad to occupy as a bedroom, we heard that Kataley's Guard division along with Dandeville's detachment from Bunovo was to continue the pursuit of the fugitive Turkish army by the Petricevo road, and two Guard cavalry brigades were to move by another road in the hope of taking it in flank. A day or two later came the news that General Kataley and one of his brigade commanders had been killed in a skirmish with some stragglers of the Turkish rear guard.

CHAPTER XIV

FROM SOPHIA TO ADRIANOPLE

NEXT morning (January 3rd) we accompanied a reconnaissance made by General Gourko towards the northern vicinity of Sophia, in the course of which we were within a few hundred yards of its outskirts. No opposition was visible here; but the earthworks on the slope eastward of the town were seen to be full of men, the fortifications were manned, and there were no signs whatever of impending evacuation. Gourko did not at all like the attitude of the Turks, and Naglovski muttered ominously that "Sophia might become another Plevna." It was believed that the garrison of the place was about 15,000 men with about twenty guns, and the redoubts and entrenchments seemed very strong. "Well," said Gourko, "the longer we look at it the worse we shall like it!" He determined to attack on the 5th, and made his dispositions on the spot. Prince Oldenburg's command of eight battalions and sixteen guns was ordered up; Wilhelminoff with the same strength was to operate from the north; and Rauch with twenty battalions and forty-two guns was to make the main attack along the Plevna-Sophia high road. Prince Tzeretleff was very glum as we rode back to quarters. "The place," he remarked, "will cost us 5,000 men even if the attack succeed, and that seems to me doubtful enough."

For once we were in comfortable quarters, in a large farm-house belonging to a wealthy Turk, near the covered bridge across the Isker about five miles short of Sophia. We lived at rack and manger on the Turk's livestock; but the thirty-six hours of suspense which we reckoned on rather damped our spirits. It was near noon of the 4th when a Cossack brought the welcome news that the Turkish troops had evacuated Sophia during the night, and that Rauch's advance guard had been in the town for the last two hours. We mounted and rode rapidly past the main column tramping on steadily with uncased banners, marching to the ringing songs of the platoons heading each battalion. Gourko sat on horseback close to the entrance of the town, sternly warning the troops as they passed him that plundering would be punished with the utmost severity. They fully understood when they saw the uplifted forefinger and heard the curt ringing tones, that their general was a man of his word and that marauders would have from him a short shrift. The inhabitants of Sophia did not prepossess us in their favour. They were the reverse of enthusiastic, and seemed languidly curious rather than excited by what the Russians called their "deliverance." Sophia may be said to have been one great hospital, crowded with the helpless wounded whom Osman Pasha had sent away from Plevna in the early weeks of October. The mortality among them had been awful, both during the long slow rough journey and after their arrival in Sophia. Such of them as could walk or even crawl had been ordered to accompany the departing Turkish troops, who had been marching away by the southern road to Dubnitza during the whole of the previous night. It was told us that some 6,000 of those hapless wounded had limped away with the soldiers, of whom a terrible percentage were sure to die of cold and hunger within the next few days. The hospitals had been fairly well managed, but when the *débâcle* set in the Bulgarian attendants had robbed the patients who were too ill to move, and then had deserted in a body. There was a wretched interval of three days between the time of the departure of the Turks and the first issue of food to the hospitals by the Russians. This was sheer carelessness, for Sophia was full of available supplies, only it was made the business of nobody to distribute them, and meanwhile the unfortunate patients in very many instances died of hunger. It was far different in the hospitals which were in English hands — those of Lady Strangford, the Red Crescent Society, and the surgeons and administrators of the Stafford House organisation. The personnel of all those establishments remained loyally in execution of their duties, and saved many lives. After the general evacuation about a thousand wounded remained in Sophia too ill to be moved, and those who survived the interval of utter neglect were well cared for by the surgeons of various nationalities. Lady Strangford was treated with the utmost consideration, and transport was placed at her disposal should she have chosen to follow the Turkish retreat; but she preferred to carry out her task of humanity in Sophia, where also the surgeons of the Stafford House organisation and of the Red Crescent elected to remain.

I believe that Sophia is now quite a handsome city. When you wrote to me from it during your recent travels, you mentioned that you were living in a comfortable hotel, that boulevards were being built, a theatre was open, and in short, that Sophia was a stirring place — almost, I remember you said, to be named alongside of Bucharest. The Sophia of 1878 was a shabby and dilapidated Turkish town, swarming with Jews, its Bulgarian population more objectionable even than the Bulgarians of the Danube provinces. They disliked the Russians, and the Russians loathed them. There was nothing in common between the deliverers and the delivered, except some similarity in language and religion. We stayed in Sophia for five days and were dead sick of the place. The Turks in leaving had done Gourko a good turn; they had abandoned in Sophia about eight million rations of flour, rice, sugar, coffee, salt, etc., and there was abundance of sheep and cattle in the Sophia plain. A supply-train loaded with biscuit was brought over the mountains from Orkanie, and the troops were served out with six days' rations of "hard tack."

I had known from General Todleben before I left Plevna that Gourko's instructions after reaching Sophia were that he should advance from that place by the old Roman road through Philippopolis to Adrianople, driving the Turks before him as he marched. But I also learned from Prince Tzeretleff that the general was a good deal in the dark as to the probable positions of the enemy. He knew that in crossing the Balkans he had driven Shakir Pasha's army of about 20,000 men away over the Little Balkans through Petricevo and probably to Otlukioj, and that the 15,000 men who had constituted the garrison of Sophia had taken the circuitous route by Dubnitza round the huge mountain mass of Rilo towards Samakovo.

But there had also to be reckoned with the army of Suleiman which had been withdrawn from the Quadrilateral, and was now marching up from Philippopolis towards Trajan's Gate by the Roman road. Its strength was reported to be over 20,000 men. Gourko, leaving a brigade in Sophia, divided his marching army into four detachments. On the left Krüdener with 24 battalions, 16 squadrons and 58 guns was already following Shakir by Petricevo towards Otlukioj. This force constituted the Russian left. Gourko himself left Sophia on the morning of the 9th with the centre (main) column commanded by Count Schouvaloff, consisting of 30 battalions, 12 squadrons and 76 guns, all of the Guard. This body was to follow the Roman road, in the expectation of finding and beating Suleiman in the Trajan Gate position. Wilhelminoff had left Sophia on the 7th, marching towards Samakovo by the direct road, with orders to cut off the retreat of the Sophia garrison and then operate against Suleiman's flank and rear at the Trajan Pass. Wilhelminoff had only a brigade of infantry, another of Caucasian Cossacks, and 12 guns. Schilder-Schuldner with a small force was to descend the valley of the Topolnica between Otlukioj and Trajan's Gate. I have bothered you with these details which you may follow out at your leisure on the map, that you may the better understand Gourko's comprehensive strategy.

During the march of the 10th the tidings reached us that Radetski's army had crossed the Schipka Pass, and that the whole of Vessil Pasha's Turkish army had surrendered to Skobeleff on the previous day. You should have heard the cheering as the good news ran along the column, betokening for the home-sick soldiers the beginning of the end. A snow-storm had set in, the road was a sheet of ice and the cold was bitter and cutting; but the men, elated by the intelligence of the day, made light of a bivouac in the snow and sang round their fires till the night was far advanced. Next day at Ichtiman we heard that the whole of the Turkish forces which had been in Gourko's front were on the run, having abandoned all their positions; and the same afternoon there presented himself an aide-de-camp of Suleiman with a message that "the war was over," orders having been received from the Minister of War at Constantinople to cease hostilities, as an armistice had been arranged with the Russian Commander-in-Chief. This was a bit of bluff on Suleiman's part in the hope of delaying the Russian advance, but Gourko was not to be deceived by it; and presently telegrams from the Grand Duke Nicholas arrived stating that negotiations merely were in progress, and ordering that active operations were to be vigorously prosecuted. General Wilhelminoff, who was frequently unfortunate, alone fell into the trap and thereby lost twenty-four hours, of which the astute Osman Noury Pasha, commanding the Turkish force which had garrisoned Sophia, skilfully availed himself. The rest of the Turkish forces had gone and left him to his own resources, but Osman Noury was a gallant soldier and a man of no little resource. But for the difficulties which Schouvaloff's people experienced in getting their artillery up and then down the ice-bound road over the lofty pass of Trajan's Gate, Osman and his detachment of some 15,000 men would have been cut off. As it was, the Russians had the chagrin of watching from

Vejtrenova his rear guard disappear on its march to Tatar-Bazardjik. He had wisely crossed from the left to the right bank of the Maritza, leaving to us the high road but moving with great celerity along the tracks on the south bank. On the 13th we pushed on with all possible vigour to within a few miles of Tatar-Bazardjik, and that afternoon looked down into the great plain of Philippopolis. As the heads of the Russian columns converging simultaneously on Tatar-Bazardjik, by the Ichtiman and Otlukioj roads, moved forward threateningly, two Turkish divisions formed line of battle behind the Topolnica near its confluence with the Maritza, but no serious collision occurred, and Osman Noury's column marching towards the town on the south bank was not molested by the Russians.

During the night between the 14th and 15th, the whole of Suleiman's army which had completed its concentration by the arrival from Samakova of Osman Noury's detachment and was now 40,000 strong or thereabouts, evacuated Tatar-Bazardjik having burned the bridge across the Maritza between the two sections of the town, and marched towards Philippopolis. The line of route of both armies was parallel, the Turkish on the right bank, the Russian on the left. The former army was hurrying on to reach Philippopolis, where it was to find a reinforcement of twenty-six battalions which would raise Suleiman's strength to nearly 55,000 men. The Russian infantry columns were preceded by the cavalry which was sent forward to occupy Philippopolis in the expectation of finding that city unoccupied by Turkish forces, but was disappointed in that hope. Late in the afternoon, after a long march, Schouvaloff's advance forded the Maritza and occupied the village of Adakioj on the south bank. Suleiman's army spent the night in Kadikioj, a village three miles further east on the same side of the river. Fuad Pasha had skilfully conducted the Turkish retreat from Tatar-Bazardjik, and in the morning his division, about 12,000 strong, was found in position behind a deep affluent of the Maritza along a front that seemed too much extended. The fighting lasted most of the day, but had little earnestness; the Russians aiming at delaying the Turkish retreat, Fuad's people quite content to be held where they were while the retreat of the main force was being prepared. During the day Suleiman skulked out of Philippopolis with some 20,000 men, marched to Stanimaka, and left the rest of his army to its fate. Fuad and Shakir fought out the issue with a valiant desperation which commanded the admiration of their enemies. Gourko made the most of his superior numbers; I counted that in the course of the day he employed forty-six battalions: taking a battalion at this stage of the campaign at 600 men, he was using 27,600 men against Fuad's 15,000, Schouvaloff's estimate of that Pasha's strength. The Russian losses on that day amounted to about 300. Fuad's were probably about the same, and as he had to abandon the villages on which both his flanks rested, he fell back into a position at the base of the mountains in front of the village of Demendere.

Wilhelminoff had come up during the night, and on the morning of the 16th he followed Fuad along the base of the mountain. Schouvaloff deployed in Fuad's front, and Schilder-Schuldner was to have closed on the Turkish right flank; but that supine person, one of the Czar's many "bad bargains," halted in a village on his march on the pretext that his troops were fatigued. Gourko must have wished that his commission gave him the right to shoot imbeciles like Schilder-Schuldner, to be commanded by whom was an insult to good soldiers. Fuad in the afternoon made a savage attack on Wilhelminoff's column, which you will remember had so fiercely repulsed the Turkish onslaught at Gorni-Bugaroff on January 1st. His troops repeated now the tactics which they had found so successful then, lying down behind a rocky ridge until the Turkish charge was within 100 yards of their front, and then meeting and crushing it with steadily-aimed volleys. This onslaught cost the Turks about 600 men, and Wilhelminoff's loss did not amount to sixty.

Schilder-Schuldner's torpidity had allowed Fuad to move nearer to his line of retreat by the Stanimaka road on the night between the 16th and 17th. On the morning of the latter day his left flank, thrown back to oppose Wilhelminoff, was found to be close to the village of Markovo. His front rested on the village of Tchiflick, with Schouvaloff and the crack regiments of the Russian Guard directly opposite to him. His right was pivoted on the village of Belesnitza, beyond which further to the right was the division of Shakir Pasha, who had come to give the hand to his gallant comrade. Shakir found opposed to him in his front and on his right flank the 3rd Division of the Guard which Dandeville had been commanding since the death of General Kataley. After two days' fighting Gourko had become impatient to end the business, and since the Philippopolis bridge had been burned by the Turks he had sent Dandeville down stream several miles to a ford, where that commander's division was carried over on the horses of one of the Guard cavalry brigades. In the late afternoon of the 16th the leading brigade of the division advanced to the attack of the village of Karagach, which was found occupied by a part of Suleiman's rear guard. This village was at the mountain-foot, not far from the Stanimaka road. It was carried by the Russian brigade with rather a smart loss, and the Turks lost there 18 guns. Next morning Dandeville moved up into the left of the Russian line facing and flanking on its right the Turkish division commanded by Shakir Pasha, and took part in the long and bitter fighting of the day. The offensive was with the Turks. In the morning Shakir made a furious effort to hurl back Dandeville's division and so open his way to the Stanimaka road; but the Russian Guardsmen stoutly repulsed him, and becoming the assailants in their turn seized and held a number of his guns. In the afternoon Schilder-Schuldner struck Fuad's front at Tchiflick at the same time that Wilhelminoff rolled up his left. Fuad had fought a long and stubborn fight and Shakir was worthy of his comrade. Dandeville's people told of a Turkish colonel who hacked his way into the thick of the fighting and struck down seventeen Russians with sword and revolver before a final bayonet-thrust did for him. The Turks retreated sullenly from terrace to terrace up the mountain-side, still striking viciously back at their pursuers, till at last, after a heroic but hopeless resistance, the disorganised, exhausted, famished, half-frozen remnants of the two divisions broke into groups, and under cover of darkness groped their way up into the

Rhodope mountains, to the road by which the recreant Suleiman was heading for the Ægean. His army had been all but shattered. It had lost 5,000 men in battle, the Russians held of it 2,000 prisoners, all its guns (114 in number, of which 96 had been captured in open fight), its baggage, ammunition, and supplies. The losses of the Russians did not reach a total of 1,300.

In Philippopolis we were restored to comparative civilisation. I once again was really warm, in the bright and comfortable room in which we installed ourselves. I slept on a spring mattress, and nestled in an easy-chair with a sense of languid luxury which I cannot describe to you. The Philippopolis bazaar had been burned down, but there were excellent shops, and the English consul was kind enough to introduce me to a club where I found a file of *The Times* and read up about six months of the world's doings.

That was a ghastly march from Philippopolis to Adrianople on which we set out on January 23rd. It had been a subject of curiosity with us all the way from Plevna what had become of the Turkish population in the Balkans and in Roumelia. Before reaching Philippopolis we passed no fugitives; there was not a Turk in Sophia, and the whole region we had traversed had been Christian of a sort. Scarcely had we left the outskirts of Philippopolis when the dread solution to our oft-discussed problem presented itself in all the horror of death, blood, and misery unspeakable. Our first day's ride was full thirty miles long, and not a kilometre of it was there that did not lie among corpses, dead animals, broken arabas, piles of rags and stray tatters of cast-off clothing.

The two antagonistic races, Turk and Bulgarian, had
found here an arena wherein to work off the blood-feuds
of generations. The vendettas had been intensely fierce.
There lay side by side the bodies of Bulgarian peasants
with gaping wounds, often abominably mutilated; and
side by side with those, corpses of dignified old Turks,
their white beards clotted with blood, their hands closed
on their bare breasts. Between the races there evidently
had been war to the knife: the men had died violent
deaths; but it had been cold and privation which accounted for the dead women and children who had been
frozen to death, and now lay in the snow as if still alive.
From the muddy water of the ditches tiny hands and
feet were visible, and baby-faces looked out from the
snow that half covered them. We rode by the interminable procession of miserable arabas full of human
beings and household effects, dragged by gaunt oxen.
Women and children rode alongside on asses, and behind
stretched the long miles of stragglers, wretched, famine-
stricken, utterly worn out; grandfathers and old crones hob-
bling wearily, mothers with infants at the parched breasts
— all this after months of a fugitive life, constant exposure,
never-ceasing dread of the hated Bulgarians. I watched a
mother slowly leading a miserable sick child which lagged
continually. Both were half naked, and both were ema-
ciated to the last degree. The last vehicle of the araba train
was nearly out of sight. The mother tried to urge on the
child, fast losing patience as the dusk began to fall.
With a sob and a gasp she caught the child to her breast,
then threw it from her into the snow on the roadside, and
hurried on without daring to glance over her shoulders.

We spent the night in a miserable village which had been pillaged to the very bone by three successive relays of marauders — only the day before the Russian cavalry had eaten the sordid place bare. When we were leaving the next morning, the village street was blocked by a train of Turkish refugees which the resident Bulgarians were systematically looting. In the village of Haskioj there lay bodies of Turkish soldiers who had been stoned to death by the Bulgarians, and whose corpses were half buried under the stones and bricks with which they had been killed. Things were worse beyond Haskioj. The country was one great abandoned bivouac, littered with all manner of household effects. We rode trampling in the snow-mire over carpets, bedding and bundles. Then we saw before us in the distance a vast park of closely-packed arabas stretching far away over the fields and slopes on both sides of the road. I believe that there could not have been fewer in the mass than 15,000 arabas, the oxen of which still remained in the yokes. There had been a recent skirmish in which two or three Russians had been killed and several Turkish soldiers. But the inhabitants of this bivouac — there must have been many thousands of them — had all but utterly disappeared. Bulgarian plunderers swarmed through the vast laager, making their perquisitions with a hungry greed and gloating over their spoil. The great company of wayfarers had been seized with a sudden access of panic as the advance guard of Russian cavalry approached. The Turkish villagers, fugitive soldiers, and half-maddened refugees had fired on the horsemen while they were passing through the successive villages. Reprisals naturally occurred and men on both sides suffered. The bivouac, it seemed, had a sort of convoy in the shape of a battalion of Turkish infantry. This force dispersed at sight of the Russians, of whom a squadron rode forward into the throng of vehicles to ascertain what this strange gathering meant. Suddenly from all sides came a burst of firing by which several Russian cavalrymen were struck down. This could not be endured and preparations were made for an attack. The fugitives in the bivouac saw a couple of guns unlimber, and at the sight a thrill of panic darted through the mass. There was a universal rush to the mountains and a wholesale abandonment of all the property remaining in the great bivouac, to the material advantage of the ready-handed Bulgarians. It was afterwards ascertained that the immense caravan consisted of over 20,000 vehicles and had a population of 200,000, of whom all the able-bodied fled, leaving the old, the sick, and the infants to be massacred by the Bulgarians or to perish in the snow.

If I remember correctly, it was on the 26th January that we rode into Adrianople behind General Gourko. Skobeleff, hurrying down from the Schipka by forced marches, had entered Adrianople on the 22nd, and there we found him and congratulated him on his great triumph. He was too busy to tell us much, and he was off again in a day or two, following the railway towards the lines of Buyuk-Tchekmedje, which he had instructions to assault with the utmost energy if the armistice should not have been previously signed by the Turkish Commissioners. Skobeleff had to submit to a disappointment, for which I confess I was not sorry. It was rather a close thing.

Skobeleff's cavalry commanded by the brilliant and dashing Stroukoff was at Tchorlu, within a march of the lines, on the 29th, having captured that village after a skirmish the last shot of which was also the last shot of the war; and at that date Skobeleff was at Lule-Bourgas, only one march behind Stroukoff. The armistice was signed in the evening of the 31st, on which day Gourko and his army quitted Adrianople for Rodosto on the Sea of Marmora, whither neither Millett nor myself accompanied him. We dined with him on the evening previous to his departure, and took farewell of him with sincere acknowledgment of many kindnesses and good offices. I myself could never forget his conduct to me on the evening of the fighting at Gorni-Dubnik. He was not a lovable man in the sense that dear old Todleben was, nor had he the fascination of Skobeleff, but he had the respect and esteem of his staff and of his army; and I should regret deeply if the things are true which have been said and written of him while governor of St. Petersburg and afterwards of Poland. If they are, all that I have to say is that his nature must have greatly deteriorated since I knew and admired him.

With the accomplishment of the double passage of the Balkans by the Sophia road and over the Schipka Pass, the whole Turkish defence had come down by the run. With the exception of the army of the Cesarevich and Zimmermann's corps in the Dobrutscha, nearly the whole of the Russian forces were now south of the Balkans. We were told that about 125,000 Russian soldiers were around or eastward of Adrianople. The Grand Duke Nicholas and his staff had arrived in Adrianople on the 27th, ac-

companied by the Turkish Commissioners, Server Pasha
and Namyk Pasha. MacGahan came in the same day,
still limping, but bright and cheery as ever. A day or two
later Villiers arrived, complaining of having been almost
frozen to death on the Schipka, having forgotten to keep
himself warm while engrossed in his interminable sketching. We four lived together comfortably in a good house,
resting after our hardships. We ate, drank, smoked and
were merry, and the voice of MacGahan was again uplifted
in song. He had come over the mountains with Skobeleff,
and in his own phrase we "swapped stories," he recounting to us the adventures of the Schipka, Millett telling him
of what had happened with Gourko. You know all about
what we saw and endured when marching with that chief,
but the story of the Schipka crossing as told by MacGahan you will find worth listening to, for it was an extraordinary feat. I give you merely a summary of MacGahan's
account, and do not pretend to give his own words.

Staunch old Radetski had made good his resolution to
hold the Schipka "come Turk, come devil," and his long
steadfast endurance was now to have its reward. When
Mirski and Skobeleff had come to reinforce him, the gallant old fighting man had at his disposition an army of
56,000 infantry, besides cavalry and artillery. One of his
divisions, the 24th, was of no use to him; for it had suffered so dreadfully up on the mountain summits from exposure that one-half of it was entirely unfit for duty. He
divided his army into three separate columns, one of which,
his own particular command, was to remain on Mount St.
Nicholas, while the other two were to cross one on either
flank and attack simultaneously in reverse the Turkish

army beyond the pass in the lower ground about the village of Schipka. The left column, under the command of Prince Mirski, consisting of 26 battalions, some cavalry and 22 guns, was to make the crossing by the Travna Pass, debouch into the valley at Gusevo, then wheel to the right and attack the eastern face of the works defending the Turkish positions. Skobeleff commanded the right column of 22 battalions and 12 guns. He had the more arduous task; for whereas Mirski had a road, rugged indeed in places but still a practicable road, by which his column was to traverse the mountain ranges, Skobeleff had for his guidance a mere footpath which for a great part of the way was buried under many feet of snow. Both columns started on January 5th and Radetski's reckoning was that they should reach the Tundja valley on the evening of the 7th and be in position to attack on the following morning. Mirski, having the easier although the longer journey, fulfilled his part of the programme. About noon of the 8th he deployed his command, and advanced to the attack of the Turkish positions in accordance with his instructions. At first he prospered, and after some sharp fighting carried a couple of outlying villages; but then he came in face of a low ridge lined with tiers of rifle pits which gave him pause. Mirski, although a gallant soldier, was a nervous man, and there were no strong men on his staff. His troops with a rush captured the Turkish line of trenches, but were then brought up all standing by the chain of redoubts south of Schipka village. It fell dark; the Russians were tired and dispirited and they had run short of ammunition. The Turks seized the opportunity, charged them vigorously, and drove them back some little distance.

It was for poor Mirski a sufficiently unpleasant situation, and he was very unhappy. As he wrote to Radetski, he had been confronted by superior numbers, he had lost heavily, he was all but run out of ammunition, there were no signs of Skobeleff, and unless some help came to him he would be compelled to retreat. Radetski replied, begging him to hold on, assuring him that Skobeleff would soon arrive, and promising to relieve him by a direct attack from St. Nicholas on the following morning. Fog blinded the scene then, but Radetski heard the sound of heavy firing down in the valley and loyally struck in to make a diversion in favour of Mirski. Through the thick snow and fog he hurled a couple of regiments against the Turkish defences in front of St. Nicholas. The effort succeeded so far that two of the Turkish trench-lines were carried, but at the formidable cost of a loss of 1,700 men. Meanwhile Mirski was doing better than on the previous day. He had been assailed on both flanks, but had repulsed both attempts. Then he had hardened his heart and betaken himself to the offensive, with the result of capturing a redoubt and occupying the village of Schipka. During a lull in the afternoon fighting Mirski's men suddenly heard loud cheering on their left about the village of Shenova. The cheering came from the throats of Skobeleff's soldiers making the assault which, as Captain Greene, the American military attaché, pointedly remarks, "decided at once the battle and the fate of the entire Turkish army of Schipka."

Skobeleff did not keep tryst with his brother commander. Skobeleff, I may here interpolate, like every successful man, had many enemies, and his nature was not conciliatory. He was accused of fighting too much for his own hand and of not being loyal in co-operation. When I called on Prince Mirski in Adrianople to pay my respects to one who had been kind to me in the early days of the campaign, I may tell you that he broke out very vehemently against Skobeleff, and frankly accused him of having been guilty of deliberate treachery for the sake of increasing his own prestige. There was with Mirski an ex-Prussian officer, whom the general introduced to me as a member of his staff, and for whom, because of his manner, I conceived a great dislike. This officer permitted himself to assert in as many words that Skobeleff had "deliberately sold" Prince Mirski,—that was his expression,—and further charged him with having pillaged the Turkish military chest of several heavy bags of gold. I was sorry that a grand seigneur like Mirski should not have exercised more self-restraint than to give heed to the irritating expressions of this coarse German condottiere. This is a digression: I return now to the summary of MacGahan's narrative. Skobeleff was a day behind his prescribed time; he had started later by several hours than Mirski because the latter had to cover nearly twice the distance of the former. While descending the mountain on the 7th he met with resistance from the Turks holding a line of trenches commanding his route, in dislodging whom he was a good deal delayed, and it was with only his advance guard that he reached the village of Imetli that evening. He would probably have suffered much more heavily but for the wise precaution he had taken before leaving Plevna of arming a battalion of the Ouglitski regiment with Peabody-Martinis taken from the

Turks. On the morning of the 8th some slight opposition near Imetli was brushed away. Skobeleff declined to believe the testimony of his pickets that on this morning Mirski, acting on his instructions, was advancing single-handed to the attack; and he expressed his belief that the sound of firing which was heard came from the direction of Mount St. Nicholas. He had sent word to Radetski that he could not be up to time, and the reply came that he was to attack on the 9th, but not do so until his force should be concentrated. It seemed an unwise omission not at this juncture to have opened communication with Mirski, to whom information of Skobeleff's dispositions would have been valuable; but Skobeleff might have held that if Mirski desired to have intelligence of him, he might take the trouble to send for it. Skobeleff stood by the letter of his instructions, and would not descend into the valley until his whole force had reached Imetli. By the morning of the 9th all of it was over the summit except the rear-guard regiment, which was delayed by dragging the guns up the steep ascents. Skobeleff sent it word to leave the guns and hurry forward. When it was in sight on the descent, he fronted to his left and marched eastward on the double line of Turkish redoubts covering on the west the village of Shenova.

Some distance had to be traversed, there were a few preliminary skirmishes, and the deployment, according to Skobeleff's habit, was effected with a deliberation and punctiliousness which he held indispensable to give the men steadiness and composure. The first line consisted of the Ouglitski regiment and the Bulgarian legion seven battalions strong; in the second were the 61st and 64th regiments and the Rifle Brigade. The banners were unfurled, the regimental bands filled the air with their music, and Skobeleff gave the word. The serried line moved forward to the assault with dressed ranks and without firing a shot. The casualties were very heavy, but as men went down the ranks closed in and pushed on steadily and silently. As the redoubts were approached, the soldiers with a rattling "hurrah!" sprang forward at the double and stormed the faces of the Turkish redoubts. Then there was a short but fierce fight, for the most part with the bayonet, between the enemies pressed together in the confined spaces in mortal conflict. In the issue, of the Turks who outlived that stern strife some surrendered, some fled towards Schipka. Skobeleff was organising the pursuit when a *parlementaire* rode up to him, and in the name of the Turkish Commander-in-Chief surrendered to Skobeleff the whole Schipka army. It numbered in all 36,000 men, of whom about 6,000 were sick or wounded; and with it 93 guns became prize of the conquerors. But their victory was not cheaply attained. The Russian losses were about 5,000. The proportion of casualties to the strength actually engaged was 1 in 5. Mirski's command suffered most severely.

The Tundja valley — in peace time the loveliest tract I have ever seen, with its rose gardens, its vineyards, its clear streams, its hanging woods and fertile farms — was now a howling desolation and could yield no supplies to troops on the march. A delay occurred before the Schipka Pass could be opened; and it was not until the 13th that General Stroukoff, commanding Skobeleff's cavalry, left Kezanlik on the march to Adrianople. On the evening of the 14th he was on the Maritza in front of Tirnova, after a ride of sixty miles. Next day he attacked a Turkish detachment of regulars and a horde of armed peasants who held the village and the bridge, drove them away, made himself master of the bridge, and cut the railway and the telegraph wires. On the 19th, when near Adrianople, tidings came to Stroukoff that the city was in a wild chaos of panic, its Turkish garrison having fled after blowing up the powder magazines. Stroukoff acted promptly. He galloped into Adrianople, took possession of it in the name of the Czar, and restored order with resolution but discretion. Skobeleff's infantry could travel as fast as Stroukoff's cavalry. His march from Kezanlik began on the 15th, and his troops were in Adrianople on the 22nd. Todleben was right — Adrianople might well have become another and a stronger Plevna. It had a garrison of 10,000 men, and if Suleiman had been of any account that force could have been increased to 50,000, a strength sufficient to man the formidable works which surrounded it. Yet Stroukoff took possession of Adrianople without firing a shot, and a few days later that beautiful and venerable city was the headquarters of a Russian Grand Duke.

I cannot tell the difference between a ravelin and a bastion — for aught I know, indeed, they may be the same thing. But the Russian officers were full of admiration for the skill and ability with which Blum Pasha, a Prussian Engineer officer in the Turkish service, had fortified Adrianople. The Turks when they evacuated that city left an immense quantity of military stores and more than 200 Krupp siege-guns, all of which were now Russian property. Properly garrisoned and with all that wealth of stores, munitions and guns, Adrianople, it was said by the experts, would have been impregnable. The detached forts which surrounded the city were most elaborate constructions, each with a high central "cavalier" — whatever that may mean in military engineering phraseology. There was some talk of bringing General Todleben over the Balkans to inspect the Adrianople fortifications. I may tell you that on February 21st the grand old chief took formal possession of Rustchuk in terms of the armistice. Todleben's fire had made a complete smash of the fortifications of Rustchuk, as I was informed by an officer who had recently left that neighbourhood. The houses in the town had also been badly battered and the whole Grande Place was one dismal wreck. I was told that after an inspection of the outlying forts General Todleben returned to his quarters in Giurgevo, — this house, you will remember, — and that next day he left for Bucharest on his way home to Russia. I had hoped to meet him at my father's table before his departure, but I had the honour of being his guest when I visited Russia after the war.

Now and then we became acquainted with incidents which went to prove that, notwithstanding their superficial gloss of refinement and civilisation, the Russians had in their blood a strong strain of sheer savagery. You will remember me telling you of the pleasant evening I enjoyed with the English surgeons at Strigli on the day after the fight at Tashkessen. I could not give much hope to Baker Pasha, but I had ventured, from what I had heard of the Grand Duke Nicholas' courtesy to Messrs. Douglas

and Vachell, to assure the Strigli surgeons that they need
apprehend no detention at the hands of the Russians.
The provisions of the Geneva Convention, against infractions of which on the part of the Turks the Russians
protested to the nations with a vehemence so great, were
perfectly definite in regard to surgeons volunteering to
give their services to the sick and wounded in war time,
their character being proved by their papers and by the
Red Cross brassard on their arm. I myself heard General
Gourko say that the Strigli surgeons could not for a
moment be regarded as prisoners of war; and I further
heard, although this was at second-hand, that they were
to be free at their convenience either to go west into
Servia on their way home or to cross the Danube into
Roumania. You can imagine my surprise, then, when
one morning at the British Consulate in Adrianople I
found those gentlemen in Mr. Blunt's waiting-room, looking extremely pulled down and forlorn. It was with indignation and disgust that I heard them tell that they were
still prisoners of war in charge of a Russian corporal
whom I had seen on the pavement outside, and that they
had been subjected to cruel sufferings and hardships
which made one's blood boil. Prince Oldenburg had
left at Strigli a certain Captain Baranoffsky, who gave
them into the custody of a corporal's guard with orders
to march them to the Commander-in-Chief's headquarters
at Bogot. For three weeks had those English gentlemen
been tramping through Bulgaria as common prisoners of
war, roughly treated by the rude soldiers who guarded
them, compelled to walk afoot and lead their horses, and
during the nights incarcerated in some wretched cellar.

They had to live for the most part on bread and water, for among them they had scarcely any money and the two roubles apiece of marching money which Baranoffsky had handed to them lasted for only the first few days. They crossed the Balkans twice in their compulsory tramp, trudging in the bitterest days of winter from Strigli by way of Orkanie, Plevna, Loftcha, Selvi, Gabrova, and over the Schipka to Kezanlik, where for the first time they found a friend in the commandant of that place who gave them some money and otherwise befriended them. On the representations of the British consul they were at once set at liberty and went off to Constantinople immediately. The Grand Duke, probably with his tongue in his cheek, not only instructed the commandant of Adrianople to apologise for what he thought proper to designate as a misunderstanding, but intimated his intention to have the conduct of Captain Baranoffsky strictly investigated. I never heard that anything came of this investigation, and if the captain is still alive probably his most amusing after-dinner story is the manner in which he treated the English surgeons in the war time.

CHAPTER XV

SAN STEFANO AND HOME AGAIN

I CONFESS that I got extremely tired of Adrianople after a fortnight's stay in it. Millett, too, had enough of that city, and was well content that we should travel further and get to the front. We had sold our horses and were now travellers by the railway. I think it was on February 10th that we reached the smiling village of Tchataldja, consisting chiefly of pleasant country-houses belonging to rich Greeks and Turks of Constantinople. The Greeks had remained, but the Turkish houses were empty and in them Skobeleff and his staff found excellent accommodation. Tchataldja is about thirty-five miles from Constantinople and within four miles of the famous lines of Kuyuk-Tchekmedje. These had been occupied by some 30,000 of Suleiman's forlorn soldiers brought up by sea from Enos and by the troops that had been the garrison of Adrianople, commanded by Mukhtar Pasha who had previously lost an army in Asia. In terms of the armistice Mukhtar had to evacuate this commanding position, which was declared to be neutral ground, and to withdraw behind the inner line of Kuyuk-Tchekmedje, only about ten miles from the Turkish capital. Skobeleff had experienced some trouble in enforcing on Mukhtar the conditions of the armistice, and his heavy guns, we were told, were still in position but had been dismounted from their carriages. On the 12th came the ominous intelligence that the British fleet had forced its way through the Dardanelles, when the Grand Duke Nicholas immediately received an authorisation from St. Petersburg to enter Constantinople. For once Nicholas showed moderation, and contented himself with occupying with the permission of the Porte the village of San Stefano on the Sea of Marmora about six miles from the capital. When this arrangement was arrived at the headquarter staff, accompanied by a Cossack regiment and the body-guard, left Adrianople by train on February 23rd and reached Tchataldja the same evening. Skobeleff's command was drawn up to receive the Grand Duke, who reviewed and praised the troops, and he was on the point of starting for San Stefano when Tahir Bey, the Turkish delimitation-commissioner, saluted his Highness and informed him that Mukhtar Pasha had no orders to withdraw his troops from Kuyuk-Tchekmedje. This intimation prevented the Grand Duke from going on to San Stefano, and he became exceedingly angry.

Shaking his finger at Tahir, he shouted in a voice that made the Turk shake in his boots:

"Go and tell Mukhtar Pasha that when I give him an order he must obey and that at once, or he will repent it. Go!"

Tahir sprang on a locomotive and sped along the line to Kuyuk. It became known that unless the Turks abandoned their positions before then they would be attacked at daylight, and there was any quantity of thunder in the atmosphere. Skobeleff was in high spirits, for he was burning for another fight. The Grand Duke, who never thoroughly liked Skobeleff, asked him what he thought of the situation. Skobeleff in his most reckless manner replied :

" For my part, Monseigneur, I hope we are going to have a war with England ! "

" Oh, but you are a madman ! " exclaimed the Grand Duke in a passion, as he turned from Skobeleff and spat viciously on the ground. Skobeleff shrugged his shoulders.

Tahir was back by midnight with the intimation that Mukhtar was withdrawing and that Russian troops were marching into the evacuated positions. So the journey was resumed, and early on the morning of the 24th the Grand Ducal train was at San Stefano. Millett and I travelled by it, and had to walk about till daylight. We all found San Stefano delightful — clean and bright, with a pleasant esplanade, a pier, and charming little painted houses looking out on the sea. Life was very gay in San Stefano ; and the fine bands of the regiments of the Guard, of which the first and second divisions were in camp close to the village and the third only a short distance away at Kuyuk-Tchekmedje, played on the esplanade all day long. The weather was perfection, and it was very restful to look out on the Sea of Marmora through the glimmer of the sunshine with Mount Olympus in the misty distance. But though cheerfulness was the *mot d'ordre* among the Russian sojourners in San Stefano, what with the English ironclads looming over against us, the Turkish troops gathering fast behind the rising earthworks encircling Constantinople, and the impatience of the hot-heads in the Russian army to end the business with a final Armageddon, thinking men realised that we might be dancing on a volcano. The Turkish ambassadors pottered on, interposing delays and hesitation at every stage. At length the terms of the treaty of peace were reported to have been settled, and there remained but the formalities of engrossing and the signatures. I had a touch of fever and was unable to witness the dramatic celebration of the announcement of peace. You will not in the least regret my absence from that scene and my consequent inability to describe it to you, when I quote to you the letter to the *Daily News* which was the admirable combined work of MacGahan and Millett, and which presents to you vividly a scene not less picturesque and romantic than memorable because of its historic interest and importance —

". . . In General Ignatieff's house by the seaside at San Stefano, shaken by the increasing gale that tore across the Sea of Marmora, were busy all night long the secretaries of both diplomatic bodies copying and arranging for the signatures the Treaty of Peace, the result of the now concluded negotiations. All night long Prince Tzeretleff dictated the treaty to his colleague Chebachoff, who wrote and wrote through the long hours until the document was finished. Although wearied by continual labour, these two secretaries, appreciating the value of their work, kept at their task, only stopping for refreshment and to listen to the scratch of the reeds of the Turkish secretaries in an adjoining room busy with their own copy, until the dawn found them still at the table. Then, the last word being on paper, they slept amidst the confusion of documents, maps, and volumes, as a soldier sleeps in his harness.

"Scarcely was it daylight when, notwithstanding the storm, there was an unwonted stir in the village. Steamers from Constantinople came rolling along over the rough sea, overladen with excursionists attracted by the review which had been announced to take place in celebration of the anniversary of the Czar's accession to the throne. Greeks, Bulgarians, Turks and Russians crowded the little place, besieging the restaurants and impatiently awaiting the hour of two, the appointed time for the spectacle. The horses of the Grand Duke and his staff were gathered about the entrance to his quarters, and keen-eyed spectators ready to interpret the slightest movement of the Russian Commander-in-Chief formed unbroken ranks around the group of horses in the street.

"One o'clock passed. Two o'clock passed; and still no movement. People began to grow serious, began to feel that something was in the air, gradually assured themselves that the decisive moment was near, that peace and war were trembling in the balance; and one man said to another, 'This is an event in history.' At length word was given out that the review was postponed until three, but that time came and went, and brought only a postponement for another hour.

"At length patience was rewarded. About four o'clock the Grand Duke mounted and rode to the Diplomatic Chancery, where he asked at the door 'Is it ready?' and then galloped towards the hill where the army was drawn up. Here we halted again for a few moments, wondering what would happen next. Finally a carriage came whirling out of the village towards us. General Ignatieff rose from his seat in it and said in a loud voice:

"'I have the honour to congratulate your Highness on the signature of peace!'

"There was a long loud shout. Then the Grand Duke, followed by about a hundred officers, dashed forward to where the troops were formed up on rising ground close to the seacoast, and began to ride along the lines. As he passed the soldiers did not know that peace had been signed, for it was still unannounced; but soon the news spread and the cheering grew louder and more enthusiastic. Very different indeed was the appearance of these soldiers now and that of the same men two months ago. During their interval of rest they had patched and cleaned their clothes, repaired and polished their boots, and washed and brushed up generally, so that they looked as trim and neat as need be.

"After riding the lines the Grand Duke halted on a little eminence whence all the troops could be seen, and made the formal announcement of the peace:

"'I have the honour to inform the army that with the help of God we have concluded a Treaty of Peace.'

"Then another great shout burst forth from 20,000 throats, rising, swelling, and dying away. The feeling of relief and satisfaction was universal. There stood the famous regiment of Peter the Great, the Preobrazhensky, which often headed the attack in the later battles of the war. There were the troops which had faced the enemy on the bleak summit of the Balkans above the Baba-Konak Pass for a long, cold, terrible month. These were the men who had toiled over the slippery mountain-paths, scantily fed, thinly dressed, dragging the heavy guns up the steep mountain-sides, and finding after their struggles with hunger, cold and fatigue, a desperate enemy ready to oppose them on every hill-top. These were the same brave fellows who had made the long march from Sophia to Philippopolis, who had run that race for enormous stakes with Suleiman's army, had finally hurled it against the precipices of the Rhodope mountains, and had smashed it to pieces. These were the men whose courage, devotion, and unparalleled endurance will go down in history and legend.

"And there, gathered scarcely more than a rifle-shot distant, was the enemy they had found worthy of their steel. For on the crests of the neighbouring hills stood the Turks in groups, interested spectators of the scene; those very men who had kept the snowy ridge of Shandarnik, who had defended the great gate of Roumelia, and who at last, after a memorable retreat, had fought as heroes fight, on the hills of Stanimaka. These two armies stood looking at each other in this hour of final peace; like true soldiers they had learned to respect and esteem each other, and welcomed peace as an honourable finish to the fight which they cared not to prolong. It was the beginning of a new friendship formed on the basis of actual mutual experience of qualities that had previously been unrecognised.

"After the review,—gathering his officers about him where the priest stood ready for the *Te Deum*, the Grand Duke spoke briefly and emphatically, saying:

"'To an army which has accomplished what you have done, my friends, nothing is impossible.'

"Then all dismounted and uncovered and a solemn service was conducted, the soldiers all kneeling. Never

THE "TE DEUM" AFTER THE PROCLAMATION OF PEACE.

could a peace have been celebrated under more dramatic and picturesque conditions, or with more impressive surroundings. The two armies face to face, the clearing storm, the waning light of day, the rush of the wind and the near wash of the wave mingling with the chaunt of the priests and the responses of the soldiers and the roar of the sea swelling and falling. The landscape, always of great beauty, now formed a wonderfully appropriate background to the picture. Across the chafing waters of the Marmora the dome and minarets of St. Sophia rose up sharply against the sky, the dominant points in the broken silhouette of Stamboul. Away to the south the Prince's Islands rose like great mounds, dark and massive, against the distant Asiatic shore, and behind them we knew was the English fleet. Above and far beyond the white peak of Mount Olympus unveiled for the moment its majestic summits as the rays of the ruddy sunset were reflected from the snow-clad flanks.

"The religious ceremony over, the Grand Duke took his stand, and the troops began to file past with a swinging rapid stride, in forcible contrast to the weary pace with which they used to drag themselves along at the end of that long and exhausting race, scarcely at times able to put one foot before the other. The night was falling and darkness was settling over the scene. As we left the spot the Grand Duke was still sitting immovable in the saddle, and the troops were still passing. As we rode down into the village we could hear the joyful shouts still ringing in the air and the measured tramp moving away into the darkness."

My long story is very near its ending. The memory of that eventful year breaking the peaceful monotony of my quiet life would not be other than pleasant, notwithstanding the hardships I had endured, but for the sorrow that came as that year drew to its close. When peace time had come I was needed at home, where commerce had begun to revive along the Danube and where I could be of service to the house of Carnegie. Well do I remember that pleasant last night in the Pera Hotel, where the gentlemen who had been so kind to me and had treated me as one of themselves — MacGahan, Millett, and Villiers — came together to eat with me for the last time. When the time came to break up, and MacGahan led off the old song of farewell, there was a lump in my throat that hindered me from joining in the "Auld Lang Syne!" The oldest and dearest of my three friends, the wise, genial, and high-souled MacGahan, rode with me as far as San Stefano. The grip of his hand was still on mine as the train carried me off and left him standing on the platform. I was to see that kindly face no more. He was under orders to attend the Berlin Congress when his countryman Captain Greene sickened of typhus fever. MacGahan nursed him, took the infection from him, and died in Constantinople after a few days' illness. Frank Millett and Frederic Villiers, — the former a New Englander, the latter an Englishman, — both of whom had begun and finished the campaign with him, helped to lower him into his far-off foreign grave, around which stood mourners of a dozen nationalities, and over which his true and constant friend, Lady Strangford, placed a stone with an epitaph as true as beautiful. Another friend who could not stand by his graveside, while life and memory remain to him will never forget him, his wisdom, his sagacity, his frank courage, his loyal manliness, his cheery lovableness, his noble genius.

FINIS.

Norwood Press:
J. S. Cushing & Co. — Berwick & Smith.
Boston, Mass., U.S.A.